Terrorism and democratic stability

MANCHESTER
UNIVERSITY PRESS

PERSPECTIVES ON DEMOCRATIZATION

The series presents critical texts on democratization processes and democratic theory. Written in an accessible style, the books are theoretically informed and empirically rich, and examine issues critical to the establishment, extension and deepening of democracy in different political systems and contexts. Important examples of successful democratization processes, as well as reasons why experiments in democratic government fail, are some of the issues analysed in the series. The books in the series make an important contribution to the ongoing debates about democracy, good governance and democratization.

SHIRIN M. RAI AND WYN GRANT   series editors

already published

Funding democratization
PETER BURNELL AND ALAN WARE (editors)

Globalizing democracy
KATHERINE FIERLBECK

Democracy in Latin America
GERALDINE LIEVESLEY

Democratization in the South
ROBIN LUCKHAM AND GORDON WHITE (editors)

Terrorism and democratic stability

JENNIFER S. HOLMES

MANCHESTER UNIVERSITY PRESS
Manchester and New York

distributed exclusively in the USA by Palgrave

Copyright © Jennifer S. Holmes 2001

The right of Jennifer S. Holmes to be identified as the author of
this work has been asserted by her in accordance with
the Copyright, Designs and Patents Act 1988.

Published by Manchester University Press
Oxford Road, Manchester M13 9NR, UK
and Room 400, 175 Fifth Avenue, New York, NY 10010, USA
http://www.manchesteruniversitypress.co.uk

Distributed exclusively in the USA by
Palgrave, 175 Fifth Avenue, New York,
NY 10010, USA

Distributed exclusively in Canada by
UBC Press, University of British Columbia, 2029 West Mall,
Vancouver, BC, Canada V6T 1Z2

British Library Cataloguing-in-Publication Data
A catalogue record for this book is available from the British Library

Library of Congress Cataloging-in-Publication Data applied for

ISBN 0 7190 5959 3 hardback

First published 2001

10 09 08 07 06 05 04 03 02 01   10 9 8 7 6 5 4 3 2 1

Typeset in 10/12 pt Trump Medieval
by Graphicraft Limited, Hong Kong
Printed in Great Britain
by Biddles Ltd, Guildford and King's Lynn

To my husband Brian

Contents

List of tables	*page* x
List of figures	xi
List of abbreviations	xii
Acknowledgements	xiv

1 Introduction — 1

The question	1
Organization of the book	2
The case studies	3
Traditional explanations	5
The military	7
Case selection	8
Conclusion	9

2 Aristotelian concepts applied to a comparative study of violence and democratic stability — 12

Introduction	12
The limitations of conventional contemporary comparative politics	12
The Aristotelian approach defined	15
How the Aristotelian approach differs from conventional comparative politics	16
What concepts and tools the Aristotelian approach offers	18

Aristotle's contemporary applicability and possible objections to the approach	22
The theory	26
Conclusion	31

3 A historical overview of Uruguay, Peru and Spain — 36

Introduction	36
Terrorist groups	54
Economic crisis	62
Conclusion	69

4 Terrorist violence — 78

Introduction	78
The theory in three case studies	78
Hypothesis one	80
Summary	88

5 State repression and violence — 90

Hypothesis two	90
Uruguay	90
Peru	98
Spain	105
Summary	110

6 Testing of hypotheses one and two — 115

Introduction: the hypotheses	115
Rudimentary purpose of the state: security	116
Rudimentary purpose of the state: integration	124
Purposes of the state: summary	131
Citizen confidence	133
Citizen confidence: summary	147
Democratic stability	150
Democratic stability: summary	161

7 Conclusion 171

Introduction 171
Alternative explanations 172
The treatment of violence in the literature 187
Why the purposes of the state is an
appropriate concept 188

8 Epilogue 203

Introduction 203
Uruguay (1973–98) 203
Peru (1992–99) 205
Spain (1986–2000) 216

Select bibliography 227
Index 239

List of tables

3.1	Uruguay: economic indicators, 1965–73	page 63
3.2	Peru: economic indicators, 1980–92	67
3.3	Spain: economic indicators, 1974–86	68
4.1	Peru: victims and those responsible, 1991	85
5.1	Peru: state violence with categories of victims and those responsible, 1991	104
6.1	Peru: four principal problems	119
6.2	Spain: top problems facing the country, 1977–86	122
6.3	Peru: average or good rating of institutions, 1990–92	143
6.4	Spain: summary table of terrorist attacks and impression of terrorism	149
6.5	Peru: choice of regime, 1982–92	157
8.1	Uruguay: economic indicators, 1980–99	206
8.2	Peru: economic indicators, 1988–99	209
8.3	Peru: actions by armed groups, 1989–98	211
8.4	Spain: economic performance, 1987–98	217
8.5	Spain: people killed by ETA, 1987–2000	218

List of figures

4.1 Uruguay: total incidents of terrorist violence, 1963–73	*page* 81
4.2 Uruguay: terrorist incidents by category, 1963–73	82
4.3 Uruguay: monthly terrorist incidents by category, 1972	83
4.4 Peru: terrorist violent incidents, 1980–95	84
4.5 Spain: number of attacks with victims, 1968–86	87
4.6 Spain: number of kidnappings by ETA, 1976–86	87
4.7 Spain: deaths attributed to the extreme right, 1976–82	88
5.1 Uruguay: state violence, spring and summer 1973	97
5.2 Peru: number of 'disappeared', 1982–91	105
6.1 Peru: view of what the National Police inspire	120
6.2 Peru: deaths due to state violence and terrorism, 1980–92	120
6.3 Spain: deaths and those responsible, 1968–86	123

List of abbreviations

AAA	Alianza Apostólica Anticomunista
AP	Popular Alliance
APRA	Alianza Popular Revolucionaria Americana
APRODEH	Asociación pro Derechos Humanos
CIA	Central Intelligence Agency
COMISEDH	Comisión de Derechos Humanos
CONAE	National Council on Education
COSENA	Consejo de Seguridad Nacional
CRF	Comando Rodrigo Franco
DEA	Drug Enforcement Agency
DSV	double simultaneous vote
EE	Euskadiko Eskerra
ELP	National Liberation Party
ETA	Euzkadi ta Askatasuna
ETA-m	ETA-militar
ETA-pm	ETA-político-militar
FBIS	Foreign Broadcast Information Service
FONCODES	Fondo Nacional de Compensación y Desarrollo Social
FREDEMO	Frente Democrático
GAL	Anti-Terrorist Groups of Liberation
GRAPO	Grupos de Resistencia Antifascista de Octubre (Antifascist Resistance Groups of the First of October)
HB	Herri Batasuna (People's Unity)
IMET	International Military Education and Training Programme
IMF	International Monetary Fund
IPA	InterAmerican Police Academy
IU	United Left
JNE	National Electoral Board
JUJEM	Joint Chief of Staffs
JUP	Juventud Uruguaya de Pie
MANO	Movimiento Armado Nacional Oriental
MIR	Movement of the Revolutionary Left

MPS	*medidas prontas de seguridad*
MRTA	Movimiento Revolucionario Tupac Amaro
OAS	Organization of American States
PCE	Spanish Communist Party
PCP-SL	Communist Party of Peru in the Shining Path
PNV	Basque Nationalist Party
PPC	Popular Christian Party
PSOE	Spanish Socialist Worker Party
SIDE	Argentine Information Service
SIN	Servicio de Inteligencia Nacional
SINAMOS	National System of Support for Social Mobilization
UCD	Union of the Democratic Centre
USAID	United States Agency for International Development

Acknowledgements

I would like to acknowledge the assistance and support of many people and organizations who made the successful completion of this work possible and enjoyable. The generous support of the University of Minnesota Graduate School in the form of the Doctoral Dissertation Special Grant provided funds for the purchase of public opinion data. I would also like to acknowledge the support of my family. In addition to bountiful encouragement, Theodore and Carolyn Smith, Jessica and John Klingler, Natina and Tedd James, and Rebecca and Willem Bastiaens graciously allowed me to stay with them, enabling me to return to Minneapolis to teach and to research the last three years of graduate school while I commuted from Arkansas. Rebecca Bastiaens should also be recognized for the countless hours spent photocopying Peruvian magazine articles while I was away. While in Arkansas, I was fortunate to meet Jaime Malamud Goti, whose encouragement, friendship and intellect made me a better scholar and citizen. Finally, I would also like to acknowledge the support of my dissertation committee, Professors Robert T. Holt, Mary Dietz, Carla R. Philips, Norman Dahl and August Nimtz. These faculty members have demonstrated exemplary professionalism and personal integrity in both teaching and research. It has been an honour to work with them. At the University of Texas at Dallas, I would like to thank my colleagues in the School of Social Sciences for their support, encouragement and advice. I appreciate the advice and guidance of Brian J. L. Berry, Sheila Amin Gutiérrez de Piñeres, Edward J. Harpham and John Peeler. A special thanks to Douglas Dow, whose many helpful comments on the manuscript only served to improve it.

1
Introduction

The question

Can terrorist and state violence cause democratic breakdown? Typically, the origins of violence are studied, but rarely are the consequences. For example, Ted Gurr states, 'on the basis of the record to date, the revolutionary potential of political terrorism is vastly overrated. Where it has had any impact at all, other powerful political forces were pushing in the same direction'.[1] When the consequences of violence are studied, its effects are usually limited to a reflection of the preexisting conflict that originally spawned the violence. In this study, the claim is made that to understand the consequences of violence on democratic stability, violence coming from terrorist groups and violence emanating from the state must be studied together. Instead of asking what unleashed the violence in Uruguay, Peru and Spain, the consequences of the violence are examined. Violence is considered as a cause of further instability, instead of merely a manifestation of preexisting conflict. In my initial examination of this question, the conventional social science concepts of legitimacy and order appeared to be inadequate for my analysis. Because of this, I shall proceed from what might seem an unusual starting point, Aristotle's political philosophy and contemporary proponents of his work. The use of these concepts in conjunction with the three case studies articulates both a persuasive defence of the usefulness of the Aristotelian framework and a greater understanding of the three case studies.

Organization of the book

The first part of the book will be conceptual. The reintroduction of Aristotle's political philosophy into current political thought by contemporary philosophers has introduced new concepts and questions for comparative politics. The pathways linking these two subjects, further explored in chapter 2, provide a framework of analysis to investigate the consequences of violence on democratic stability. The Aristotelian framework replaces 'legitimacy' with an evaluation of the state, and ultimately the constitution, based on its rudimentary purposes, and 'order' with the concept of the political community. Aristotelian concepts help to illuminate the effects of violence and its consequences on democratic stability, resulting in an approach that works well in a comparative analysis.

The rest of the book is a comparative, empirical analysis of the effects of violence (terrorist and state) on democratic stability in three countries: Uruguay (1965–84), Peru (1980–92) and Spain (1975–86). Chapter 3 provides a short historical discussion of the challenges facing all three democracies, including terrorism and economic crisis. Chapter 4 examines the consequences of terrorism on democratic stability. It is theorized that terrorist violence threatens democratic stability by undermining both rudimentary purposes of the state: security and integration. As the purposes of the state are unfulfilled, then citizen confidence in the state should decline. As citizen confidence decreases, increases in democratic instability are expected. Chapter 5 examines the consequences of state repression and violence on democratic stability. It is hypothesized that state violence also undermines the rudimentary purposes of the state. A decrease in citizen confidence is expected to follow the decrease in the rudimentary purposes. Chapter 6 concludes the testing of the two hypotheses by examining changes in citizen confidence in the state and in democratic stability. Overall, this inquiry seeks to explain, with reference to Spain's successful democratic consolidation, the demise of Uruguayan and Peruvian democracies. Specifically it aims to understand the initial popular support for the military takeover in Uruguay and the support for Alberto Fujimori's *autogolpe* in Peru.

Chapter 7 presents the conclusion that although terrorism is a threat to democratic stability, the state reaction to that violence is at least as important to influencing the ultimate outcome of continued democracy or democratic breakdown. Alternative explanations are discussed. In addition, the conclusion of this study is presented in a brief comparison to the conventional wisdom on counter-terrorism policies.

Chapter 8 is an epilogue of the three cases. In this chapter, the cases are discussed up to May 2000. Moreover, the literature on democratic consolidation is engaged to decide whether or not 'consolidation' is a helpful concept, independent of democratic stability. In addition, the role of international influence on democratic stability after the attempted and successful coups is examined.

The case studies

Uruguay

Uruguay was 'one of the world's friendliest, most progressive, and most democratic countries' according to Russell Fitzgibbon.[2] Shockingly, in 1973 the peaceful, progressive country crumbled into authoritarian rule. Strategically located between Brazil and Argentina, Uruguay, the 'Switzerland of South America', was considered one of the most stable democracies in Latin America. The small, tranquil country of approximately three million people, which prior to the coup did not even have compulsory military service, became a victim of widespread, military-led torture and repression under authoritarian, military rule from 1973 to 1984. How did the military change from an institution that 'played only a marginal role in the public arena and were mildly despised and indulgently tolerated by a populate that considered them good only for disciplining the unruly sons of the middle classes or for providing relief during natural disasters' to an institution that assumed power with the support of the citizenry?[3] In 1965 the Tupamaros began their violent protest, disrupting society and publicizing corruption. As early as 1966, the dismantling of democracy began, including severe censorship of the media. These first steps towards tyranny were mostly unchallenged by the people. In 1973 the military directly assumed power by issuing communiqués and later by occupying the National Assembly (the Uruguayan legislature). Democracy was not restored until 1984. In a country with such a pervasive history of participatory democracy, why the absence of popular protest of the military takeover?

Peru

Unlike Uruguay, Peru experienced numerous changes of constitution in the twentieth century. Politics of the early part of the century were plagued by factions within the old oligarchy and shifting, unstable political alliances. The military was directly involved in many of these changes. Two early military interventions resulted in the relatively effective rules of President Benavides (1933–39) and President Odría (1948–56). When these leaders were elected by citizens, few Peruvians were eligible to vote. A majority of Peruvians remained excluded from any meaningful participation in politics. A revolutionary coup, led by General Velasco, replaced the elected President Belaúnde in 1968. Velasco attempted radically to reform Peruvian society. He succeeded in some agrarian reform but his proposals were opposed by many. Eventually he was ousted and replaced by General Morales Bermúdez in 1975. The country was returned to democratic rule in 1980. For the first time, illiterates were granted the right to vote.[4] Newly democratic Peru faced economic crisis and rampant violence. Sendero Luminoso, or the Shining Path, emerged in 1980 and MRTA, the Tupac Amaru Revolutionary Movement, began violent activities in 1984. In 1990 Alberto Fujimori was elected president in an atmosphere of public cynicism, economic crisis and widespread violence. On 6 April 1992, Fujimori, with the support of the military, committed an *autogolpe* or self-coup, dissolving Congress, dismissing the judiciary and restricting the press. His action was widely supported by the Peruvian people. What role did violence, both state and terrorist, play in preparing the people to support Fujimori's *autogolpe*?

Spain

Early twentieth-century Spain was chaotic. In a short number of years, Spain had a constitutional monarchy, a benign dictatorship, the re-establishment of a republic and a civil war. The victorious Nationalists, under the command of General Francisco Franco, imposed calm after the civil war. Franco's rule was sanctified by the Catholic Church in the 1953 Concordat and was supported by the military until his death in 1975. Under the guidance of Franco's successor, the new King Juan Carlos, Spain began a transition to democracy. Nonetheless, the military remained a potentially powerful institution. The new democracy was tested and challenged by violent attacks which spanned the ideological spectrum. In addition to the violent threat, Spain faced economic crisis. Violent activity increased between 1975 and 1980. However, the state largely refrained from a broad repressive response. During this time, military conspiracies and plots flourished within the barracks, culminating in an almost successful coup attempt on 23 February 1981. In response to this attempted coup, citizens demonstrated in favour of democracy.[5] Why did Spaniards remain loyal to their democracy, in spite of such troubles?

Traditional explanations

There are three dominant explanations for democratic breakdown: economic, political and foreign. First, some scholars blame economic crisis and tension for democratic breakdown. Both Peru and Uruguay experienced prolonged economic crisis preceding democratic breakdown. Uruguay began having negative economic growth in the mid 1950s. Peru had declining growth from 1975–92 with a 50 per cent decline between 1988 and 1992. Both countries had high inflation, Peru experiencing hyperinflation of up to 7,650 per cent in 1991. Spain's economy also suffered from inflation and higher unemployment in the late 1970s. A sophisticated example of this type of argument can be found in Adam Przeworski, Michael Alvarez, José Cheibub and Fernando Limongi's 'What Makes Democracies Endure?'. They state:

> democracy is more likely to survive in a growing economy with less than $1,000 per capita income than in a country where per-capita income is between $1,000 and $4,000, but which is declining economically ... When poor countries

stagnate, whatever democracies happen to spring up tend to die quickly ... we have found that once a country is sufficiently wealthy, with per-capita income of more than $6,000 a year, democracy is certain to survive.[6]

Two years after the coup, in 1975, Uruguay had a per capita income of $2,144. Two years before Fujimori's *autogolpe*, in 1990, Peru's level was $849. Spain's level in 1980, one year before the attempted coup, was $6,657.[7] Indeed, at first glance this looks consistent with the economic situations of the three countries. In this study, I do not deny the importance of economic factors, nor do I claim violence to be a monocausal explanation of breakdown. However, an exclusive focus on economic factors cannot explain democratic breakdown or lack thereof. Economic problems need to be considered in a broader context to understand their effects on democratic stability.[8]

Second, others focus on explanations of leadership as a prime factor in democratic breakdown.[9] Juan Linz focuses on leaders and their behaviour, stating that no regime is ever fated to fail from deterministic factors. Although he believes that the actions of leaders have a cumulative effect on the probability of regime survival, he claims that even to the end leaders have the opportunity to act meaningfully to save the regime. Leadership was important in the following cases. In Uruguay, many officials in the Bordaberry government and within the major parties courted military intervention. In Peru, Fujimori committed an *autogolpe* and dissolved Congress. In Spain, the King played a crucial role in the consolidation of democracy. The problem with this style of analysis is that it is very difficult to craft a definition of good leadership. Juan Linz's definition of good leadership is tautologic in the sense that good leadership is leadership that prevents breakdown, while poor leadership is leadership that results in breakdown.

Finally, other scholars have focused on the power of foreign intervention or demonstration effect to explain breakdown.[10] In both Uruguay and Peru there was some foreign influence, but the evidence is contradictory. In Peru, beginning in 1983, the Peruvian army emulated the US army's strategic hamlet campaign plan used in Vietnam. However, this plan only succeeded in allowing Sendero to exploit the economic dislocation. Later, however, the United States pressured for investigation of human rights violations. In Uruguay, the Central Intelligence Agency (CIA) was involved in aid and training programmes in regard to the anti-communist National Security Doctrine; however these ended in 1973. Others argue that forces, such as the National Security Doctrine, in the Southern Cone countries, were so pervasive that Uruguay was unable to resist democratic breakdown; for example in Brazil in 1964, in Chile in 1973 and in Argentina in 1976. However, of all the countries it seems reasonable to expect that Uruguay, with its treasured history and tradition of participatory democracy, would have been able to withstand such pressures for change.

The military

In each of the three cases, the military played an important role. In Uruguay, the military directed dismantled democracy. In Peru, Fujimori conducted his *autogolpe* with the support of the military. In Spain, the military remained a threat to the new democracy throughout the democratic consolidation. Historically, a major issue in Latin American politics has been figuring out how to stop politicians from 'knocking on the barrack doors' and how to convince the military that they are not the ultimate protectors of the constitution, as they interpret it.

The problem of military intervention is not limited to Latin America or to the Iberian Peninsula. This has been the subject of discussion since antiquity and the issue remains salient today. What motivates a military institution or particular officer to move against the state and to seize power? I recognize that the framing of the debate on stability in terms of internal military factors is important, although it is not my main concern. In Uruguay, Peru and Spain, some military officers viewed the armed forces as a source of power to be used to assume control of the country or to promote someone who could. This propensity towards power among some in the military was present in all three cases and should not account for the differences in outcome among the cases. Instead of analysing internal factors within the military to explain military intervention, this study asks what makes public support for military intervention possible, by focusing on the problems facing the state which could undermine citizen support for democracy. In the cases of authoritarian takeovers of democracies, the military entered the political scene because the officers believed the civilian politicians to be incompetent. Something about the performance of the previous state was unacceptable.[11] Considering that many interventions are popularly supported, it appears that some citizens also believed that the performance of the state was lacking. The successful coups in Uruguay and Peru were supported, at least initially, by the people. Instead of merely focusing on the actors in the destruction of a state, it is also necessary to ask why they lost the support of a large number of citizens.

Case selection

The design incorporates two types of analysis: the parallel demonstration of theory and a most different design. In the parallel demonstration of theory, it is my intention to show the usefulness of my concept of citizen support in understanding these cases. In the most different design, the questions are examined in Uruguay and Peru. There are three main similarities between the two. First, both countries experienced violence followed by a change of constitution. In Uruguay, the Tupamaros began their violent protest in 1965. In 1973, the military assumed power. Democracy was not restored until 1984. In Peru, the most recent violent political movement is Sendero Luminoso (the Shining Path), which emerged in 1980. President Fujimori conducted his *autogolpe* in 1992. Second, neither country had extensive United States intervention in their national politics. Third, both states responded to the threat with repression. In spite of these similarities, the two countries differ in respect to features that are speculated by some to be related to stability. The violent movement in Uruguay was mostly urban, whereas in Peru it was mostly rural. Uruguay has had a much more stable history of democratic governance than Peru. The level of industrialization in Uruguay was higher than in Peru. The Uruguayan population includes the original

Spanish settlers, plus a large proportion of later Spanish and Italian immigrants, creating a generally homogeneous population.[12] On the other hand, Peru has a large population of indigenous Indians, in addition to people of African and Chinese descent, creating a heterogeneous population. Not only is the country heterogeneous, but it is geographically divided. Twelve per cent of the population is white, Catholic and lives on the coast. Of the remaining population, in general 45 per cent is Indian, 37 per cent is mestizo and 6 per cent is black. Two-thirds of the population lives in the Andean mountains and consists mostly of non-Spanish-speaking, impoverished peasants who adhere to Incan faiths.[13] In total, there are fifty-seven ethnic groups[14] and approximately thirty-one spoken languages.[15] Uruguay has had a very well-established, almost consociational, two-party system of the Colorados and Blancos since 1904. Peru has an extensive history of military intervention and unstable political parties. Its most popular party, APRA, was excluded from electoral competition for much of the twentieth century. In addition, the coup and *autogolpe* occurred in very different time periods.

Spain is introduced as an exploratory case. Spain, like Uruguay and Peru, faced terrorist violence. However, the outcome was different. Spain's democracy was consolidated. The case of Spain is important for illustrating an alternative state response to terrorist violence. The new democracy was challenged by a plethora of violent groups from across the ideological spectrum. Spain did not implement policies of indiscriminate state violence and repression. Spain has a high level of industrialization and literacy. The country is composed of different autonomous regions, many of which are historically recognized regions with their own culture and language. In addition to a threat from violence, Spain faced an economic crisis and a politicized military. Nonetheless, Spanish democracy survived.

Conclusion

This study is a comparative study of the consequences of state and terrorist violence on democratic stability in Uruguay,

Peru and Spain. How do people react to attacks and threats of state and terrorist violence? Does violence affect the citizen support of democracies? What is the basis of the citizen support of democracies? These are compelling questions. The Aristotelian approach I will sketch in the following chapter promises to illuminate these issues in ways that other approaches to violence have not. The Aristotelian approach can explain how state and terrorist violence has effects more insidious and long lasting than previously thought, by referring to the purposes of the state and to the importance of the political community.

Notes

1 Ted Gurr, 'Some Characteristics of Political Terrorism in the 1960s', in Michael Stohl (ed.), *The Politics of Terrorism* (West Lafayette: Purdue University, 1988), p. 51.
2 Russell Fitzgibbon, *Uruguay: Portrait of a Democracy* (New Brunswick: Rutgers University Press, 1954), p. vii.
3 Carina Perelli, 'From Counterrevolutionary Warfare to Political Awakening: The Uruguayan and Argentine Armed Forces in the 1970's', *Armed Forces and Society*, Vol. 20, No. 1, Autumn 1993, p. 35.
4 David Scott Palmer, 'Rebellion in Rural Peru', *Comparative Politics*, Vol. 18, No. 2, January 1986, p. 130.
5 Most of the literature on the early years of the current Spanish democracy focuses on the successful transition to democracy. Little attention is paid to why Spanish citizens did not support the attempted coup in 1981. Most credit for the successful transition to democracy is given to political factors, good leadership, modernization and foreign influence.
6 Adam Przeworski, Michael Alvarez, José Cheibub and Fernando Limongi, 'What Makes Democracies Endure?', *Journal of Democracy*, Vol. 7, No. 1, January 1996, p. 49.
7 United Nations Development Programme, *Human Development Report 1999* (New York: Oxford University Press, 1999), pp. 151-2.
8 Kurt Weyland, in 'Latin America's Four Political Models', *Journal of Democracy*, Vol. 6, No. 4, October 1995, p. 137, highlights this connection. 'Poverty and inequality thus pose more urgent problems for democratic stability ... The quality of democracy and indeed its very survival in the long run may require that poverty be reduced and popular hopes for social improvements be satisfied'. Nancy Bermeo concurs, stating, 'economic crises might be a necessary though not sufficient incentive for the breakdown of authoritarian regimes'. Nancy Bermeo, 'Rethinking Regime Change', *Comparative Politics*, April 1990, p. 366.
9 Juan Linz, *Breakdown of Democratic Regimes: Crisis, Breakdown and Equilibration* (Baltimore: Johns Hopkins, 1978).

10 See Richard Millet, 'Beyond Sovereignty: International Efforts to Support Latin American Democracy', *Journal of Interamerican Studies and World Affairs*, Vol. 36, No. 3, Autumn 1994, pp. 1–23.

11 An excellent, recent example of a study of military intervention is Peter Calvert and Susan Milibank, 'The Ebb and Flow of Military Government in Latin America', in William Gutteridge (ed.), *Latin America and the Caribbean: Prospects for Democracy* (Aldershot: Ashgate, 1997).

12 In Uruguay, approximately 90 per cent of Uruguayans are of either Spanish or Italian heritage. The original Indian population fled or was killed off during colonization; no pure Churrúa and Chana Indians were left by 1850. Approximately 5–8 per cent of the population is mestizo, and this population is clustered along the northern border. Another small ethnic group of about forty to sixty thousand blacks live in the north and are employed mainly in the meat packing 'Cerro' area. Martin Weinstein, *Uruguay: Democracy at the Crossroads* (Boulder: Westview Press, 1988), p. 3.

13 Cynthia McClintock, 'The Prospects for Democratic Consolidation in a "Least Likely" Case: Peru', *Comparative Politics*, Vol. 21, No. 2, January 1989, p. 129. See also Peter Klaren, 'Peru's Great Divide', *The Wilson Quarterly*, Vol. 14, No. 3, Summer 1990, p. 29.

14 Alberto Adrianzén, *Democracia, etnicidad y violencia política en los países andinos* (Lima: IEP, 1993), p. 111.

15 *Statistical Abstract of Latin America*, Vol. 23. Edited by James W. Wilke (Los Angeles: UCLA Latin American Center Publications), p. 151.

2
Aristotelian concepts applied to a comparative study of violence and democratic stability

Introduction

Some scholars in the philosophy of science argue for an Aristotelian approach to politics.[1] Although the more ambitious claims for social science are appealing, the reader may be convinced more readily by the appropriateness of a number of Aristotelian concepts to the study of the consequences of terrorism and state repression on democratic stability. Certain Aristotelian concepts and categories are useful to examine instability and are applicable to a comparative study of violence and democratic stability in Uruguay, Peru and Spain. Without rejecting the importance of studies on the origin of violence, this study focuses on the possible consequences of the violence, once established.[2]

The limitations of conventional contemporary comparative politics

In terms of conceptualizing citizen support, most scholars of contemporary comparative politics operate within the general framework outlined by Max Weber. Contemporary comparative politics typically defines the state by process or means, instead of ends or purposes. Max Weber provided a general definition of the state that has continued to influence contemporary scholars:

> Sociologically, the state cannot be defined in terms of its ends. There is scarcely any task that some political association has

not taken in hand ... Ultimately, one can define the modern state sociologically only in terms of the specific means peculiar to it, ... we have to say that a state is a human community that claims the monopoly of the legitimate use of physical force.[3]

An example of a contemporary scholar following this tradition is Juan Linz. He defines the state in the following manner: 'A chief characteristic of the modern state is the monopoly of legitimate force in the hands of police and the military under the direction of political authorities'.[4]

According to Weber, there are three basic legitimations of domination: traditional, which would include habit and 'ancient recognition'; charisma; and virtue of legality, which includes a 'belief in the validity of legal statute and functional "competence" based on rationally created rules'.[5] Today, the three main contemporary concepts of legitimacy, socialization, and procedural and evaluative, fit within the bounds espoused by Weber.

Robert A. Dahl, in *A Preface to Democratic Theory*, defines legitimacy 'not in an ethical but in a psychological sense, *i.e.*, a belief in the rightness of the decision or the process of decision making'.[6] He identifies three areas of consensus necessary for a functioning polyarchy: procedural rules, scope of policy options and range of legitimate political activity. He views legitimacy as a belief in the procedures of rule.

David Easton's definition of legitimacy typifies concepts that are based on socialization. He identifies the objects of legitimacy, the political authorities or the regime. Easton identifies three sources of legitimacy: ideological, structural and personal.[7] Legitimacy is transmitted through socialization.

In the literature that deals with democratic breakdown or democratic consolidation, the concept of legitimacy used by Juan Linz in his 1978 *Breakdown of Democratic Regimes* dominates the discussion. In general, legitimacy is considered to be a positive attitude towards the particular democracy and a belief that the democratic form of constitution is most appropriate for that nation.[8] Linz identifies three ways to anchor legitimacy: through a belief in the legitimacy of a regime, through habit or through rational calculation. He highlights the fact that belief in a regime's legitimacy is particularly important in times of crisis. Habit in obeying a particular regime grows with time. Rational calculation involves evaluations of a regime's basic functions of efficacy and efficiency. These evaluations of a regime's effectiveness and efficacy seem to be biased 'by initial commitments to legitimacy'.[9] Linz defines the relationship between legitimacy and effectiveness and efficacy as circular. Efficacy is the 'capacity of a regime to find solutions to the basic problems facing any political system'. Effectiveness is the 'capacity actually to implement the policies formulated, with the desired results'. The basic functions are economic and social policies, the 'maintenance of civil order, personal security, the adjudication and arbitration of conflicts, and a minimum of predictability in the making and implementation of decisions'.[10] The public evaluates a regime and awards legitimacy on the basis of these two functions: regime efficacy and effectiveness. In this discussion, there is no statement of why some things seem to matter more than others. Mentions of the need to 'maintain public order' and 'promote economic growth' are fragmentary and unconnected.

The strength of process-based concepts of legitimacy is in helping to explain the origin of violence. In most of the studies that discuss terrorism, the discussion is normally focused on explaining the origin of this violence, not the consequences of it. Perhaps this is a function of 'legitimacy'. In one example, Juan Linz addresses the issue of political violence. He states that, typically, a challenger to a regime will dispute a regime's authority and its ability to maintain order. Linz suggests that political violence is usually not enough to explain regime breakdown, although he believes that the cause and effect overlap. In another example, Nef and Vanderkop cite a system of violence to explain Peruvian conflict:

> In Peru, and for that matter in most of Latin America, violence is a manifestation of profound conflicts that exist in the society, the international system and within the state itself. It involves the inability of the contending social forces to reach political consensus – a lack of legitimation – as well as the incapacity of the government to exercise effective control. In this context, violence should not be perceived necessarily as abnormal or irrational, but as a particular form of conflict management coexisting with other non-violent forms.[11]

They believe that Peruvian society 'has tended to nurture ideologies which justify violence'.[12]

Within the contemporary concepts of legitimacy, exactly what the state is supposed to be doing is not touched upon.

The concept of legitimacy fits with a notion of a state without ends. Within these contemporary definitions, there is little independent basis for the evaluation of whether a state, legitimate or illegitimate, is good or bad. In the initial examination of these questions, the conventional concepts of legitimacy and the state appeared to be inadequate for this analysis. The socialization-based concepts do not help with questions of citizen evaluation of the state. The efficiency-based concepts cannot satisfactorily explain what functions the state is expected to fulfil. The concept of legitimacy, while attempting to measure degrees of acceptance or rejection of authority which is helpful in understanding the emergence of terrorist groups, does not aid in understanding the consequences of violence. Legitimacy rarely includes standards of evaluation necessary to understand these consequences. Evaluation becomes a critical foundation for state, and ultimately constitutional support, when history provides a choice of constitutional type and when habit-based legitimacy is not strong. The Aristotelian approach provides a purpose- or end-based concept that is essential to understanding the consequences of terrorist and state violence.

The Aristotelian approach defined

Stephen Salkever describes the Aristotelian approach to politics not as a particular method, but rather as a series of questions which define the task of the social scientist. He states that the approach stems from three fundamental questions which 'have to do with how, given our specific nature and the various environmental circumstances we confront, communities can best solve the three great problems, which as *problems* are unique to the experience of human being: living, living together and living well'.[13] In order to answer the three questions, the scholar must call on many resources, philosophical and empirical, to pursue answers.

The Aristotelian approach, with its aim of achieving the highest good possible and its requirements of virtue, is inherently purpose or end oriented. In sum, Aristotle's approach acts 'in response to descriptions of observed phenomena relational propositions of two distinct kinds – predictive hypotheses and functional or teleological placements are set out; and on the basis of these propositions, action orienting evaluative conclusions are drawn about institutions, policies and ways of life'.[14] These conclusions are then presented in a non-dogmatic way, in the manner of a discussion or persuasion.

Salkever presents the approach as deliberation oriented; accordingly, the Aristotelian approach is a way of thinking about political problems, a way of thinking that encourages a conversation from various forms of inquiry. 'Aristotelian social science is oriented towards thinking about our own action – rather than towards predicting or narrating the action of others – in a way that modern alternatives are not'.[15] The approach is a type of practical philosophy, which is 'necessarily imprecise and in the form of an outline, and thus should be treated not as a source of definite answers to definite questions about how to act but rather as a preparation for informed deliberation in cases where no such answers are available'.[16] What this challenges the scholar to do is to consider problems and solutions within broader goals, such as a healthy, stable state, not just focusing on ending terrorism by any means.

How the Aristotelian approach differs from conventional comparative politics

According to Aristotle, the most practicable form of constitution is not always a form of rule by the many. This idea is rejected by many contemporary scholars.[17] He also believed that there were good forms of rule by one and rule by few. His standard is absolute justice, 'those constitutions which consider the common interest are right constitutions, judged by the standard of absolute justice. Those constitutions which consider only the personal interest of the rulers are all wrong constitutions, or perversions of the right forms' (*Pol.*, p. 112). In cases of a corrupt form, instead of advocating revolution, Aristotle advocates reform. (He also suggests self-imposed exile.) Aristotle counsels us to examine each particular state, as is, and to try to improve it in order to achieve the most possible stability, even if the best possible in that case is an inferior type.

This notion that there are better and worse forms of different forms is more acceptable in Latin America. For example, as Guillermo O'Donnell noted, there is a differentiation between the terms *dictadura* and *dictablanda*. A *dictadura* is a dictatorship that is particularly repressive. On the contrary, a *dictablanda* is seen as a more benign, sometimes even a partially good, form of constitution. In the cases of Uruguay and Peru, the people abandoned their loyalty to their democratic constitutions in favour of a change to what they hoped would be a more practicable form of rule. In Peru, they supported Fujimori, who forcibly reformed their democracy with his *autogolpe*. In Uruguay, they supported the military, at least initially. Peruvians and Uruguayans had different expectations for the alternative constitutional forms; however, they had one thing in common: hopes for a more practicable form of rule. There was an optimism that the new forms would be better. These hopes can be betrayed. Citizens can be misled or misunderstood. These hopes were betrayed in the case of Uruguay. There were hopes that the Uruguayan military would act as an aristocracy not as a tyrannous oligarchy that ruled by fear. In Peru, Fujimori has made some reforms and reduced terrorist violence, although recently more Peruvians have been viewing him as an authoritarian leader. It seems that the concept of acceptable forms of rule other than democracy is well established in many countries.

Instead of labelling states as corrupt based on principles of rule, Aristotle asks if they are oriented to the good. The teleological vision of the good orients the Aristotelian approach.[18] Can this conception be compatible with a political science that predominantly believes that the science of politics should be value-neutral? Is an inquiry of the problems and possibilities of politics, guided by such a conception, merely an idealistic pursuit of a subjective whim? Can a conception of the good be defended? Most contemporary scholars reject the teleological vision based on three objections: that the teleological end cannot be demonstrated scientifically; that the teleological vision is hopelessly idealistic and therefore irrelevant to actual politics; and that the teleological vision will lead to dogmatism and oppression. If something cannot be demonstrated scientifically, does that necessarily mean that it cannot be supported rationally? Even though the first principles may not be deduced from other principles, the teleology may be supported by argument, by inference or by reason. Without falling back on dogmatism, it can be shown through reason or argument that some conceptions of the good are better or worse than others. Reason, argument and deliberation are always welcome in an Aristotelian approach. Moreover, it is entirely possible that most, if not all, political scientists are committed to some conception of the good that implicitly guides their work. This can be shown by asking political scientists why they are interested in politics. If the practice of political science is only one intellectual curiosity among others, then the Aristotelian approach is not appropriate. However, if one believes that political science may be useful, perhaps that some genuine good may come out of it, then the individual probably has some conception of good behind their work and this approach may not seem so inappropriate. Some conception of the good may already guide political scientists in their own work, even if they do not include it in a description of their studies. Alasdair MacIntyre argues that teleology is not as uncommon as one may first suspect: 'there is no present which is not informed by some image of some future and an image of the future which always presents itself in the form of telos – or of a variety of ends or goals – towards which we are either moving or failing to move in the present'.[19]

Other critics may reject Aristotelian teleology on the basis that it is idealistic and irrelevant to the everyday imperfect politics and societies. Bernard Yack, in *Problems of a Political Animal*, counters this charge. The Aristotelian approach 'shows how even the imperfect politics of actual political communities can make human flourishing possible, it encourages us to use our understanding of the problems of a political community to identify the real possibilities for a good human life'.[20] Aristotle himself, in book IV, chapter 1 of the *Politics*, stresses the need to look for the practicable and the appropriate, as well as what would be ideally best in general and best given the circumstances (*Pol.*, pp. 155–6).

What concepts and tools the Aristotelian approach offers

Certain Aristotelian concepts and tools can help to illuminate the consequences of terrorism and state repression on democratic stability in the political community. The evaluation of whether or not a state works for the common good and aims to help its citizens flourish are issues that move to the forefront of the discussion when legitimacy is replaced by a more Aristotelian notion. This Aristotelian concept of the purposes of the state provides explanatory power to understand the consequences of terrorism and state repression on democratic stability.

The concept of a *polis* leads the scholar to look at a state in terms of its purposes. The political community upon which Aristotle bases his discussion is the *polis*. It is 'an association of households and clans in the good life, for the sake of attaining a perfect and self-sufficing existence ... The end and purpose of a *polis* is the good life, and the institutions of social life are means to that end' (*Pol.*, p. 120). The *polis* is necessary for the development and perfection of human capacities by supplying self-sufficiency, inculcating healthy habits, educating citizens and enabling leisure time. These are all necessary to a good life, to the development of virtues and the development of justice.[21] Aristotle criticizes those who view the state as an end for factors other than the cardinal factor of the good life, while still acknowledging the importance of the rudimentary purposes of the state. Aristotle recognizes that the rudimentary purposes of the *polis* are also necessary. While the *polis* '*grows* for the sake of mere life, it *exists* for the sake of a good life' (*Pol.*, p. 5).

In addition, Aristotle (*Pol.*, p. 156) asks three questions of the constitution of a *polis*: what kind of authority is used, what is the end of the constitution and is it well ordered? In asking these questions, he seems to incorporate the other two factors (authority and end) and matches those factors with the particular body of people that makes up the state. Whether or not a state is well ordered is indicated by at least two factors: general approval and stability.

> The maintenance of a constitution is the thing which really matters ... Legislators ... must be on their guard against all the elements of destruction; ... they must believe that the true policy, for democracy and oligarchy alike, is not one which ensures the greatest possible amount of either, but one which will ensure the longest possible life for both. (*Pol.*, p. 267)

Again, Aristotle stresses citizen approval: '... the proper policy, wherever it can be pursued, is to keep all citizens alike attached to the constitution and the government under it, or at any rate, failing that, to prevent any citizen from regarding the government as his enemy' (*Pol.*, p. 268). Even though it is difficult to measure the balance of forces within a state to determine whether or not the state is well balanced, stability and general approval are user-friendly indicators of a well-balanced state. In times of violence, a nation is not stable.

In most societies, the predominant notion of justice is based on reciprocity. Aristotle recognizes that the vast majority of political associations are not true *poleis*; that is, they have not progressed to the second level of achieving human flourishing or complete virtue. Instead, these societies are based on exchange instead of virtue. Aristotle acknowledges that many people think that mere reciprocity is, without qualification, just (*NE*, 1132b21–22, p. 117). Aristotle states:

> in associations for exchange this sort of justice does hold men together ... Men seek to return either evil for evil – and if they cannot do so, think their position mere slavery – or good for good – and if they cannot there is no exchange, but it is by exchange that they hold together. (*NE* 1132b31–34, p. 118)

In these exchange-based societies, the justice common, reciprocal, to them is also less stable and whole than other types of justice.

Instead of focusing on legitimacy, the notion that is so central to contemporary accounts, to explain political stability and instability, the Aristotelian approach looks to the purposes of the state to understand popular support, or lack thereof. This approach fundamentally differs from a process-oriented understanding of legitimacy. This approach does not just ask whether or not the majority of the people acquiesce to authority or to an agreed-upon process, but it attempts to introduce some broad standards, the purposes of the state, in terms of which to understand support of the state, and ultimately of the form of constitution. The notion of purposes of the state introduces two questions: are the rudimentary purposes being fulfilled and is the state attempting to move beyond the rudimentary purposes to achieve human flourishing? I propose to substitute the notion of the purposes of the state for the contemporary concept of legitimacy.

In the *Politics*, Aristotle draws a distinction between living and living well in political life. Stephen Salkever, in his commentary on the *Politics*, identifies two levels of the purposes of the *polis*. In the first level, some rudimentary conditions must be guaranteed before more ultimate purposes are even proposed. Salkever states, 'before it is possible to live well, it is necessary for us to live and to live together'.[22] To achieve this, stability and integration are necessary. 'Survival and internal tranquility ... are only necessary conditions of virtue, but they are very necessary'.[23] The first level of purpose involves the achievement of the proximate goals of security and integration. As Leo Strauss says, 'the most urgent and primary task is self-preservation'. The second level entails achieving the goal of developing flourishing and virtuous citizens, or self-improvement.[24] For an Aristotelian, the second threshold needs to be achieved, or at least attempted.[25] However, Aristotle acknowledges that fulfilling even just the first threshold is important: 'for perhaps there is some simple element of the good in just living, so long as the evils of existence do not preponderate too heavily' (*Pol.*, p. 111). In his emphasis on the second threshold, he does not minimize the importance of the first.

Sometimes the requirements of each level conflict with one another. Salkever characterizes the tension in Aristotelian thought as a conflict between stability and virtue, stating:

> Political organization and authority are not fully justified unless the laws and customs of that organization are reasonable means toward the development of healthy personalities, but the organization cannot continue to exist unless those same nomoi (laws and norms) are also reasonable means toward the stability and integration of the *polis*.[26]

More importantly, these purposes are not independent, tradable commodities. One cannot make up a lack of liberty, or any other benefit, with an excess of order, or vice versa. To have a healthy state, one needs an appropriate balance of all these features.[27] Comparative judgments can be made among different goods, but certain tradeoffs between various goods are unacceptable. When it is a matter of the ends that constitute the good for human beings, it is not satisfactory to the Aristotelian to imagine a tradeoff between them in purely quantitative terms. For example, indiscriminate repression can usually quell terrorism. However, it can do much more than just eliminate 'subversives'; it can also destroy community, friendship and justice and prevent any possibility of promoting the common good. This distinguishes the concept of purposes of the state from merely a list of functions necessary to maintain legitimacy.

It is possible to ask whether or not most people believe that their form of constitution is most appropriate. But can scholars assess how well the state is fulfilling its rudimentary purposes? Although human flourishing is not precisely quantifiable, questions of justice and flourishing can still be raised. The rudimentary purposes of the state are security and integration. These can be quantified. This conceptualization enables the scholar to see the effects of terrorism and state repression on the fulfilment of the rudimentary purposes of the state.

The concept of purposes of the state attempts to conceptualize citizen support. Instead of other concepts that look to procedural grounds or to belief, this concept relates to purposes instead of processes. Using these ideas, it can be shown that if the state is not fulfilling its rudimentary purposes and making no effort to fulfil its ultimate purpose, then the citizens look to other forms of constitution that can. The good in politics implies asking what the state is supposed to be doing. Does the state exist to maintain a monopoly of the forces of coercion, or is it supposed to do something for its people? If a state should be doing something, what then should it be doing? What do its citizens expect of the state? An idea of a well-ordered constitution, the purposes of the state and competing notions of justice are all important things to examine when studying instability. The Aristotelian approach provides a coherent framework within which to ask these questions. Aristotle recognizes that most political associations will never become true *poleis*; however, that does not mean they can abrogate their attempts to progress towards the ultimate end.

Aristotle's contemporary applicability and possible objections to the approach

Some scholars, political theorists and others have argued that the Aristotelian approach is inappropriate for incorporation into the contemporary study of politics. First of all, some charge, it is old and thus, presumably, out of date. Aristotle wrote approximately twenty-five hundred years ago. How could his theory be relevant today, in a context much different from that in which Aristotle lived and wrote? In addition, isn't such a theory too hampered by all the normative concepts and ethical notions inherent in the approach, possibly leading to dogmatism? Finally, by calling an approach Aristotelian, isn't one really just falling back on an authority (i.e. Aristotle) to make and defend some general points?

Stephen Holmes, in 'Aristippus In and Out of Athens', claims that classical Greek political theory has become anachronistic because of the massive changes in society. He states that the changes that began in medieval times and accelerated in modern times have simply erased the relevance of classical Greek political theory. Specifically, he attacks two claims of classical thought: that there are 'true' purposes and that 'individuals, being thoroughly "political animals" can fully realize themselves in political participation'.[28] Holmes extends his criticism beyond charges of mere anachronism, arguing that the incorporation of these 'outdated' concepts can become 'flagrant and despotic archaisms when transported, even with the best of intentions, into the institutional context of modern society'.[29] One of the main reasons why Holmes believes that classical Greek concepts do not travel well through time is that they are 'inseparably linked to descriptive postulates about the institutional framework of the city state'.[30] Things have changed. For example, the separation of the social from the political, the theological from the political, the difference of scale, and the differentiation within modern society when compared with that of ancient society, all mark off the context of contemporary political thought and action from that of classical Greece. Holmes defines modern politics as 'electioneering, lobbying and bureaucracy, it cannot also be conceived of as a whole, much less as a society-encompassing whole, which could give moral security and "warmth" to its constituent parts'.[31]

Undeniably, the ancient definition of politics was more encompassing than the modern. To the ancients, politics was more than just casting a vote or sending a cheque to a favourite political action committee. However, that does not mean that the connections which the ancients more readily recognized do not exist in modern life. James H. Nichols responds to the charges of Holmes in his article 'On the Proper Use of Ancient Political Philosophy: A Comment on Stephen Taylor Holmes's "Aristippus In and Out of Athens"'. He first responds to Holmes by elaborating three levels of political thought set out by Leo Strauss in 1964. They are 'philosophic principles, analysis of a given society, and immediately available prescriptions for political action'.[32] Nichols claims that any failure to recognize these different levels would make any political theory, from any foreign or temporally distinct context, obsolete. In short, Nichols dismisses Holmes's claims as misleading since he conflates the different levels, losing the relevance of the first. 'Relying simply on differences between the contemporary society and the Greek *polis*, it does not address the issue of the adequacy of the fundamental principles of Greek political philosophy on the level on which they are presented'.[33] Nichols defends proposing philosophical principles from other times and contexts as possibly helpful. This illumination is not automatic, but relies on the analysis of given societies and an analysis of their principles. Whether or not prescriptions for action can be drawn from them is a matter of prudence, moderation and empirical analysis.

Stephen Holmes, in his dismissal of Aristotelian concepts in modern life, underestimates one key historical similarity between the time of Aristotle and the historical situation in parts of the contemporary world. Aristotle wrote in times of political turbulence and tried to formulate a political theory in the context of this instability. Finley characterizes the typical politics of Aristotle's day as unstable. 'In city after city there was an oscillation between oligarchy and democracy, accompanied by civil war, wholesale killing, exile and confiscation. Sometimes tyrants intervened, adding another dimension'.[34] Political instability was prevalent during Aristotle's time, as it has been in much of the world in the twentieth century.

Other scholars, specifically John Wallach, criticize the neo-Aristotelians as disingenuous in their use of Aristotle. He resents how many of the neo-Aristotelians, such as Martha Nussbaum, Alasdair MacIntyre and Stephen Salkever, attempt to separate the 'essential' Aristotle from the aspects of his thought which are historically conditioned or unacceptable to them. He claims:

This means that the identity of Aristotelian *politike* is an interpretive construct. Whatever then serves as the 'essential' Aristotle in the contemporary theoretical discourse is necessarily a construction of a construction ... As a result, invocation of Aristotle that transports the foundations of ethical and political reflection from the present to the past, from contemporary theorization to 'Aristotle', is typically, even if unintentionally, disingenuous. Contemporary Aristotelians do not acknowledge either the ambiguity of their theoretical authority or the constructive character of their own project.[35]

Wallach doubts that some aspects of Aristotle's works that are unacceptable to modern sensibilities, such as slavery and the domination of women, can be separated from other aspects of his thought. The elevation of some aspects of his thought as essential and the demotion of others as dispensable troubles Wallach. Wallach characterizes 'Aristotelian' authors as using Aristotle as an authority and as a philosophical anchor instead of as an inspiration.[36]

Calling a work Aristotelian does not entail a claim that the work embodies the one and only true interpretation of Aristotle. Contrary to Wallach's claims, the scholars do acknowledge their interpretations as such; for example, Salkever calls Aristotelian social science 'my reconstruction of that social science'.[37] It is true that these interpretations do differ from Aristotle's political thought in issues not considered essential to his political thought. The question of whether or not aspects considered essential can be separated from those aspects that contemporary Aristotelians would prefer to disavow is a legitimate question to ask. I am confident that the concepts that contemporary Aristotelians take from Aristotle can be separated from some of Aristotle's more controversial views, such as on women and slavery. However, this is something the reader will have to decide for him- or herself, by examining the concepts that are included by the contemporary Aristotelians and then asking whether these can be held without embracing Aristotle's beliefs on women and slavery.

Another possible objection to using an approach inspired by Aristotle and contemporary commentators on his work is that contemporary democracy is significantly different from ancient democracy. Aristotle broadly defines democracy as a constitution in which 'the freeborn and poor control the government – being at the same time a majority' (*Pol.*, p. 164).

In a democracy, according to Aristotle, the principle of justice is equality (*Pol.*, p. 117). Although the modern democracy is different in that citizens do not directly rule but instead vote for representatives, the modern democratic state would still be considered a democracy for Aristotle since the poor majority has the same rights to vote and participate in the government as do the rich. It is consistent with Aristotle's statement that 'in this variety [of democracy] the law declares equality to mean that the poor are to count no more than the rich' (*Pol.*, p. 167). This definition is similar to Lord Bryce's definition in his *Modern Democracies* and that used by Russell Fitzgibbon in his 'The Pathology of Democracy in Latin America'. The definition reads, 'that form of government in which the ruling power of the state is legally vested . . . in the members of the community as a whole'.[38] More typical, contemporary process-oriented definitions of democracy can be found in Robert Dahl's *Polyarchy*.[39] Juan Linz, in his classic *Breakdown of Democratic Regimes*, defines democracy in the following manner:

> Our criteria for democracy may be summarized as follows: legal freedom to formulate and advocate political alternatives with the concomitant rights to free association, free speech, and other basic freedoms of person; free and nonviolent competition among leaders with periodic validation of their claim to rule; inclusion of all effective political offices in the democratic process; and provision for the participation of all members of the political community, whatever their political preferences.[40]

Although contemporary scholars of Aristotle differ in their interpretation of what an Aristotelian social science would be, they agree that Aristotle deserves another examination to determine how his approach and concepts may be helpful to contemporary politics. It is not my intention in this work to craft the one and only true interpretation of Aristotle. This work is an interpretation of Aristotle and of his commentators, with attention focused on the topical subject of violence and democratic stability.

The theory

Instead of legitimacy, this approach provides a notion of purposes of the state. It is theorized that violence attacks the first level of rudimentary purposes of the state, preventing progress towards the second level. In addition, attacks of violence create fear and mistrust. Safety becomes a good in high demand. More and more people react by becoming less active politically and more isolated, further weakening the political community. As violence undermines the purposes of the state and as citizen confidence decreases, more opportunities for groups or individuals to act against the state emerge. And, as citizens become frustrated with the lack of fulfilment of the rudimentary purposes, they are more likely to support attacks against the state.

I theorize that terrorist and state violence is a cause of democratic breakdown (see box). Resulting instability, however, is not automatic. Instead, violence creates opportunities for others to act against the state. Whether or not those opportunities are realized is influenced by other factors. Before attempting to identify the consequences of violence, certain historical and contextual issues must be clarified. Acceptable levels of violence and forms of authority need to be determined to distinguish when levels have become critical and what other models of authority and governance are available. The military must be studied, since most attacks against democracy involve indirect or direct military support and action.

Hypothesis one

Terrorist violence threatens democratic stability by undermining both rudimentary purposes of the state: security and integration. As the purposes of the state are unfulfilled, citizen confidence in the state declines. As citizen confidence decreases, democratic instability increases.

Hypothesis two

State repression and violence also undermine the rudimentary purposes of the state: integration and security. Decreases in citizen confidence should follow a decrease in the fulfilment of the rudimentary purposes. Finally, as citizen confidence in the state decreases, increases in democratic instability should be identifiable.

Acceptable form of authority

First, if the current state, and ultimately constitutional form, cannot fulfil its state purposes, people are likely to search for options to replace that state, and ultimately constitutional form, with some form that is capable of fulfilling its rudimentary purposes. After an erosion of citizen support, the possibility exists for people to attempt to destroy the constitution with popular support.[41] The available choices depend on each country's history and circumstances. If democratic leaders are perceived to be incapable of ending society's ills, then a different type of constitution, such as a military regime or rule by one, could be considered. Previous constitutional forms present themselves as handy, accessible options. Habits and norms inculcated during a previous constitutional form linger. However, it is worth noting that it is difficult to replace military rule if the military leadership is unwilling to relinquish power or if there is not a sub-group in the military that is willing to initiate a coup against the current leadership. It must be acknowledged that the military has the coercive capabilities to resist attempts to remove them from power, unlike civilian leaders who rely upon the military to obey them and who are vulnerable to military intervention.

Level of violence

Second, although it is ideal to have a political association that is free of all violence, many times that is not possible. In most countries, a certain level of violence is expected and almost impossible to eliminate within normal means. Throughout history, some countries have been afflicted more than others and some times are more turbulent than others. The reason behind different acceptable thresholds is not my concern. What appears to be salient is a marked increase in the violence or the reaching of a new plateau, beyond what is expected.

The military

Third, the military is especially important in areas plagued by political instability. Many times it is the only institution with a permanence extending past the last constitutional form. In every case of this study, those who successfully act against the state do so with the blessing of the military.

Security

In Aristotelian terms, both state and terrorist violence can create further instability. Specifically, violence creates fear and a desire for safety. If the state does not successfully respond to violence, fear and a lack of safety undermine the state, and possible ultimately the constitutional form, at the rudimentary level of state purposes. Specifically, in situations with rampant violence, fear is a common emotion. Wrongdoers fear punishment, and law-abiding citizens fear victimization. Fear indicates a lack of safety, or at least a perception of a lack of safety. Fear of becoming a victim and contempt for those in power for their inability to deal with the problem provide potential support for people to attempt to overthrow the state. If a significant portion of the community believes it is the victim of injustice, then additional support for change could develop within the affected group. This can be seen with the emergence of violent groups on the right, in response to the groups on the left. Attitudes of superiority and concern for safety or honour can result in contempt for those in power, and ultimately support for change by the affected group.

Integration

Violence also undermines the second rudimentary purpose of the state: integration. It is expected that violence will encourage mutual suspicion and enmity and discourage people from attempting to achieve common goals, from deliberating in common affairs and from actively engaging in politics. In healthy communities, in the Aristotelian sense, peers deliberate, participate and act to further both individual and common goals. Violence encourages fear, creates intolerance and becomes a hindrance to participation.

The treatment of justice is extremely complex in Aristotle's work. For the purpose of this study I am only interested in the type of justice applicable to exchange-based societies. In exchange-based societies – societies that Aristotle defines as societies that are not bound by a common pursuit of the good – reciprocal justice is used. Reciprocal justice is based on the idea of a proportionate return, somewhat like the idea of 'tit for tat'. Violence can undermine political stability by creating situations of unequal exchange (*NE* 1130a15–

1132b20, pp. 110–16). The victims and those who feel they could be victims desire a response to restore balance to this exchange. But, in a situation where it is not always known who is responsible, it is not easy to restore the reciprocity. As Aristotle states, 'the well-being of every *polis* depends on each of its elements rendering to the others an amount equivalent to what it received from them' (*Pol.*, p. 41). Random acts of violence, such as the detonation of bombs in crowded civilian areas or indiscriminate repression, begin to unravel social ties. State-sponsored repression isolates people, making mutual distrust common. Participation in politics becomes dangerous. The focus on indiscriminate repression and violence is essential to capture the concept of an uneven exchange. If the state uses limited violence targeted only at those who practise it, then it is acting to render an equivalent response. This would not be acting against reciprocal justice. Aristotle's discussion of tyrants provides a way of understanding repressive responses to political dissension, real or feared. A repressive response is one in which the state punishes in an indiscriminate manner. Indiscriminate repression is also an uneven exchange in terms of reciprocal justice. This way of understanding repressive responses helps one to understand how they can undermine democratic stability. The effects of violence then spread. 'An offense against the laws destroys those possible relationships which make common pursuit of the good possible; defective character, while it may also render someone more liable to commit offenses, makes one unable to contribute to the achievement of that good without which the community's common life has no point'.[42] Violence, an uneven exchange in terms of reciprocal justice, can undermine the political association at the very first level of stability. The concept of the purposes of the state helps to illuminate the specific causality behind this. Indiscriminate repression might be effective in eliminating attacks on the state, but it is also very successful in eliminating the conditions necessary for a healthy community.

Both terrorist and state violence erode citizen confidence. If the state unsuccessfully deals with the initial violence, other factions within society start to believe that they could handle the situation better. In many cases, the other faction is the military. Moreover, if the military is handed this role and succeeds, then there is the risk that this will change the composition of the state, and open up the possibility that some may act against the state. Aristotle warns that 'constitutions may also be changed ... as a result of the growth in reputation or power of one of the magistracies, or of some other part of the state' (*Pol.*, p. 213). This problem becomes especially salient during times of internal conflict, in which the military may be called in to suppress a violent insurrection. Success of the military and growth of its prestige increase the possibility of the emergence of some military men to seize power. The rule of the military or one leader can be viewed as a more practicable form of constitution, if the existing form has demonstrated its inability to fulfil its two rudimentary purposes. This implies that it is conceivable that citizens would support the rule of the one or the few over rule by the many. The appeal to people in these cases is not whether or not the military will act democratically but whether or not the military will act effectively to fulfil the purposes of the state. Of course, the hopes of the people can be betrayed. The new constitutional form might turn out to be worse than an ineffective, enfeebled democracy.

Conclusion

The incorporation of certain Aristotelian concepts promises to illuminate the issues of violence and democratic instability in ways that other approaches to violence have not. Terrorist and state violence have effects more insidious and long lasting than previously thought. The Aristotelian approach can explain this by referring to the purposes of the state and to the importance of the political community.

To begin such a study, an assessment of the constitution is necessary. Upon what kind of authority is the state based? What is the end of the constitution, common or private benefit? Is the state well ordered? Aristotle provides two indicators for a well-ordered state: general approval and stability. Stability is identifiable, but what about general approval? Understanding public opinion within the context of the political community and using the purposes of the state as guideline allows a better understanding of seditious violence and its consequences.

How do terrorist and state repressive violence threaten the fulfilment of state purposes? The effects of violence can be understood given Aristotle's account of the purposes of the state. How well a state is achieving its purposes provides a basis for this understanding and appraisal, rather than to what extent the state had achieved legitimacy as it is currently understood in most of social science. The concept of the purposes of the state illuminates the way in which terrorist and state repressive violence challenge the stability of democracy. The two levels of purposes of the state give insight into how an exclusively military and indiscriminate response to terrorist violence can succeed in eliminating terrorism and providing security, but at the expense of harming the integration of the community. Destruction of the first level makes progress towards the second level, that of achieving living well or the good, impossible. In addition, this perspective allows us to understand why many times authoritarian regimes initially enjoy popular support.

The purpose of the inclusion of Aristotle is not to place his thought on a pedestal to be revered as an authority, but to use some of his key concepts as the inspiration for the formulation of an analytical framework and hypotheses to study the consequences of terrorist and state repressive violence. This study is a work of comparative politics, informed by Aristotle's political thought. It is called 'Aristotelian' because of the Aristotelian origin of the disposition of the study and the origin of many of the concepts. The hypotheses that arise in my comparative analysis are capable of empirical testing within the bounds of my three case studies. At least within this limited context, the adequacy of the Aristotelian framework in formulating interesting hypotheses can be empirically confirmed.

The application of the Aristotelian approach to the question of the consequences of terrorist and state repressive violence on democratic stability yields clarity for the cases of Uruguay, Peru and Spain. In Uruguay, the military began assuming more power to respond, in a repressive manner, to the terrorist violence. Ultimately, it took power in 1973. In Peru, Fujimori, in 1992, responded repressively and consolidated control by dissolving Congress and suspending the judicial process, with the blessing of the military. In both these countries, a predominantly repressive response to terrorism was chosen. Subsequently, with their success in suppressing the terrorist violence, came an initial growth of reputation for the military and contempt for the democratic form of rule. Ultimately, this led to democratic breakdown. Spain resisted the repressive response to terrorist violence and successfully consolidated its democracy.

Notes

1 See the works of Stephen Salkever, Martha Nussbaum, Leo Strauss, Bernard Yack and Alasdair MacIntyre, listed in the select bibliography. Unless otherwise noted, all citations from the *Politics* are from Earnest Barker's translation, *Politics* (London: Oxford University Press, 1958); and citations from *Nicomachean Ethics* are from David Ross's translation (New York: Oxford University Press, 1992). The following abbreviations will be used when referring to works by Aristotle: *Pol.* = *Politics*; *NE* = *Nicomachean Ethics*.

2 Most studies of seditious violence, revolution, terrorism and insurgency view violence primarily as a symptom of other problems. Correspondingly, much emphasis is given to the origins of violence. Typically, if terrorist violence is considered to be a strain on democratic stability in its own right, it is considered a threat to legitimacy.

3 Max Weber, 'Politics as a Vocation', in H. H. Gerth and C. Wright Mills (eds), *From Max Weber: Essays in Sociology* (New York: Oxford University Press, 1946), pp. 77–8.

4 Linz, 1978, p. 58.

5 Weber, 1946, p. 79.

6 Robert A. Dahl, *A Preface to Democratic Theory* (Chicago: University of Chicago Press, 1960), 46n.

7 David Easton, *A Systems Analysis of Political Life* (New York: John Wiley and Sons, 1965), pp. 289–310.

8 Linz, 1978, p. 16.

9 Linz, 1978, p. 18.

10 Linz, 1978, p. 20.

11 Jorge Nef and J. Vanderkop, 'The Spiral of Violence: Insurgency and Counter-Insurgency in Peru', *Canadian Journal of Latin American and Caribbean Studies*, Vol. 9, No. 17, 1988, p. 56.

12 Nef and Vanderkop, 1988, p. 59.

13 Stephen Salkever, 'Aristotle's Social Science', *Political Theory*, Vol. 9, No. 4, November 1981, p. 503. It should be noted that Salkever is using 'method' as in the different methods that are associated with specific disciplinary divisions, such as moral philosophy, specific social sciences

and political theory. Some scholars may insist that Aristotle used the method of dialectic in his own studies. Salkever is not referring to Aristotelian dialectic in this statement.

14 Stephen Salkever, *Finding the Mean: Theory and Practice in Aristotelian Political Philosophy* (Princeton: Princeton University Press, 1990), p. 58.

15 Salkever, 1990, p. 7.

16 Salkever, 1990, p. 4.

17 It is not uncommon to find normative references such as Guillermo O'Donnell and Philippe Schmitter's statement that 'political democracy constitutes per se a desirable goal'. In O'Donnell *et al.*, *Transitions from Authoritarian Rule: Tentative Conclusions about Uncertain Democracies* (Baltimore: Johns Hopkins University Press, 1986), p. 3.

18 The *polis*, like an individual, does not automatically progress towards its final end. Aristotle states, 'the *polis* belongs to the class of things that exist by nature, and that man is by nature an animal intended to live in the *polis*' (*Pol.*, p. 5). The *polis* is not strictly natural, in the sense that its capacities will automatically be realized if nothing interferes with the realization, much like an acorn developing into a tree. The *polis* is natural in the sense that it exists in virtue of human beings whose natures require the *polis* to fully develop their capacities.

19 Alasdair MacIntyre, *After Virtue* (Notre Dame: University of Notre Dame Press, 1984), p. 215.

20 Bernard Yack, *The Problems of a Political Animal: Community Justice and Conflict in Aristotelian Political Thought* (Berkeley: University of California Press, 1993), p. 10.

21 Is the *polis* the same as the state? In Barker's translation '*polis*' and 'state' are used interchangeably – see, for example, Aristotle's *Pol.*, p. 92 – but caution should be used not to confuse the modern concept of the state with the ancient Greek *polis*. Among other things, the ancient state was a city-state, unlike the current definition of a state.

22 Stephen Salkever, 'Aristotle's Social Science', *Political Theory*, Vol. 9, No. 4, November 1981, p. 492.

23 Salkever, 1981, p. 492.

24 Leo Strauss, *The City and Man* (Chicago: University of Chicago Press, 1964), p. 6.

25 The component of attempting to achieve the good is inseparable from the Aristotelian approach. It would be inconsistent to call an approach Aristotelian that denied the value component. However, this does not mean that the approach needs to be disregarded by those who disagree with the incorporation of empirically unverifiable aspects. The orientation of the study is directed by the quest for the good; however, an empirical component remains, one that may still be examined by those who disagree with the approach in general.

26 Salkever, 1981, p. 492.

27 Martha Nussbaum, 'Human Functioning and Social Justice: In Defense of Aristotelian Essentialism', *Political Theory*, Vol. 20, No. 2, May 1992, p. 131.

28 Stephen Holmes, 'Aristippus In and Out of Athens', *APSA*, Vol. 73, March 1979, p. 113.

29 Holmes, 1979, p. 114.
30 Holmes, 1979, p. 114.
31 Holmes, 1979, p. 126.
32 James H. Nichols, 'On the Proper Use of Ancient Political Philosophy: A Comment on Stephen Taylor Holmes's "Aristippus In and Out of Athens"', *APSA*, Vol. 73, March 1979, p. 129.
33 Nichols, 1979, p. 130.
34 M. I. Finley, *Politics in the Ancient World* (Cambridge: Cambridge University Press, 1991), p. 101.
35 John R. Wallach, 'Contemporary Aristotelianism', *Political Theory*, Vol. 20 No. 4, November 1992, p. 628.
36 Wallach, 1992, p. 614.
37 Salkever, 1981, p. 503.
38 Russell Fitzgibbon, 'The Pathology of Democracy in Latin America: A Political Scientist's Point of View', *American Political Science Review*, Vol. 44, 1950, p. 118.
39 Robert Dahl, *Polyarchy* (New Haven: Yale University Press, 1971).
40 Linz, 1978, p. 5.
41 Aristotle defines a constitution as 'the organization of the *polis*, in respect of its offices generally, but especially in respect of that particular office which is sovereign in all issues', *Pol.*, p. 110.
42 MacIntyre, 1984, p. 152.

3
A historical overview of Uruguay, Peru and Spain

Introduction

This chapter presents a brief historical overview of the three cases studies. The presentation is organized to provide the necessary background to understand the consequences of state and terrorist violence on democratic stability. Specifically, acceptable forms of authority, historical precedent of violence, prior role of the military, violent groups and economic crisis are explored in the cases of Uruguay, Peru and Spain.

Introduction to Uruguay

Although Uruguay was stable during the first fifty years of the twentieth century, nineteenth-century Uruguay was chaotic. Uruguay's independence was wrested from neighbouring Brazil and Argentina and the colonizing powers with the help of the gaucho chieftain José Gervasio Artigas and the 'group of thirty-three'. After independence in 1828, Uruguay was embroiled in intrigue among Paraguay, Brazil and Argentina. The intrigue culminated in a five year War of the Triple Alliance (Uruguay, Brazil and Argentina) against Paraguay. With the end of the war, Uruguay was able to focus on domestic affairs. During the rest of the century, Uruguay experienced conflict between the Church and state, civilians and military officers, and the two main political parties, the Blancos and the Colorados. The conflict between the two parties continued with intermittent struggles until they agreed to an 1872 pact of cooperation that followed two years of intense conflict. This pact guaranteed the Blancos some of the advantages of office, through control over four of the country's departments. However, the peace between the parties was broken with the Blanco revolt of 1897 which was led by Aparicio Saravia. The revolt turned into a civil war. During the war, José Batlle y Ordóñez was elected president, serving from 1903-7. The civil war ended with the death of Saravia at the battle of Masoller in 1904.

After the end of the civil war in 1904, Uruguay enjoyed a period of peace. Elections were without violence, the military stayed out of politics, the parties shared power and cooperated, and labour relations were good.[1] Claude Williman succeeded Batlle as president (1907–11) and continued with Batlle's basic policies. Batlle was then reelected president and served from 1911 to 1915. Batlle's innovative policies included many reforms, including free primary and secondary education, the eight hour workday, pensions, and the rights to strike, to organize and to vote.[2]

The spirit of participation in the 1872 agreement reemerged in the constitutional form of the *Colegiado*. During part of the twentieth century (1919–33 and 1952–67), the Uruguayan executive was a *Colegiado*, an executive council formed of nine members. The nominal positions of president and vice-president were rotated among the members. Of the nine, six were from the majority party and three from the minority party. Administrative positions were also similarly divided between the two parties.[3]

In 1931, President Gabriel Terra broke the political calm. Terra faced strong opposition from the National Assembly and the *Colegiado* for his Depression era economic and social policies. In 1931, Terra responded by dissolving both bodies, ruling by decree and creating a new constitution. The 1934 constitution eliminated the *Colegiado* and returned Uruguay to a single executive. Martin Weinstein calls the coup a response by heavy-handed politicians, 'driven by personal vendetta and ambition' to an economic crisis. This period has been called a dictatorship, but it must be noted that freedom of speech and most individual rights were respected. There was no torture, murder or political prisoners. Moreover, the military was not involved.[4] Shortly after, in 1935, part of the army attempted a coup, but it failed.[5] In 1950, with the election of Andrés Martínez Trueba, a Colorado Batllista, the country returned to the executive council.

In 1954 scholar Russell Fitzgibbon described Uruguay as a 'staunch little democratic outpost'.[6] The small country was renowned for its high standard of living, democratic commitment, education, social services and stability. Its experience was unique in Latin America. As Charles Gillespie points out, the military was not seething, waiting for democracy to fail. Instead, there was a strong, stable party system, a long history of avoidance of ideological polarization, the sharing of power among the major parties and a high level of political learning.[7] The two traditional parties of Uruguay, the Blancos and the Colorados, are as old as modern Uruguay. The party system is one of the two oldest in Latin America (Chile has the other). Its party system even predates many European party systems.[8] The Colorados are typically urban notables, Italian immigrant descendants, lawyers, intellectuals and businessmen. The Blancos are usually traditional elites and large landowners.[9] In addition to a stable party system, Uruguay had an impressive public education system. From 1877, under the Lorenzo Latorre administration, public education was free, secular and compulsory. During much of the twentieth century, Uruguay had the largest expenditure on education in Latin America. The University of the Republic is free and all may enrol provided they finish secondary school.[10]

In the twentieth century, the Uruguayan military was known for its apolitical attitude, small budget and size, and the strict civilian control over the organization.[11] This attitude of military subservience to civilian authority was communicated as late as 1966, when the Inspector-General of the army, Hugo Tirobochi, stated in response to uncertainty about the lawful change of the 1966 constitution:

> I am firmly disposed to respect and to make respected all electoral acts and pronouncements derived from those acts as the supreme expression of the will of the citizens and sovereign will of our nation recognized by the Constitution of the Republic. Nothing or no one can wrest us from the norms that guide us, we have contracted a commitment of honor and we will honor it to the end, giving anew an example to the world of the pride of the nation and to all of you to make us worthy of your respect and admiration.[12]

However, this attitude of subservience to civilian authority soon dissipated. Only seven years later, the military dissolved the National Assembly and took control.

As Uruguay moved into the 1970s, the country's constitution (in the broad Aristotelian sense) appeared to be less well ordered. To an Aristotelian, a constitution is well ordered if it enjoys general approval and if it is stable. Due to labour disputes, a state of siege (or *medidas prontas de seguridad*) was declared in 1965. The first four invocations of the state of siege were in response to labour disputes. This new strategy for dealing with strife was applied later to the disorder caused by the guerrilla group, the Tupamaros. In the 1970s, general approval of the government sagged and terrorism became more prevalent. The democratic principle of authority became overshadowed by recourse to a tyrannical style of governance with presidential decrees and the limitation of citizen participation. In response, fewer Uruguayans felt attached to the Uruguayan state and more began to view it as the enemy.

The military also began to issue policy demands to the civilian authorities. For example, in April 1972 the military demanded that President Bordaberry and the National Assembly decree a state of internal war with a cancellation of individual liberties, which they did.[13] One month later, in May 1972, the military demonstrated more independence. As the state of internal war was about to expire, the joint command of the armed forces and the police, both generals, demanded that it be extended. Rumours circulated that a coup may have resulted had Bordaberry not agreed. Bordaberry bolstered his support within the National Assembly by forming a coalition with the Blanco Echegoyen faction, a faction whose members fully approved of the state of internal war. This deal, however, fell apart with the pressure from some constitutionalist military officers who preferred a political solution to the problem. The constitutionalist faction of the military was concerned about the demoralization of some troops and the undisciplined behaviour of others; for example, the use of torture and some anti-terrorist groups.[14]

The military also began to defy orders from the civilian authorities. For instance, in April 1972 some in the National Assembly called for public exposure and punishment of those responsible for the most visible abuses in allegations of torture. Six hundred military officers responded with a resolution to prevent public censor.[15] The response demonstrates the increased politicization of the military. The military's growing independence and its defiance of civilian authority grew more serious in the autumn of 1972. In response to strikes, Bordaberry wanted to use the military to crack down on labour. The military refused and pushed for an increase in wages, siding with the workers. The military did not want to be implicated in an economic policy that it did not create.[16]

The military openly defied Bordaberry twice in October 1972. The colonel in charge of a base where four doctors were held prisoner refused to release them, despite court orders to do so. In response, Defence Minister Legnani directly ordered the colonel to release the men, but still the colonel refused. Minister Legnani resigned in frustration. The second incident occurred after an inquiry into an illegal financial dealing. The military had led an investigation that resulted in the arrest of over one hundred people. Senior officers and Bordaberry agreed that the findings and further inquiry should be turned over to a special committee. The investigating officers, many of them captains and their superior colonels, refused to hand over the documents or terminate their investigation.[17]

What had been known as Uruguayan exceptionalism came to an end in 1973, and with it one of the most stable and prosperous democracies in the Western hemisphere. Military intervention occurred in what has become known as the 'slow coup'. The military assumed power in two steps. In February 1973, branches of the military revolted. On 7 February Bordaberry had replaced Dr Armando Malet with retired General Francese as Minister of Defence. The commanders-in-chief refused to recognize Francese's authority. Bordaberry wanted a new minister of defence to break up the 'commands of the more independent minded military branches'. Instead, he faced a rebellion.[18] On 8 February, Minister of Defence Francese informed Bordaberry that the army and air force were to be confined to the barracks, as a precaution against disturbances. After the meeting, Bordaberry ordered the commander of the marines to confine marine troops to the barracks as well. The general command of the army, General Hugo Chiappe Posse, and air force commander General José Peréz announced their reasons for ignoring the orders of Francese. Shortly after, they demanded his resignation. Army General Esteban Cristi directed the army to take control of some television stations. Francese offered his resignation to Bordaberry, who refused to accept it. That night, Bordaberry appealed to the public over radio and television to defend the institutions. Less than a hundred people showed up to protest the military defiance.

The army continued to occupy more and more radio and television stations. On 9 February, it occupied the old city of Montevideo, isolating the other ministers and most of the judges, and assumed combat positions near the canal. The marines proclaimed themselves loyal to the president. Late on the ninth and early the tenth, communiqués four and seven were released by the rebel forces. Communiqué four demanded the elimination of unemployment, subversion and calls for land reform. Communiqué seven called for the preservation of sovereignty and security, the pursuit of development and modernization, and further benefits for the citizens, such as better health care. The document denied any partisan affiliation.[19] On Sunday 11 February communiqué five was released. It announced control of the country by the police, the army and the air force. The commanders of the army and air force demanded that Bordaberry remove the loyal commander of the marines. Bordaberry complied. On Monday the 12th, Bordaberry announced that he was essentially in agreement with the goals of the armed forces. The next day he met with the military commanders at the Boiso Lanza air force base. The meeting concluded with a pact among them and a new Defence Minister, Dr Walter Ravenna, was announced. Bordaberry, on 14 February, stated:

> The armed forces, who have repeatedly shown testimony of a great spirit, of a great capacity, could not stay away from national life, because of its anxieties and pains, its hopes and sacrifices ... Today I can announce that following this thought, the executive will create the appropriate institutional ways for the participation of the armed forces in the national task, within the framework of law and the constitution.[20]

The Boiso Lanza agreement between Bordaberry and the armed forces aimed to restructure foreign relations, public spending, development plans, subversion, services and organizations, social security, the relationship between the state and the military, the internal organization of the military, jail management and unemployment. Part of this agreement was the establishment of the Consejo de Seguridad Nacional (COSENA). COSENA was composed of the president, his main ministers, and the commanders of the army, air force and navy. Other members serve in a consulting capacity. COSENA had an 'advisory' role for the president to help integrate all the aims of the state and military. In addition, a permanent secretary was established, ESMACO, to advise the president and to help integrate the armed forces into the decision-making process. The military claimed that it was indispensable that they participate in this task. The Junta de Comandantes en Jefe was also formed.[21]

These concessions did not permanently appease the military. In mid June, the military attempted to rescind the immunity of two senators it suspected of subversive activity, Senator Vasconcellos and Senator Erro. The National Assembly refused the military's requests.[22] Undaunted, the military continued to pursue leftist politicians. However, this time the head of the largest Blanco faction, Senator Dardo Ortiz, defended Erro and joined with the Frente Amplio against the military and attempted to refute the accusations. Ortiz claimed that the evidence against Erro was unreliable since it had been obtained by torture of a Tupamaro.[23] Finally, Generals Gregorio Alvarez and Esteban Cristi commanded the dissolution of the National Assembly on 27 June 1973.[24] Bordaberry nominally remained president. During the subsequent authoritarian rule, Uruguay had the highest number of political prisoners per capita in the world. What happened to the 'Switzerland of the South'?

Introduction to Peru

Peru is an ethnically diverse, poor country with a history of severe instability. Peru gained independence in 1821 with the help of legendary Generals Bolivar and San Martin. Shortly thereafter, the country became embroiled in competition among chieftains for the presidency with the result of many coups and counter-coups. This early instability continued into the twentieth century. Historically, Peru has excluded many popular groups from political participation. The Alianza Popular Revolucionaria Americana (APRA), the historically populist party, established in 1930 by Haya de la Torre, was illegal until the government of Odria (1948–56). The Communist Party was legal only under the governments of Bustamante y Rivero (1945–48) and General Velasco Alvarado (1968–75) before 1980.[25] The military intervened often to protect the 'political and economic prerogatives of the upper class against the growing challenge from the popular classes'.[26] From 1930–68, the military ruled for eighteen of the thirty-eight years.

During the 1960s, Peru was also faced with guerrilla movements. In 1963, a group organized by Hugo Blanco operated in Cuzco. The police quickly quashed the movement. Later, in 1965, two new groups, the Movement of the Revolutionary Left (MIR) and the National Liberation Army (ELP) were formed. MIR was founded by Luis de la Puente. ELP was founded by Héctor Béjar. MIR was active in the departments of Junín, Cuzco and Piura. ELP was active in Ayacucho. The tenure of these groups was short lived. Within six months both groups had been destroyed by a massive army counterinsurgency campaign. In spite of the presence of these groups, guerrilla activity was not pervasive at the time.[27]

The aim of military interventions changed in 1968 with the Revolutionary Government of the Armed Forces led by General Velasco. In 1968, a group of officers became aware of the 'peasant problem' (i.e. inequitable land distribution, exclusion from politics and poverty) through their education in the Centro de Estudios Militares del Peru (centre of high military studies). According to Victor Villanueva, 'since the end objectives of the institution was to produce officers to direct and preserve the national defense, it was also necessary to prepare these officers for intervention in the general politics of the state where the roots of the problem of national defense were to be found'.[28] Military officers perceived military intervention to be a legitimate act of patriotism.

Velasco's land reform reduced the land disparity. Before his reform of the early 1970s, 69 per cent of privately held Peruvian land was composed of plots larger than 2,471 acres (1,000 hectares). After his reform, only 42 per cent of privately held land was composed of plots larger than 1,000 hectares.[29] Velasco's agrarian reform in 1973 created SINAMOS, or the National System of Support for Social

Mobilization, a national organization created to transform expectations of reform into reality by creating a network of state-supported organizations.[30]

The military controlled Peru from 1968 until 1980. However, the military regime faced difficulties as protest increased. The revolutionary regime was unable to absorb the politically activated populations. Moreover, the national deficit reached high levels. For example, in 1974 45 per cent of the budget was financed by debt. In 1975, General Morales Bermúdez replaced General Velasco and slowed the pace of reform. Slowly, Morales Bermúdez began to liberalize the regime because of growing discord within the military, domestic opposition and pressure from international banks. The military negotiated with APRA and eventually allowed elections to create a constitutional assembly. The transition to democracy was completed in 1980.[31]

Peru's experience with democratic governance has been limited. Although the constitution has been formally democratic, in the modern sense, until 1980 illiterates could not vote and many Peruvians rate the democratic leaders as authoritarian. Integration to the political community is also limited because of the extreme heterogeneity of the society and historical racism against indigenous peoples. Extreme income disparity also limits integration. Raúl González, a sociologist from the Centro de Estudios y Promoción del Desarrollo, believes:

> No teníamos un Estado legítimo. En este país el Estado no llegaba a muchas zonas; y en las zonas donde llegaba, llegaba mal. Para utilizar una metáfora, este país no terminó nunca de ser colonizado y es país porque existen unos límites que nos dicen que somos un pais. Pero este país nunca fue una nación, sino muchas naciones juntas.[32]

Corruption and the treatment of indigenous people have fed a cynicism and the belief that the state exists for the benefit of the few, as opposed to the common good. Indeed, many Peruvians have rejected the notion that Peru is a real democracy. For example, Rodrigo Montoya charges that none of the democratically elected leaders have really governed democratically.[33]

The newly democratic state faced many challenges. In spite of attempts at reform, Peru's most stubborn problems remained. Approximately 70 per cent of the people were impoverished. In 1990, life expectancy was less than fifty years. One out of every eight infants dies in the first year. Eighty per cent of Peruvian homes lack running water, sewage and electricity.[34] In addition to these fundamental problems, Peru also faces the challenges of severe economic crisis and rampant terrorist violence.

Was the Peruvian constitution well ordered, in Aristotelian terms? The two indicators of general approval and stability suggest that it was not. Approval ratings of the democratically elected Presidents Belaúnde and García had sunk to extremely low levels by the end of their terms. The approval rating of Congress and the political parties hit a nadir before the coup. Only President Fujimori and the armed forces maintained support before the *autogolpe*. Moreover, during the twelve years of Peruvian democracy, rumours of possible coups were not uncommon. Coup rumours circulated at the end of Belaúnde's term and during numerous occasions after García's first year as president, particularly during the last year of his presidency.[35]

As President, Fujimori did not alienate the military. According to Enrique Obando, this can be done in one of two ways: by being a member of APRA or by being grossly ineffective. Fujimori is neither.[36] However, Fujimori did have to act to consolidate support in the military. He had difficulties with certain sectors of the military at the beginning of his term. For instance, in the 1990 election there were rumours that the navy would conduct a coup if Fujimori were elected. The navy at the time supported Vargas Llosa. After Fujimori's election, he promptly retired the navy's commander-in-chief.[37]

Whereas the military had become frustrated with a lack of state support to help them comply with their mandate to end the terrorist violence, Fujimori expanded their powers. Fujimori reorganized the system of national defence, expanding the military role. A 1991 law also allowed military involvement in areas not under a state of emergency, for example in prisons and universities. Within some universities, the military established permanent bases. The Universities of San Marcos, Huamanga and La Cantuta were notorious for Sendero activities.[38] Many students welcomed the increased presence. Senator Enrique Bernales stated: 'Yo no soy estudiante, pero pregunto, ¿qué estará pasando en las universidades para que los estudiantes sean los primeros en pedir que los tanques, las tanquetas y los soldados no salgan de ellas'?[39] The intent was to reassert control over universities in which Sendero had established a presence. Fujimori also expanded military power by granting the military protection from charges of human rights violations.[40]

Fujimori acted to consolidate his control over the military and to curry their support. He forcibly retired officers who opposed him, like the previous navy commander-in-chief, and promoted those who supported him. Top-ranking military officers who disagreed with Fujimori's policies were rooted out and retired. He involved the military in the decision-making process of creating a strategy and granted them new powers and protections. Fujimori tightened his control of the armed forces with the help of his 'intelligence czar', Vladimiro Montesinos.[41] Montesinos keeps files on all of Peru's influential military officers.[42] In 1991, Fujimori and Montesinos pushed for and received a law that changed the procedure for the selection of new commanders-in-chief. Previously, selection had been made according to rank. Under Fujimori's reform, the president could pick his commanders from the top-ranking officers and forcibly retire officers at will. He used his powers to craft a more loyal service. 'Following Montesino's advice, he used the new process to remove high-ranking officers linked to the "institutionalist" current within the military, which advocated maintaining the military's independence and avoiding its political manipulation'.[43] With his new powers, Fujimori retired the officers who posed a threat to him and promoted those who supported him.[44] By September 1990, President Fujimori seemed to have consolidated support from the military. On this date, he received two important military decorations: the Peruvian Cross of Military Merit and the Francisco Bolognese Military Order in the grade of grand cross.[45]

By following a policy of eliminating officers he suspected of being disloyal, Fujimori succeeded in creating a military much more loyal to him than before, thus guaranteeing military support for his coup. Fujimori committed his *autogolpe*, or self-coup, on 5 April 1992, one day before Congress was set to reconvene. All three branches of the military supported Fujimori and his coup.[46] He also received the backing of the business community, in spite of the risk of jeopardizing international economic assistance in the short term.[47] On 6 April 1992, the armed forces joint command released communiqué number one. It stated that the armed forces 'have unanimously agreed to give their most decided support and endorsement to the decision adopted on this date by the president of the republic and supreme commander of the armed forces and Peruvian national police'.[48]

Fujimori explained his reasons for his April 1992 *autogolpe*. 'What I have tried to apply are some pragmatic strategies and measures to gain good control of the country by confronting the three social diseases of corruption, inefficiency of the state and *Sendero Luminoso* violence'.[49] Fujimori stated his goals of amending the constitution, restoring morality to the judicial branch, modernizing public administration, pacifying the country, struggling with the drug problem, rooting out corruption, promoting a market economy, reorganizing the educational system, decentralizing the state and increasing the standard of living. Fujimori stated that he was acting to rebuild democracy, not to destroy it. 'What I have been trying to do is reconstruct this weakened democracy so that it can stand up to the challenge of terrorist violence and to other challenges that may come in the future'.[50] According to Fujimori, he was acting to create a legal and effective democracy instead of what he characterized as a demagogic, obstructionist, inefficient and corrupt system.[51]

Introduction to Spain

Spain's democratic tradition is as old as it is turbulent. This tradition began in 1812 with the drafting of the first constitution. It reemerged in the First Federal Republic of 1873–74 and again in the Second Spanish Republic of 1931–36.[52] In spite of this democratic tradition, nineteenth-century Spain was violent and unstable. Between 1814 and 1886, there were forty-six military uprisings. Between 1923 and 1936 there were another eight.[53] Stanley Payne characterizes nineteenth-century Spain as a 'search for a viable structure of government'.[54] Factions of the Spanish army were involved in almost every constitutional change. The character of these *pronunciamientos* began to change in the early twentieth century. David Bell characterizes the earlier *pronunciamientos* as 'mostly liberal; that is anti-absolutist and in favor of a constitution'.[55] Moreover, none of the *pronunciamientos* led to a military dictatorship until Miguel Primo de Rivera in 1923. Primo de Rivera ruled until stepping down in 1930.

After Primo's rule ended, the Second Republic was proclaimed on 14 April 1931. The Second Republic was established 'through an unusual electoral and civil process that involved remarkably little disturbance'.[56] This calm beginning did not last. Shortly after the municipal elections in which the conservative and monarchist parties were defeated, King Alfonso XIII left Spain with the statement that 'we are out of fashion'.[57] The 1931 constitution was progressive, including provisions for universal suffrage, accommodation of some regional calls for autonomy, expanded state education and a rejection of the special status of the Catholic Church within the state.[58] However, the process that created the 1931 constitution was not cooperative. The leftist coalition that dominated the process made little effort to appease those with other views.[59] Recovering from its electoral defeat in 1931, the right won the general elections in 1933. Two and a half years later, the socialists, communists and leftist republicans created the Popular Front and regained control in the general elections of 16 February 1936.

In general, the period was marked by severe polarization and violence. During the short experiment of the Spanish Second Republic, more than two thousand lives were lost. Both the right and left resorted to violence, although Payne notes that most of the violence can be attributed to the left.[60] By 1934, the political situation had become polarized and the number of deaths increased dramatically.[61] There were 2,045 political killings from 1931–36, with a peak of 1,525 in 1934. According to Payne, the last straw was the assassination of rightist leader Calvo Sotelo. Socialist activists and some leftist police were implicated.[62]

Many in the military and on the right could not tolerate the rule of the Popular Front. A military revolt was planned. The Nationalist military uprising of 17–18 July 1936, against the Republic, was conceived as a *pronunciamiento*. Instead, it escalated into a bloody three year civil war against the Republican forces.[63] At the last minute, General Franco[64] joined the Nationalist rebellion. The civil war was bloody and chaotic. The civil war ended in victory for the Nationalist forces and Franco was later chosen as commander-in-chief and head of the Nationalist state by his fellow Nationalist generals.[65]

General Franco's rule imposed stability on to Spain. Although brutal in the beginning, it matured into a benign authoritarianism that most Spaniards came to accept, waiting for Franco's death for an opportunity for change. His rule was supported by the Catholic Church, the Falange and the military. Most Spaniards did not want to return to the bloody chaos that characterized Spain before and during the civil war. After Franco, a 'broad consensus soon developed in a large part of political opinion, and ... all major and nearly all minor political groups have firmly rejected any tactic of violence'.[66] However, not everyone subscribed to the ideal of consensus. Violence was chosen as a means by some groups. For example, Euzkadi ta Askatasuna (ETA), a Basque separatist group, assassinated Franco's most trusted Prime Minister, Admiral Carrero Blanco, by blowing up his car after mass on 20 December 1972.

On 20 November 1975, Francisco Franco, Generalisimo of Spain, died. Two days later, Juan Carlos was sworn in as King of Spain. Juan Carlos, grandson of King Alfonso XIII, was named Franco's heir in 1969 and had been raised under Franco's supervision since his youth. Franco's plans for an orderly succession appeared to be working. The King reappointed Franco's Prime Minister Carlos Arias Navarro. However, the King became frustrated with Arias and asked him to resign, which he did on 1 July 1976.[67] The King then chose Adolfo Suárez as Prime Minister,[68] a selection which disappointed those who wished for reform. They were not disappointed for long.

The King and Suárez moved quickly. Less than one year after Franco's death, the Cortés passed the Law of Political Reform in November 1976, formally ending the dictatorship and creating a new elected bicameral legislature. A referendum was called in December to approve or disapprove of the Law of Political Reform. Seventy-eight per cent of the Spanish people affirmed the new law. The old Francoist Cortés approved the reform by 425 votes to 59 with 13 abstentions. In February 1977, some political parties were legalized; in March free trade unions were allowed and the right to strike was granted.[69] In April 1977, the Communist Party was legalized.[70] Two months later, in June 1977, the first democratic elections since 1936 were held. One month later, the new Cortés opened.

Unlike the previous round of elections, moderation and peace characterized this election. Participation was high. Almost 80 per cent of the electorate voted. Two parties, the Union of the Democratic Centre (UCD) and the Spanish Socialist Worker Party (PSOE), emerged as the dominant parties. The UCD had been formed by a group of smaller centre parties in May 1977, just in time for the elections.[71] The UCD candidate was Adolfo Suárez. Many of the UCD members were former Francoist officials. The other major party, the PSOE, had defined itself as Marxist in its twenty-seventh party congress in 1977. However, before the first general elections, party leader Felipe González publicly retracted the statement of Marxist orientation.[72] In general, the political atmosphere was marked by cooperation. Most of the parties, even the Spanish Communist Party (PCE), supported the monarchy.[73] The conservative Popular Alliance (AP) responded to its electoral defeat by revamping its image from the 'ogre of the country' to a more moderate law-and-order party that supported national unity.[74]

In addition to the main national parties, some Basque and Catalan regional parties won seats in the Cortés. In the Basque country, the Basque Nationalist Party (PNV) had much support. The party, which was founded in 1895, emerged from the Franco period with immediate electoral success in the Basque country. Another party, Herri Batasuna, or People's Unity (HB), the political wing of ETA, did not do well enough to gain seats in the Cortés. In Catalonia in 1977, the Catalan Democratic Union and the Catalan Democratic Convergence Party were the main regional parties. These two parties joined to create the Catalan Convergence and Union in 1979.[75]

The transition process, characterized by many as a process of pacts and agreements, has been called one of a negotiated break with the former regime.[76] In addition to the elections, the year 1977 was marked by two grand events: the Moncloa pacts and the establishment of a new constitution. Representatives of all the major political parties and the Prime Minister met in the Moncloa palace in October to craft an economic policy to respond to the economic crisis. The agreement among parties of the right, left and centre specified reforms within the existing market economy: wage ceilings, moderated union demands, a continued state intervention and a tightening of the money supply. The pact dealt with potentially divisive issues in a conciliatory manner. Drafts of the constitution were completed in September 1977 and voted on by the Cortés on 31 October 1978. Eighty-seven per cent of the Spanish people ratified the constitution in a 6 December 1978 referendum.[77]

The nascent Spanish democracy was vastly different from the Spanish state under Franco. Although Franco's state was supported, or at least tolerated, by many Spaniards, by the end of his rule many people were ready for change. The desire for democracy was strong even before Franco's death. The new constitution appeared to be a good match for the Spaniards. It was based on a democratic principle of authority, with universal suffrage. The new constitution was well supported both formally in the plebiscite and informally in public opinion polls. The Spanish democracy enjoyed basic stability. However, dissension among the military and some violent groups existed.

In Spain, the newly democratic state faced an already politicized military. For forty years, the conservative, nationalist ideals of Franco were supported by the military and taught in the military academies. Historically, the military was not uniformly conservative. However, the civil war of 1936–39 forced a split within the Spanish armed forces. After the civil war, many of the leftist or liberal officers were simply eliminated by the victorious Nationalist forces. Approximately five thousand of them were either shot, imprisoned or exiled. They were replaced by nearly eleven thousand Falangist and Carlist men who were admitted into the army as *'alféreces provisionales'*, or provisional lieutenants. Many of them remained in the military after the end of the war. The military became more conservative as it was incorporated into the new Franco state.[78] This trend towards conservatism continued even though many later officers did not fight in the civil war, because they were educated by those who did. They were taught that democracy was vulnerable to the chaos that erupted during the Second Republic. This military ideology resisted change because of the isolation and the distinct education of the military families.[79]

The transition to democracy troubled many in the military. Promises made to the military during the transition were broken. Not only was the Communist Party legalized in April 1977, but regional autonomy was granted.[80] In addition, certain aspects of military reform irked top officers. Reformist General Manuel Gutiérrez Mellado became Minister of Defence. He supported the creation of a civilian minister of defence, abolished the social investigation brigade, and reformed the military code of justice and the military ordinances. He changed the promotions and retirement procedures, replacing seniority with merit in promotions above the rank of major.[81] In February 1977, JUJEM, the joint chiefs of staff, was formed. JUJEM was subordinated to the minister of defence.[82] The military had lost many prerogatives. In an effort to appease the military, it was given one new role. In the new constitution, the military was granted the duty of defending the constitutional order.[83]

Suárez's UCD government had to act carefully with regard to reform. Many in the military had to be placated and reassured, especially in light of the challenges facing the new democracy. In the words of Carolyn Boyd and James Boyden,

> Terrorism, particularly but not exclusively in the Basque Provinces, made it difficult for the UCD to pursue further reforms with vigor. On the one hand, the party dared not offend officers already outraged by the frequent assaults on military personnel; on the other hand, the right wing of the party opposed the rapid and generous resolution of the autonomy question that might have undercut the terrorists.[84]

The new ruling coalition had to balance the pressures for reform with the reality of awakening sedition on the right or in the military. In addition, divisions within the military were weakening its power.[85]

There were many conspiracies against the new democracy within the military. The first major rumble of trouble erupted in 1977. Rumours of a military coup followed the legalization of the Communist Party.[86] Months later some of this discontent developed further. In September 1977, the 'Játiva conspiracy' was formed. General Milans de Bosch and former ministers of the army and navy gathered to celebrate a wedding. At this gathering, they discussed what is widely believed to have been a conspiracy against the new democracy. Sentiments for a military intervention remained high. In May 1978, the new chief of the High General Staff, Lt General Tomás de Liniers, publicly endorsed the legitimacy of the Argentine military dictatorship. A few months later, in November 1978, another conspiracy, 'Operation Galaxia', was discovered. Captain Ricardo Sáenz de Ynestrillas and Lieutenant Colonel Antonio Tejero Molina planned to seize Prime Minister Suárez and his cabinet while the King and Queen were in Mexico and other high officials were out of Madrid. The plot was foiled.[87] In the same month, General Atarés Peña was arrested for an act of indiscipline during the reunion of Minister of Defence Gutiérrez with military leaders.[88] In January 1979, after the assassination of Madrid's military governor, General Ortín, more rumbles of trouble surfaced. At the general's funeral, high-ranking officers paraded the coffin through the streets chanting 'power to the military'.[89]

In spite of the progress in elections, regional autonomy and the new constitution, not all sectors were pleased with the reform. On 20 October 1979, the ultra-conservative publication *El Alcázar* published a letter by General Santiago appealing for a military intervention.[90] In January 1981, another article appeared in *El Alcázar* stating, 'the constitution as it stands does not work. It causes the nation to be ungovernable'. The same publication warned on 8 February 1981 that Spain had reached the point of no return.[91] This followed the resignation, on 29 January 1981, of Prime Minister Suárez. He commented that he did not want 'the democratic system to be, once again, a parenthesis in Spain's history'.[92]

King Juan Carlos acted to rein in the potentially seditious military. The King was disturbed by the continued antidemocratic sentiments of the military. For example, King Juan Carlos called for discipline on the celebration of Pascua Military, an annual holiday:

> A soldier, an army that has lost discipline, cannot be saved. He is no longer a soldier, it is no longer an army. The spectacle of the undisciplined, disrespectful attitudes born in passing emotions which unleash passions that fully disregard the poise demanded of every military, is frankly shameful.[93]

The King's words were influential. He maintained good relations with all branches of the armed forces. Moreover, many officers, although reluctant to support the democracy, recognized the King as Franco's successor, and were more likely to support him.

The military discontent culminated in the attempted coup of 23 February 1981, when the entire Cortés was held hostage. After the resignation of Suárez, the Cortés had failed to approve the UCD's new candidate for Prime Minister, Calvo Sotelo. On the day of the second vote, Colonel Tejero and a company of civil guardsmen invaded and held the Cortés captive. Simultaneously, General Milans de Bosch, in Valencia, rebelled and declared a state of emergency. The King and army Chief of Staff, General Gabeiras, contacted all eleven captains-general and important commanders. Of the eleven, only one, Milans de Bosch, had openly rebelled. Only three, however, were unequivocally loyal to democracy. After successfully communicating to the military that the King would not support the attempted coup, Juan Carlos made a brief announcement on television: 'The Crown, symbol of the unity and permanence of the Fatherland, cannot in any way tolerate actions or attitudes of persons which attempt to interrupt by force the democratic process which the Constitution approved by the Spanish people determined in referendum'.[94] That night, thousands of Madrileños demonstrated in favour of the constitution. They encountered a small demonstration of pro-coup activists, who chanted, 'Tejero shoot them all'.[95] Eventually, Tejero was convinced to surrender. In addition to the King's support for the democracy, a strong majority of Spaniards continued to support the democracy. In the following days, pro-democracy marches and demonstrations filled the streets of major cities. The renegade military officers lacked support from Spanish citizens, the King and the politicians. In spite of a politicized military and a terrorist threat, Spain did not succumb to a return to authoritarianism. How did the new, fragile Spanish democracy survive?

Terrorist groups

In all three cases, the countries were challenged by well-organized and active guerrilla groups. In these cases, the terrorist groups challenged the appropriateness of the existing form of constitution, advocating change. The actions of these groups were sufficiently influential that the citizens in the countries viewed the violence and disorder as a significant challenge to the state. In addition, the presence of the groups was cited as a reason for coups and attempted coups in all three countries.

Uruguayan terrorist groups

> *O bailan todos or no baila nadie*
> (Everyone dances, or no one does)
> Tupamaro slogan painted on a raided nightclub

The most dominant and powerful terrorist group in Uruguay was the Tupamaros, or MLN-T. The Tupamaros was established by a small group of intellectuals led by Raúl Sendic, Julio Marenales and Jorge Maner Lluveras in 1962.[96] In 1967, the Tupamaros released a bulletin announcing that they had placed themselves outside of the law.[97] A Tupamaro message, broadcast on Radio Sarandi on 15 May 1969, charged that the state benefited only an oligarchy. 'Anyone is a Tupamaro if he does not merely make demands but disobeys the laws, decrees and ordinances made by an oligarchy to their interests'.[98] Until 1969, the group concentrated most of its energy on organization and ideology.[99] The Tupamaros organized their action around four principles: the exhaustion of peaceful means for change; the necessity of armed struggle; action to promote unity; and defining politics by action, not ideology. Their actions were astutely designed to increase mass support.[100] The Tupamaros were a very effective group. They were self-sufficient, effective and astutely handled public relations. In an interview in 1970, Tupamaro Urbano explained the Tupamaro position:

> if there isn't a homeland for all, there won't be one for anyone. At present, the actions the dictatorship is now undertaking are in furtherance and defense of an established order. That order means hundreds of workers fired, hundreds of teachers without a job, the government meddling in educational matters, the senior high school closed, and a steady worsening of poverty – the result of the drastic freezing of wages and a far from drastic freezing of the prices of staple goods.[101]

The Tupamaros did not believe the state to be a representative of the common interest. They viewed the state as a representative of purely private interests.

The Tupamaros were completely of Uruguayan origin. Arturo Porzencanski, in *Uruguay's Tupamaros*, stated, 'no evidence has been found that the Tupamaros ever received either money or arms from other countries or from social movements abroad'.[102] The Tupamaros were self-sufficient. They funded and stocked their organization through robberies, kidnapping and theft. The Tupamaros explained their tactics:

> We do not go outside the country to seek financing for our revolution, but seize from our enemies the money to mount the necessary revolutionary campaign ... We must make a clear distinction between what the bourgeoisie's property and the worker's property really is. The former is, beyond a doubt, the outcome of workers' exploitation; the latter is a result of work and individual effort. Therefore, the bourgeoisie's property is our natural fountain of resources and we have the right to expropriate it without compensation.[103]

Some of the more infamous Tupamaro actions include the theft of six million dollars-worth of jewellery from a branch of the Banco de la República on 12 November 1970 and the theft of four hundred thousand dollars-worth of gold from the Mailhos family mansion on 4 April 1970. The Tupamaros stole four hundred and fifty arms and a supply of ammunition from an army garrison on 29 May 1970. In addition, the Tupamaros raided industry to obtain chemical and explosive supplies. These strategies were very effective in maintaining and supplying the Tupamaro organization.

The Tupamaros were also effective in spreading their propaganda to the Uruguayan public. Before strict censorship was imposed on the reporting of terrorist actions, the Tupamaros regularly sent communiqués to the media. Later they used other strategies of communication, including the distribution of leaflets and posters. They even temporarily took over businesses to give speeches to their captive audiences. Radio stations were also stormed, including the Tupamaro interruption of a football match on 15 May 1969 and the takeover of a radio station that provided background music for all Montevidean department stores on 24 May 1969.

The Tupamaros also used kidnapping of state officials, foreign diplomats, businessmen and landowners for both political and financial gain. Notable kidnapping victims included U. Pereyra Reverbel, head of the state electricity and telephone corporations; G. Pellegrini Giampietro, a banker; D. Pereyra Manellie, a judge involved in the pro-secution of Tupamaros; Dan Mitrione, an Agency for International Development expert and adviser to the Uruguayan police force; Geoffrey Jackson, Ambassador of the United Kingdom to Uruguay; and H. G. Ruíz, President of the Uruguayan House of Representatives. The kidnap victims were held for up to eighteen months in the 'people's jail' of the Tupamaros. Only Mitrione was killed.[104]

The Tupamaros cultivated an image of an alternative state, a state which did what the real state should have been doing, but was unable to. After the March kidnapping of prosecutor-general Dr Guidi Berro Oribe, they tried him in a mock trial for his irregularities in office. Tape recordings of the trial were released to the press, all in a deliberate attempt to appear as a viable alternative to the existing state. Once released, Oribe stated that the Tupamaros seemed to be extremely well-briefed lawyers, perhaps with access to secret files. His comments led to concern that many state officials or functionaries were secretly Tupamaros.[105]

The Tupamaros also succeeded in discrediting the Uruguayan police. Not only did the police have difficulty in arresting Tupamaros, but if they did manage to arrest some they were usually released shortly thereafter or escaped from prison. There were four mass prison breaks. Through the use of police disguises, 13 women were freed from the women's prison on 9 March 1970. Later, on 20 July 1971, 38 more were freed from the same prison. At the maximum security prison Punta Carretas, 106 were freed on 6 September 1971 and 15 on 12 April 1972. In addition to bribing and intimidating prison workers, the Tupamaros constructed tunnels to escape.[106] The Tupamaros freed approximately 180 of their own members from prison.

Although almost all Uruguayans disagreed with Tupamaro tactics, many agreed with their aims. For example, in April 1971 Alberto Heber, a possible Blanco presidential candidate, announced that the state should negotiate with the Tupamaros on questions of national policy.[107] Others, including senators and representatives, agreed with some of the Tupamaro policy proposals, although they disagreed with their means of achieving them.

Although the Tupamaros were the best organized and most influential terrorist group in Uruguay, there were also other groups. Other small leftist, urban guerrilla groups included: FARO the Fuerzas Armadas Revolucionarios, and OPR-33, the Organización Popular Treinta y Tres. In addition, there were other groups, such as the Frente Revolucionario de Trabajadores; the Movimiento XXII de Diciembre (a splinter group of the Tupamaros); La Guerrilla; Grupo de Acción Unificadora (the alleged illegal counterpart to its legal faction of the Frente Amplio); the Comandos de Autodefensa del Pueblo (formed of medical students); the student groups 'Alcides' and 'Franco'; Agrupaciones Rojas; and the Frente Armado Popular.[108]

Peruvian terrorist groups

The party has a thousand eyes and a thousand ears.
Sendero slogan

The Communist Party of Peru in the Shining Path of José Carlos Mariátegui (PCP-SL) is a splinter group of the Peruvian Communist Party.[109] It was founded by Abimael Guzmán in 1970, on his return from a year in China. The split was caused by the Communist Party's rejection of the clandestine organization and armed struggle that Guzmán advocated.[110] The new Sendero organization was urban and based in Ayacucho, according to Deborah Poole and Gerardo Renique: 'The principal early base of popular support for the PCP-SL was a broad-based urban defense front which held large, public and extremely visible assemblies and marches in the Plaza de Armas of Ayacucho'.[111] In 1980, Sendero's first acts were the hanging of dogs in Lima and ballot burning in Chuschi.[112] Bombings of private companies and public buildings started later in the year. In 1982, Sendero sent a message to Lima by blowing up five high-tension electrical towers, leaving the city without power or lights.[113] Sendero had a grand plan for its actions: to turn the backwards areas into bases of revolutionary support, to attack the state and revisionist elements, to develop guerrilla war and spread violence, to expand the bases of support, to seize the cities and to cause the collapse of the state.[114]

At first, Sendero was not considered a threat. State officials thought Senderistas were common criminals or a product of an international subversive movement. For example, Peruvian President Belaúnde stated: 'it was a conspiracy against Peru within a universal strategy ... This is totally demonstrated with the discovered archives in democratic Germany and now with some notices in Moscow: the support that was given to the subversive movements for the exportation of revolutions'.[115] The left thought Sendero was part of a CIA plot to discredit them. The right believed it was merely a covert arm of the left.[116] However, Sendero was not a covert arm of the legal left, was not a group of common criminals and was not a product of international subversion. It was a violent group of domestic origin that viewed everyone who did not cooperate with them as an enemy, whether on the right, the left or without affiliation.

In addition to Sendero, another group, the Movimiento Revolucionario Tupac Amaro (MRTA) emerged. The MRTA started its violent actions in January 1984, with an assassination and an attack on a police station, in the Villa El Salvador area of Lima. The MRTA viewed itself as a movement modelled in the style of Ché Guevara and pursued a socialist revolution.[117] It publicly revealed its name in July 1984. Later, it spread beyond Lima to the province of Paucartambo in the department of Cusco. Soon after, the MRTA suffered a blow in Paucartambo on 26 November 1984, when the police captured a dozen activists and confiscated rifles, uniforms and ammunition. The MRTA responded with the kidnapping of a reporter and her cameraman to document charges of torture and mistreatment of suspected terrorists in Cusco.[118] The MRTA's presence continued to grow in Lima. Then, in October 1987, it began activity in the department of San Martín.

The MRTA attempted to gain a reputation of being the 'good guerrillas'. For example, when they took command of the city of Juanjuí, in the department of San Martín, they announced that, 'they don't come to sentence any public official or local person to death, but on the contrary, they come to have a frank discussion with the local population'.[119] At the beginning of García's term as president, the MRTA temporarily suspended actions against the state, in the hope that García would comply with his campaign promises. Two MRTA leaders, Luis Varesse and Víctor Polay Campos, demanded that the state break with the International Monetary

Fund (IMF) and declare a moratorium on debt payments, raise the minimum wage to reflect the cost of living, declare an amnesty for all political prisoners and end the 'dirty war'.[120]

Spanish terrorist groups

Euskadi ala hil

(Basque country or death)[121]

ETA originated in a small group of students who created a journal called *Ekin* (*Action*) in 1953–54.[122] In 1959, some Basque youths, frustrated with a lack of action, formed ETA. Although the history of ETA as an organization is complex, significant splits can be identified. In the early 1970s, ETA split into two groups: ETA-militar (ETA-m) and ETA-político-militar (ETA-pm). ETA-m is more committed to violence whereas ETA-pm is more inclined to negotiate.[123] Another group, Euskao Iraultzale Alderdia, the Basque Revolutionary Party, was formed as a splinter group of ETA, although it is committed to nonviolent action.[124] Two political groups emerged from within the rebel organizations. ETA-pm, which disbanded in 1981, transformed itself into the Euskadiko Eskerra (EE). ETA-m, which remains an active violent group, is represented by HB.[125]

ETA's main goals are self-determination and the reunification of Euskadi. Euskadi was the name given to the desired Basque state by Basque nationalist and founder of the PNV, Sabino de Arana, in 1865. The claimed region consists of the Spanish northwestern provinces of Alava, Navarra, Guipuzcoa and Vizcaya, in addition to three French southern provinces.[126] An ETA 1964 pamphlet called 'Insurrection in the Basque Country' compared the Basque country to a Spanish colony, as in Franz Fanon's *Wretched of the Earth*, and called for rebellion against the Spanish national state.[127] HB proposed a five-point programme which called for Basque independence, the inclusion of Navarre into the region, amnesty for all political prisoners, improved working conditions and the withdrawal of Spanish security forces.[128]

ETA continued its activities even after the democratization of Spain, calling the new democracy a 'pseudo-democracy'. ETA activists do not view the democracy as legitimate. The referendum of the constitution was not well supported in the Basque country by either the citizens or the main parties. The PNV recommended abstention and both HB and EE advocated a 'no' vote in the referendum. In the final tally, only 45 per cent of eligible voters participated, compared with 68 per cent nationally. Of those who voted, only 31 per cent approved of the constitution and 24 per cent rejected it.[129] ETA has been responsible for the vast majority of terrorist violence since the return to democracy.

Initially, ETA targeted symbols of the Franco regime and later the Spanish nation state, including the military, the police and the civil guard. ETA assassinated Franco's Prime Minister, Admiral Carrero Blanco, by detonating eighty kilos of explosives under his car after he returned from mass in 1972.[130] Later, the targets included Basque industrialists and banks.[131] ETA continued to target prominent military officers. From 1976 to 1986, ETA killed thirteen generals. Many times, the assassination of high-ranking officials coincided with symbolic occasions. For instance, on 21 July 1978, the day the constitution was approved by the Cortés, ETA killed an army general. ETA assassinated Madrid's military governor, General Ortín, in January 1979, shortly after the constitutional referendum. On the eve of Armed Forces Day on 25 May 1979, ETA assassinated the army chief of personnel and two colonels.[132] Another symbolic assassination occurred in November 1982, when ETA assassinated the commander of the elite Brunete military division, General Lago Roman. The assassination took place five days before the new socialist Prime Minister, Felipe Gonzalez, was to assume power.[133]

The activities of ETA have been varied and extensive. It has mainly operated in the Basque area and in the cities of Barcelona, Madrid and Zaragosa.[134] In addition to bombings and armed attacks, ETA has conducted kidnappings and extortion.[135] One estimate cites that ETA has been responsible for over five hundred assassinations, the maiming of over a thousand people, more than sixty kidnappings, and countless armed assaults, robberies and bombings. Its extortion, presented to the 'contributors' as 'revolutionary taxation', has been substantial, with thousands of Basque industrialists and professionals being 'taxed'.[136]

Who participates in ETA? Most ETA members are young, single men. Instead of being full-time rebels, most hold regular jobs and participate in ETA as a part-time activity.[137] One study conducted by R. P. Clark characterized ETA members as typically young men between the ages of 25 and 30. He found that most were of working-class or lower-middle-class origin with either one or two native Basque parents.[138] In addition to these part-time rebels, there are full-time leaders, whose identities, but not whereabouts, are usually known to the police.[139]

In the mid 1980s two things began to change the environment in which ETA operated. First, both the PNV and EE were less supportive of the violence used by ETA. In fact, the parties condemned ETA violence. In addition, the Spanish state began to gain the cooperation of French authorities in combating ETA, both within Spain and in France.[140]

In addition to ETA, two other groups practised violent dissension. The Grupos de Resistencia Antifascista Primero de Octubre (Antifascist Resistance Groups of the First of October; GRAPO), emerged on 1 October 1975, after a shooting in which four Madrid police officers were killed.[141] The aim of GRAPO was to create a revolutionary vanguard.[142] GRAPO never had more than thirty militants as members.[143] A few attacks attributed to GRAPO occurred in 1990.[144] The other small group was the Frente Revolucionario Antifascista y Patriótico. This emerged in the 1970s from the Communist Party. It aimed to overthrow Franco's Spain and establish a people's republic instead.[145]

In addition, Basques were targeted by other violent groups. These groups became active in 1975. For example, the Batallón Vasco-Español killed five, wounded thirty-four and kidnapped two people between 1975 and 1977. There were also urban riots started by groups of rightists who attacked Basques. These groups, called *incontrolados*, committed at least twenty attacks, killing one and wounding twenty-four, in the second half of 1977.[146]

Economic crisis

In addition to the presence of terrorist groups, each country was faced with a severe economic crisis preceding the coups or attempted coups. Moreover, citizens in each country

Table 3.1 Uruguay: economic indicators, 1965–73

Year	CPI changes (%)	GDP growth rate (%)	Unemployment (%)
1965	56.6	1	NA
1966	72.7	4	NA
1967	89.1	−4	NA
1968	125.0	1	8.4
1969	20.9	6	NA
1970	16.4	5	7.5
1971	23.9	−1	7.6
1972	76.5	−4	7.7
1973	96.8	1	8.9

Note: CPI = consumer price index.

Sources: *Statistical Abstract of Latin America*, Vol. 20, p. 332; IMF.

recognized the economic problems as severe. The importance of economic problems is not discounted. However, economic crisis needs to be evaluated in a broader context and not viewed as a monocausal explanation for democratic breakdown.

Uruguayan economic crisis

After the Korean War, in which Uruguay benefited from the increased demand for its woollen goods, the Uruguayan economy began a long period of decline (table 3.1). This crisis was manifested in a decline in wages, in the standard of living, in the value of exports and in the rate of investment. Some structural factors and the lack of innovation were to blame for the economic crisis. Henry Finch states:

> whether the form of technology incorporated was that of pedigree livestock, or wire fencing, or (most obviously) the refrigeration [of meat], the requirement on Uruguayan producers was to react to the availability of the new technology, rather than to modify or adapt it to local conditions. The pattern of production was thus broadly speaking imitative of practice elsewhere.[147]

According to Finch, this lack of innovation stalled further modernization. In addition, the level of investment was very low.[148] The ratio of gross fixed investment to GDP in Uruguay declined from a high of 16 per cent in 1955–59 to only 9.9 per cent in 1970–74. By 1970, investment in Uruguay was at half the rate of the rest of Latin America, with its rate of 20.3 per cent. As investment slowed, growth and productivity stagnated. Moreover, most of the domestic industry was costly and inefficient. The rural exporting sector, based on cattle and sheep products, with its lack of investment and primitive husbandry techniques, was forced to subsidize the industrial sector with the transfer of some of its potential earnings.[149]

Economically, Uruguay struggled in the 1960s and 1970s. The value of exports, in fixed dollars, fell 40 per cent from 1951 to 1961. Complicating the situation, the costs of imported goods and raw materials increased.[150] From 1956 to 1972 GNP fell 12 per cent.[151] In the 1960s, Uruguay had the worst growth rate in the Western hemisphere except for Haiti.[152] Wages declined while prices rose. For example, real wages for public employees fell 40 per cent from 1957–67.[153] After 1968, wages rebounded 16 per cent to 1971. However, 1972 and 1973 saw a significant decrease down to 94 per cent of 1968 wages. Inflation started increasing after 1970.[154]

Compounding these problems was the inability of the state to pare back social spending that it could no longer afford. Henry Finch, in 'The Burden of the Past', stated that, 'the country has grown accustomed to a relatively high standard of living in spite of a weak long-run economic performance, and deterioration in recent decades in that performance has found the country incapable of responding positively'.[155] Particularly unsustainable was the number of pensions, guaranteed by the state, in the country. The number of pensioners rapidly increased by 44.9 per cent from 1958 to 1962.[156] By 1969 there were 213,000 people employed in the public administration sector with 346,000 pensioners, up from 66,400 public administration employees and 196,700 pensioners in 1955.[157] This situation became more difficult considering that Uruguay had an ageing population and that many of the youngest and most highly skilled workers had emigrated.

This problem of the increase in pensioners can be traced to the pact of *chinchulín*, or the pork barrel pact, of 1931. This pact established that all *entes autónomos* (state-run businesses) would be controlled by a seventeen-member board of directors. Employment was determined by a proportion of Blanco or Colorado employees that reflected the latest election results. The resources of the state and public sector became a source of political patronage. *Chinchulín* was incorporated into the 1952 constitution. Finch blames this agreement for the consequence of a 'state apparatus and public sector whose dominant contemporary characteristic is not its extent, but its grotesque financial – but more importantly, functional – inefficiency'.[158] By 1965, the *entes autónomos* paid 40 per cent of all salaries.[159] The political parties did not dare to reform this sector, since it was a lucrative source of patronage.

Peruvian economic crisis

In addition to the fierce guerrilla threat, Peru was faced with a severe and prolonged economic crisis. Peru had declining growth from 1975–92, with a 50 per cent decline between 1988 and 1992. Concurrently with the decline in growth, Peru suffered from hyperinflation. For example, Peru experienced hyperinflation of 7,650 per cent in 1991. Although the economic situation was still bad at the time of the coup in 1992, the economy had stabilized almost two years before Fujimori's *autogolpe*. Fujimori generally succeeded in controlling inflation and in resuming growth. The cost of this stabilization was an increase in poverty, however.

Alan García, who was elected president in 1985, attempted to implement a new type of economic policy, he called 'heterodox'. In his plan, he increased subsidies to business and labour, installed price controls and used selective state intervention.[160] The unorthodox stabilization plan also included reduced foreign debt payments.

> The theory behind this reactivation program was that a sharp initial stimulus to consumer demand, particularly to that of small-scale farming peasants and shanty town entrepreneurs, would provide an impetus for growth while the modern mining and manufacturing sectors would produce import substitutes and exports, generating foreign exchange with which to recommence servicing the debt later.[161]

Initially, it seemed to work. In 1986 and 1987 GNP rose 8 per cent a year, wages increased and inflation was acceptable. However, the heterodox experiment ended when García tried to nationalize the banks. He accused the bankers of refusing to reinvest the profits.[162] In addition, the policy provoked inflation and huge deficits. For example, in September

1988 the deficit was 16 per cent of GDP and reserves fell 60 per cent to $500,000,000 in one year.[163] As early as the end of 1987, García's chief financial adviser, Carbonetto, acknowledged that the state would have to cut spending. However, García delayed any implementation until September 1988, 'one of the most disastrous delays or pieces of political cowardice in Peruvian economic history'.[164] García's popularity suffered due to the dismal economic performance. On 24 October 1988, three out of four people rejected the president and two out of three blamed García, his government and his party for the economic crisis, which was viewed as the worst of the twentieth century.[165]

The effects of García's eventual adjustment plan were harsh. The plan resulted in a 114 per cent increase in the consumer price index. In 1987–90, wages fell 75 per cent and production decreased 20 per cent.[166] In 1980 wages were half of what they had been in 1970. By 1989, real wages were half of what they had been in 1980. This drop followed an equally perilous drop.[167] The worst performance of the Peruvian economy occurred in 1989 and 1990. The economic crisis may have been a strong reason why APRA fared so poorly in the 1990 presidential elections. President Fujimori, after 1990, appeared to have stabilized the economy. The same trend can be seen in the national average of the price index and in strike data. In both cases, the worst occurred in the late 1980s, with a stabilization beginning in 1990 (table 3.2). The severe inflation was brought under control by Fujimori. Labour conflicts also became less common under Fujimori. The peak of labour troubles was in 1988, with a record number of man hours lost and the highest number of strikes since 1981. The years 1991 and 1992 demonstrated an improvement in labour relations, instead of building to a crisis point in April 1992 (table 3.2).

When Fujimori became president in 1990, he inherited a significant difficulty with the international financial community. No payments on the national debt had been made since late 1987.[168] Fujimori removed controls on foreign currency and introduced new bank laws in 1992.[169] Fujimori's economic plan, called the 'Fujishock', involved eliminating subsidies, reducing tariffs, reforming the tax structure and slashing state employment.[170] The result was a dramatic decline in inflation, from 7,650 per cent in 1990

Table 3.2 Peru: economic indicators, 1980–92

Year	Inflation rate (%)	GDP growth rate (%)	Unemployment (%)	Number of strikes	Man hours lost (millions)
1980	60.8	5	7.0	739	2.2
1981	72.7	5	6.8	871	19.9
1982	72.9	−1	7.0	809	22.7
1983	125.1	−12	9.2	643	20.3
1984	111.5	6	10.9	509	13.8
1985	158.3	2	NA	579	12.2
1986	62.9	10	5.3	648	16.9
1987	114.5	8	4.8	720	9.1
1988	1722.3	−9	NA	814	38.2
1989	2775.3	−12	7.9	667	15.2
1990	7649.6	−4	NA	613	15.1
1991	139.2	3	5.8	315	8.9
1992	56.7	−2	9.4	219	2.3

Sources: INEI, Statistical Abstract of Latin America Volume 23, 1984. Edited by James W. Wilke (Los Angeles: UCLA Latin American Center Publications), p. 415, Volume 25, 1986, p. 251; Interamerican Development Bank; IMF.

to 139 per cent in 1991, to 55 per cent in 1992 and to 27 per cent in 1993. However, the cost of the control of inflation was a doubling of poverty. For instance, in 1990 the middle class experienced a decline of 53 per cent in consumption. Social spending in 1990 was 30 per cent lower than in 1988.[171] Fujimori also normalized relations with the international financial community. In 1991, Peru negotiated a $2.1 billion financial package with the IMF and World Bank.[172] In spite of the painful adjustment, Fujimori remained popular, with 50 per cent or above approval rating through his coup and until 1997.[173]

Spanish economic crisis

Vivíamos mejor contra Franco
(We had it better against Franco)[174]

In addition to terrorist troubles, newly democratic Spain faced an economic crisis. Under Franco, Spain had achieved spectacular growth in the 1960s, which has since come to be known as the 'economic miracle'. Franco's earlier economic policy had been based around state intervention and autarky. After a cabinet shuffle in 1957, the new cabinet, distinguished by the dominance of Opus Dei technocrats, marked the transition to a market economy and integration into the Western capitalist economy. The boom continued with expansions of industry, the service sector and tourism. However, after the oil crisis of 1974, Spain began a period of economic difficulties. Growth was negative in 1975 and an anaemic 2 per cent in 1976, with rising unemployment, inflation and a fiscal deficit.[175] Unemployment had reached 10 per cent by 1979 and continued to climb. Correspondingly, the people faced high cost of living increases. Economic growth was sluggish and negative at times. After 1979, the increases in the cost of living stabilized. The unemployment rate, however, continued to increase from under 5 per cent at the time of Franco's death to 15 per cent in 1981 (table 3.3). In addition to rising unemployment levels, Spain's economic growth slowed, due much in part to the oil crisis.[176] GNP growth was negative in 1979 and in 1981. During the year of the attempted coup, Spain faced negative growth and high unemployment. Approximately one out of six Spaniards was unemployed. However, concern about poor economic performance did not convince many citizens to support the attempted coup in 1981.

Table 3.3 Spain: economic indicators, 1974–86

Year	CPI increase (%)	Unemployment (%)	GDP growth (%)	Number of strikes
1974	15.4	2.9	6	NA
1975	17	4.7	4	NA
1976	17.7	5.3	3.3	NA
1977	24.6	6.3	3	NA
1978	19.8	8.2	1.4	1356
1979	15.7	10.1	−0.1	1789
1980	15.5	12.6	1.2	1669
1981	14.6	15.4	−0.2	2556
1982	14.4	17.1	1.2	2582
1983	12	NA	1.8	2714
1984	11	18.4	1.8	3019
1985	9	19.5	2.3	2026
1986	9	21.2	3.3	2239

Sources: Joseph Harrison, *The Spanish Economy in the Twentieth Century* (London: Croom Helm, 1983), pp. 175–7; José Feliz Tezanos, Ramón Cotarelo and Andrés De Blas Guerrero, *La Transición Democrática Española* (Madrid: Editorial Sistema, 1989), p. 145; Omar Encarnacion, 'Social Concertation in Democratic and Market Transactions: Comparative Lessons from Spain', *Comparative Political Studies*, Vol. 30, No. 4, August 1997, p. 387; IMF.

Conclusion

Uruguay, Peru and Spain experienced similar national problems but under different circumstances and with different outcomes. Uruguay had a long history of cooperation between its main political parties. Its democracy had been stable for decades. Its military did not have a history of intervention. However, starting in the 1960s, the country was confronted with the emergence of terrorist groups. The Tupamaros, the group responsible for most of the violence, started their violent actions in a time when the country was already challenged by a severe and long-lasting economic crisis. Uruguay's seemingly well-established democracy was overthrown by the military with public support. Peru had a history of severe state instability and a strong tradition of military intervention. When the country was returned to democratic rule in 1980, the new democratic constitution was faced with a severe economic crisis and the emergence of terrorist groups. Peru's third elected president since the return to democracy in 1980, Alberto Fujimori, dissolved Congress in April 1992 with the support of the military forcibly to reform the state. Spain's new democracy was created after the death of General Franco. The military in the new democracy was considered a standing threat to the new state. While consolidating its democracy, Spain faced the challenges of the continuing activities of terrorist groups, an economic slowdown and frequent rumours of possible military coups. In spite of the problems, Spain's democracy survived.

Each historical outcome is surprising in its own way. It is shocking that Uruguayan citizens, with their well-developed democratic traditions, did not protest the military intervention. Although the Peruvian instability may not be surprising due to the history of extreme instability, the strong support Fujimori received puzzles many analysts. Spain, with the threat of Franco's military, economic crisis and violent terrorist groups, managed to maintain the support of its citizens, in spite of the problems and threats of a military coup. Why did the Uruguayans and Peruvians encourage and support coups and changes in constitutional form while the Spaniards rejected them? Chapters 4–6 explain these questions and present the evidence to test the hypotheses.

Notes

1. Ruth Berins Collier and David Collier, *Shaping the Political Arena* (Princeton: Princeton University Press, 1991), p. 271.
2. Paolo Mieres, 'Elecciones de 1989 en Uruguay', *Sintesis*, Vol. 13, April–June 1991, p. 211.
3. Edy Kaufman, *Uruguay in Transition: From Civilian to Military Rule* (New Brunswick: Transaction Books, 1979), pp. 21–2.
4. Weinstein, 1988, p. 22.
5. William Davis, *Warnings from the Far South: Democracy versus Dictatorship in Uruguay, Argentina, and Chile* (Westport: Praeger, 1995), pp. 24–5.
6. Fitzgibbon, 1954, p. vii.
7. Charles Guy Gillespie, *Negotiating Democracy: Politicians and Generals in Uruguay* (Cambridge: Cambridge University Press, 1991), p. 247.
8. Scott Mainwaring, 'Political Parties and Democratization in Brazil and the Southern Cone', *Comparative Politics*, Vol. 21 No. 1, October 1988, p. 108.
9. Gillespie, 1991, p. 18.
10. Weinstein, 1988, pp. 11–12.
11. Originally, the Uruguayan military was linked to the rule of the Colorado Party. Although the military was created to be opposed to military participation in politics, it was solidly Colorado. 'The armed forces were in fact not autonomous and linked as they were to a specific political family, did not regard themselves as situated above parties, with the right to set themselves up as the supreme authority and guarantor of the national interest'. L. Bethel (ed.), *The Cambridge History of Latin America*, Vol. VI: *Latin America Since 1930* (Cambridge: Cambridge University Press, 1994), pp. 261–2.
12. Sergio Jellinek and Luis Ledesma, *Uruguay: Del Consenso Democratico a la Militarismo Estatal*, Part 2, Paper No. 19, November 1979 (Stockholm: Institute of Latin American Studies, 1979), p. 30.
13. Arturo Porzencanski, *Uruguay's Tupamaros* (New York: Praeger, 1973), pp. 61–8.
14. *Generals and Tupamaros: The Struggle for Power in Uruguay 1969–1973* (London: Latin American Review of Books, 1974), pp. 43–6.
15. Porzencanski 1973, p. 69.
16. *Generals and Tupamaros*, p. 53.
17. *Generals and Tupamaros*, p. 55.
18. Servicio Paz y Justicia: Uruguay, *Nunca Más: Human Rights Violations, 1972–1985* (Philadelphia: Temple University Press, 1986), p. 35.
19. Republica Oriental del Uruguay Junta de Comandantes en Jefe, Tomo 2, *El Proceso Politico* (Montevideo: Las Fuerzas Armadas al Pueblo Oriental, 1978), pp. 87–91.
20. Kaufman, 1979, p. 33.
21. Republica Oriental del Uruguay Junta de Comandantes en Jefe, Tomo 2, pp. 100–18.

22 Senator Vasconcellos criticized the military, stating that 'a new political party has emerged; it consists of a group of generals'. Vasconcellos also criticized the state for torture and murder of prisoners. The military charged that Senator Erro was the leader of the Tupamaros. *Generals and Tupamaros*, pp. 68–70.

23 Kaufman, 1979, p. 29.

24 Kaufman, 1979, p. 59.

25 Eugenio Chang-Rodríguez, *Opciones Políticas Peruanas* (Trujillo, Peru: Editorial Normas Legales S. A., 1987), p. 217.

26 Victor Villanueva, 'Peru's New Military Professionalism: The Failure of the Technocratic Approach', in Peter Gorman (ed.), *Post Revolutionary Peru* (Boulder: Westview Press, 1982), pp. 157–9.

27 Collier and Collier, 1991, p. 717. See also Francois Bourricaud's *Power and Society in Contemporary Peru* (New York: Praeger Press, 1970); Julio Cotler's *Clases, estado, y nación en el Perú* (Lima: Instituto de Estudios Peruanso, 1978); Richard Gott's *Guerrilla Movements in Latin America* (New York: Anchor Books, 1972); and David Werlich's *Peru: A Short History* (Carbondale: Southern Illinois University Press, 1978).

28 Villanueva, 1982, p. 159.

29 Klaren, 1990, p. 29.

30 Later SINAMOS lost its influence. Peasants' organizations, as opposed to state-led organizations, became more influential. For example, the Peruvian Peasant Confederation in the 1970s became the main avenue for the pursuit of land reform. D. Poole, *Unruly Order: Violence, Power and Cultural Identity in the High Provinces of Southern Peru* (Boulder: Westview Press, 1994), pp. 225–7.

31 Susan C. Bourque and Kay B. Warren, 'Democracy Without Peace: The Cultural Politics of Terror in Peru', *Latin American Research Review*, Vol. 24, No. 1, 1989, p. 9. See also Bethel (ed.), 1994, pp. 451–91.

32 'We don't have a legitimate state. In this country, the state doesn't reach many zones, and in the zones where it is present, it is bad. To use a metaphor, this country never ceased to be colonized and it is a country because there are borders and we say we are a country. But this country never was a nation, but many nations together'. My translation. Raúl González, 'Un País Violentado', in Rolando Forgues (ed.), *Perú: entre el desafío de la violencia y el sueño de lo posible* (Lima: Minerva, 1993), p. 127.

33 Adrianzén, 1993, p. 105.

34 Americas Watch, *Peru Under Fire* (New Haven: Yale University Press, 1992), pp. 196, 2.

35 David Werlich, 'Peru: The Shadow of the Shining Path', *Current History*, Vol. 83, February 1984, p. 78.

36 Enrique Obando, 'The Power of Peru's Armed Forces', in Joseph Tulchin and Gary Bland (eds), *Peru in Crisis: Dictatorship or Democracy* (Boulder, Lynne Rienner, 1994), p. 115.

37 Enrique Obando, 'Fujimori and the Military: A Marriage of Convenience', *NACLA*, Vol. XXX, No. 1, July/August 1996, p. 31.

38 María Escalante and Ana María Vidal, *Los Decretos de la Guerra* (Lima: IDS Minilibros, 1993), p. 28.

39 'I am not a student, but I wonder what is happening in the universities to make the students be the first to ask for the tanks and the soldiers'. My translation. Enrique Bernales, 'Con la soga al cuello', in Forgues (ed.), 1993, p. 39.
40 Obando, 1996, p. 36.
41 Montesinos has a dubious background. He was discharged from the army due to allegations that he had passed classified information to the USA. In addition, in his civilian career as a lawyer, he defended drug traffickers in some high-profile cases. Obando, 1996, p. 33.
42 Daniel W. Fitz-Simons, 'Sendero Luminoso: Case Study in Insurgency', *Parameters*, Vol. 23, No. 2, Summer 1993, p. 70.
43 Obando, 1996, p. 32.
44 In spite of Fujimori's efforts at consolidating control over the military, two dissident groups formed within the military after the *autogolpe*. COMACA (Commanders, Majors and Captains) and 'Sleeping Lion' were groups opposed to Fujimori's manipulation of the military, including promotions and retirements, the low budget of the military and the low salaries. Plans for a coup against Fujimori were frustrated after the capture of Sendero leader Guzmán. Two months later, the groups were infiltrated by the Servicio de Inteligencia Nacional (SIN), resulting in the arrests of forty officers. See Obando, 1996, p. 33.
45 US Foreign Broadcast Information Service (FBIS) LAT 90 174, p. 42.
46 Tulchin and Bland (eds), 1994, p. 7.
47 Maxwell Cameron, *Democracy and Authoritarianism in Peru* (New York: St. Martin's Press, 1995), p. 145.
48 FBIS LAT 92 066, p. 31.
49 'Saving the State in Peru', *New Perspectives Quarterly*, Autumn 1993, p. 10.
50 'Saving the State in Peru', p. 12.
51 FBIS LAT 92 066, pp. 28–31.
52 Michael T. Newton with Peter J. Donaghy, *Institutions of Modern Spain* (Cambridge: Cambridge University Press, 1997), p. 1.
53 Miguel Angel Aguilar, 'The Spanish Military: Force for Stability or Insecurity?', in Joyce Lasky Shub and Raymond Carr (eds), *Spain: Studies in Political Security* (New York: Praeger, 1985), p. 49.
54 Stanley Payne, *Politics and the Military in Modern Spain* (Stanford: Stanford University Press, 1967), p. 1.
55 Pedro Vilanova, 'Spain: The Army and the Transition', in David Bell (ed.), *Democratic Politics in Spain* (New York: St. Martin's Press, 1983), pp. 148–9.
56 Stanley Payne, 'Political Violence During the Spanish Second Republic', *Journal of Contemporary History*, Vol. 25, 1990, p. 271.
57 Raymond Carr and Juan Pablo Fusi, *Spain: Dictatorship to Democracy* (London: Unwin Hyman, 1981), p. 2.
58 Newton with Donaghy, 1997, p. 1.
59 Andrea Bonime-Blanc, *Spain's Transition to Democracy* (Boulder: Westview Press, 1986), p. 124.
60 Payne, 1990, p. 269.

61 For an excellent analysis of the violence of this time, see Luis Romero's *Por qué y cómo mataron a Calvo Sotelo* (Barcelona: Planeta, 1982) and Ramiro Cibrián's 'Violencia política y crisis democrática: España en 1936', *Revista de Estudios Políticos*, 6 No. 6, November–December 1978, pp. 81–115.
62 Payne, 1990, p. 284.
63 Juan Linz, 'Church and State in Spain from the Civil War to the Return of Democracy', *Daedalus*, Vol. 120, No. 2, Summer 1991, p. 161.
64 In 1926, Franco became the youngest brigadier-general in Europe because of his service in the pacification of Morocco.
65 Carr and Fusi, 1981, p. 6.
66 Payne, 1990, p. 285.
67 E. Ramón Arango, *Spain: Democracy Regained* (Boulder: Westview Press, 1995), pp. 102–3.
68 However, it should be noted that the King could not directly choose a replacement prime minister. The King and Fernández Miranda, his former tutor, presiding chief of the Cortés and President of the Council of the Realm, arranged that Adolfo Suárez would be among the three names presented to the King as possible candidates from the Council of the Realm.
69 Arango, 1995, pp. 102–11.
70 Carolyn Boyd and James Boyden, 'Armed Forces and the Transition to Democracy in Spain', in Thomas D. Lancaster and Gary Prevost (eds), *Politics and Change in Spain* (New York: Praeger, 1985), p. 102.
71 Donald Share, *The Making of Spanish Democracy* (New York: Westport, 1986), p. 156.
72 Juliá Santos, 'The Ideological Conversion of the Leaders of the PSOE', in Frances Lannon and Paul Preston (eds), *Elites and Power in Twentieth-Century Spain: Essays in Honour of Sir Raymond Carr* (Oxford: Clarendon Press, 1990), p. 270.
73 Carr and Fusi, 1981, p. 233.
74 Richard Gunther, Giancomo Sani and Goldie Shabad, *Spain After Franco* (Berkeley: University of California Press, 1988), pp. 170–5.
75 Chris Ross, 'Nationalism and Party Competition in the Basque Country and Catalonia', *West European Politics*, Vol. 19 No. 3, July 1996, pp. 489–91.
76 José Maravall, *The Transition to Democracy in Spain* (London: St. Martin's Press, 1982), p. 11.
77 Arango, 1995, pp. 116–20.
78 Christopher Abel and Nissa Torrents (eds), *Spain: Conditional Democracy* (New York: St. Martin's Press, 1984), p. 165.
79 Julio Buaquets, Miguel Angel Aguilar and Ignacio Puche, *El Golpe* (Barcelona: Editorial Ariel, 1981), pp. 14–15.
80 Share, 1986, p. 170.
81 Arango, 1995, p. 137.
82 Boyd and Boyden, 1985, p. 103.
83 Aguilar, 1985, p. 53.

84 Boyd and Boyden, 1985, p. 108.
85 Some scholars, such as Felipe Aguero, argue that the potential power of the military was squandered by internal divisions. For example, in May 1979 the high army council was unable to decide on a chief of staff. Instead, Defence Minister Gutiérrez Mellado appointed someone. See Aguero, *Soldiers, Civilians, and Democracy* (Baltimore: Johns Hoplcins University Press, 1995), p. 140.
86 Boyd and Boyden, 1985, p. 103.
87 Boyd and Boyden, 1985, p. 109.
88 Paloma Roma Marugan, 'Cronología', in José Féliz Tezanos, Ramón Cotarelo and Andrés de Blas Guerrero (eds), *La Transición Democrática Española* (Madrid: Editiorial Sistema, 1989), p. 893.
89 Aguero, 1995, p. 141.
90 Abel and Torrents, 1984, p. 181.
91 Abel and Torrents, 1984, p. 35.
92 Share, 1986, p. 168.
93 Aguero, 1995, p. 146.
94 Aguero, 1995, p. 165.
95 Anatoly Krasikov, *From Dictatorship to Democracy: Spanish Reportage* (Oxford: Pergamon Press, 1984), p. 162.
96 *Generals and Tupamaros*, p. ii.
97 Marvin Alisky, *Latin American Media: Guidance and Censorship* (Ames: Iowa State University, 1981), p. 196.
98 Alain Labrousse, *The Tupamaros: Urban Guerrillas in Uruguay* (Harmondsworth: Penguin Books, 1970), p. 149.
99 Porzencanski, 1973, p. 52.
100 *Generals and Tupamaros*, p. ii.
101 Leopoldo Madruga, 'Interview with Urbano', in James Kohl and John Litt (eds), *Urban Guerrilla Warfare in Latin America* (Cambridge: MIT Press, 1974), p. 275.
102 Porzencanski, 1973, p. 41.
103 Porzencanski, 1973, p. 40.
104 Porzencanski, 1973, pp. 40–4.
105 *Generals and Tupamaros*, pp. 22–3.
106 Porzencanski, 1973, p. 41.
107 *Generals and Tupamaros*, p. 23.
108 Republica Oriental del Uruguay Junta de Comandantes en Jefe, Tomo 1. *La Subversion* (Montevideo: Las Fuerzas Armadas al Pueblo Oriental, 1977), pp. 349–53.
109 See José Carbs Mariátegui, *Seven Interpretive Essays on Peruvian Reality*, translated by Marjory Urquidi (Austin: University of Texas Press, 1971). Mariátegui founded the Socialist Party of Peru in 1928 and broke with APRA. He believed in a national, democratic revolution as a step towards socialism. See Julio Cotler, 'Democracy and National Integration in Peru', in Cynthia McClintock and Abraham F. Lowenthal (eds), *The Peruvian Experiment Reconsidered* (Princeton: Princeton University Press, 1983), p. 8.

110 Deborah Poole and Gerardo Renique, 'The New Chroniclers of Peru: US Scholars and their "Shining Path" of Peasant Revolution', *Bulletin of Latin American Research*, Vol. 10, No. 2, 1991, p. 141.

111 Poole and Renique, 1991, p. 157.

112 Palmer, 1986, p. 129.

113 *Equis X* (Lima), 'El gran apagon de los luminosos', No. 305, 23 August 1982, p. 8.

114 *Caretas*, 20 September 1982. The early literature on Sendero has been severely criticized by Deborah Poole and Gerardo Renique, 1991.

115 Fernando Belaunde Terry, 'El Destino Reparador', in Forgues (ed.), 1993, p. 28.

116 Philip Mauceri, 'Military Politics and Counter-Insurgency in Peru', *Journal of Interamerican Studies and World Affairs*, Vol. 33, No. 4, Winter 1991, p. 90. See also Gustavo Ellenbogen Gorritti, *Sendero. Historia de la guerra milenaria en el Perú* (Lima: Editorial APOYO, 1990).

117 Yehude Simon Munaro, *Estado y Guerrillas en el Peru de los '80* (Lima: EES Asociación Instituto de los Estudios Estratégicos y Sociales, 1988), p. 120.

118 Munaro, 1988, pp. 108–10.

119 Raúl González, 'MRTA: La Historia Desconocida', *QueHacer*, March/April 1988, p. 32.

120 González, 1988, p. 40.

121 William Douglass and Joseba Zulaika, 'On the Interpretation of Terrorist Violence', *Comparative Studies in Society and History*, Vol. 32, No. 2, April 1990, p. 252.

122 Stanley Payne, *Besque Nationalism* (Reno: University of Nevada Press, 1975), p. 242.

123 Arango, 1995, p. 225.

124 For a complete history of the numerous splits and conflicts within ETA, see Cyrus Zirakzadeh, *A Rebellious People: Basques, Protests and Politics* (Reno: University of Nevada Press, 1991).

125 Douglass and Zulaika, 1990, p. 246.

126 Edward Moxon-Browne and Peter Janke, 'Terrorism and the Spanish State', in H. H. Tucker (ed.), *Combating the Terrorists: Democratic Responses to Political Violence* (New York: Facts of File, 1988), pp. 155–6.

127 Douglass and Zulaika, 1990, pp. 238–48, 244.

128 Goldie Shabad, 'After Autonomy: The Dynamics of Regionalism in Spain', in Stanley Payne (ed.), *The Politics of Democratic Spain* (Chicago: Chicago Council of Foreign Relations, 1986), p. 149.

129 Goldie Shabad and Francisco José Llera Ramo, 'Political Violence in a Democratic State: Basque Terrorism in Spain', in Martha Crenshaw (ed.), *Terrorism in Context* (University Park: Pennsylvania State University Press, 1991), p. 452.

130 Peter Janke, *Spanish Separatism: ETA's Threat to Basque Democracy* (London: Institute for the Study of Conflict, 1980), p. 3.

131 Shabad and Llera Ramo, 1991, p. 443.

132 Aguero, 1995, p. 142.
133 Moxon-Browne and Janke, 1988, p. 161.
134 Douglass and Zulaika, 1990, p. 246.
135 Arango, 1995, p. 226.
136 Shabad and Llera Ramo, 1991, p. 441.
137 Douglass and Zulaika, 1990, p. 245.
138 Moxon-Browne and Janke, 1988, p. 159. See also R. P. Clark, 'Patterns in the Lives of ETA members', in P. Merkl (ed.), *Political Violence and Terror* (Berkeley: University of California Press, 1986), pp. 283–307.
139 Shabad and Llera Ramo, 1991, p. 438.
140 Shabad and Llera Ramo, 1991, p. 462.
141 Robert Clark, *The Basques: The Franco Years and Beyond* (Reno: University of Nevada Press, 1979), pp. 282, 58.
142 José Feliz Tezanos, Ramón Cotarelo, Andrés De Blas Guerrero, *La Transición Democrática Española* (Madrid: Editorial Sistema, 1989), p. 625.
143 Luis Alonso and Fernando Reinares, 'Conflictividad', in Salustiano del Campo (ed.), *Tendencias Sociales en España Volumen II* (Bilbao: Fundacion BBV, 1993), p. 23.
144 Arango, 1995, p. 223.
145 Alonso and Reinares, 1993, p. 22.
146 Robert P. Clark, *Negotiating with ETA: Obstacles to Peace in the Basque Country, 1975–1988* (Reno: University of Nevada Press, 1990), p. 39. See also Miguel Castells Arteche, *Radiografía de un model represivo* (San Sebastián: Ediciones Vascas, 1982) and Robert P. Clark, *The Basque Insurgents: ETA, 1952–1980* (Madison: University of Wisconsin Press, 1984).
147 Henry Finch, 'Burden of the Past', in Finch (ed.), *Contemporary Uruguay*, University of Liverpool, Institute of Latin American Studies, Working Paper No. 9, 1989, p. 14.
148 Finch, 1989, p. 16.
149 Finch, 1989, p. 17.
150 Ronald McDonald, 'Confrontation and Transition in Uruguay', *Current History*, Vol. 84, February 1985, p. 57.
151 US Government, *Uruguay: A Country Study* (Washington, DC: Federal Research Division, Library of Congress, 1990), p. 37.
152 Weinstein, 1988, p. xv.
153 US Government, 1990, p. 37.
154 Weinstein, 1988, p. 69.
155 Finch, 1989, p. 12.
156 Cesar Aguiar, *Uruguay de los setenta: balance de una decada* (Montevideo: CIEDUR, 1981), p. 38.
157 Kaufman, 1979, p. 25.
158 Finch, 1989, p. 23.
159 Weinstein, 1988, pp. 21–35.

160 Philip Mauceri, *State Under Siege: Development and Policy Making in Peru* (Boulder: Westview Press, 1996), p. 62.
161 Paul Glewwe and Gillette Hall, 'Poverty, Inequality, and Living Standards During Unorthodox Adjustment: The Case of Peru, 1985–1990', *Economic Development and Cultural Change*, Vol. 42, No. 4, July 1994, p. 691.
162 Mauceri, 1996, pp. 62–5.
163 Glewwe and Hall, 1994, pp. 691–2.
164 R. F. Watters, *Poverty and Peasantry in Peru's Southern Andes, 1963–1990* (Pittsburgh: University of Pittsburgh Press, 1994), p. 291.
165 FBIS LAT 88-207, p. 40.
166 Glewwe and Hall, 1994, p. 692.
167 Mauceri, 1996, p. 86.
168 David Scott Palmer, '"Fujipopulism" and Peru's Progress', *Current History*, February 1996, p. 70.
169 Obando, 1996, p. 27.
170 Palmer, 1996, p. 71.
171 Carol Graham, 'Introduction: Democracy in Crisis and the International Response', in Tulchin and Bland (eds), 1994, p. 3.
172 David Scott Palmer, 'Peru, The Drug Business and Shining Path: Between Scylla and Charybdis?', *Journal of Interamerican Studies and World Affairs*, Vol. 34, No. 3, Autumn 1992, p. 67.
173 Palmer, 1996, p. 71.
174 Arango, 1995, p. 134.
175 Carr and Fusi, 1981, pp. 49–79.
176 See Geoffrey Pridham (ed.), *The New Mediterranean Democracies* (London: Frank Cass, 1984), p. 160.

4
Terrorist violence

Introduction

Chapter 4 is the first of three chapters to provide evidence to test the two hypotheses. It examines the consequences of terrorism on democratic stability. Chapter 5 examines state repression and violence. Chapter 6 presents the measures of the rudimentary purposes of the state, of citizen confidence and of democratic stability. Specific measures differ in each country. In spite of these differences, it is believed that each indicator is measuring the same concept.

The theory in three case studies

The three cases of Uruguay, Peru and Spain are similar in the first stage. Although there are many differences among the countries, they all share the presence of violent, terrorist groups. With the activity of violent groups, it is expected that citizens will become disenchanted with state performance, and ultimately with the constitution, if peace is not promptly restored. Specifically, according to my hypotheses, as terrorist violence increases or reaches a critical level, the state's fulfilment of its purposes of integration and stability should decrease. As the state fails to comply with its purposes, then levels of citizen confidence in the state should decrease. As the citizens have less confidence in their state, and ultimately the constitutional form, then there should be an increase in democratic instability. Up to this point, the three cases are similar. However, only the Uruguayan and Peruvian states responded to the terrorist violence with state violence. Only the Uruguayan and Peruvian democracies were overthrown. The difference in democratic stability derives from the fact that Uruguay and Peru responded with indiscriminate state violence while Spain did not. As indiscriminate state violence is implemented, levels of the state fulfilling its rudimentary purposes will further decrease. Correspondingly, further decreases in citizen confidence, and ultimately in democratic stability, should follow. Spain did not pursue a policy of indiscriminate violence, therefore further decreases in the purposes of the state, in citizen confidence or in democratic stability, are not expected.

Uruguay

In the late 1960s Uruguay, struggling with economic troubles, was faced with a new challenge. A guerrilla movement began operating, often in spectacular form. The terrorist threat was realized by the Uruguayan people. Violence became prevalent and the state had to make a decision. How should Uruguay react to the threat? Uruguay responded to terrorist violence by suspending individual liberties, by initiating torture in police interrogations and by conducting mass arrests. Its actions added to the already existing violence. Finally, the military was placed in charge of the 'war against subversion'. Calls for military intervention emerged from across the political spectrum from politicians and civilians. The Uruguayan military, after terminating the terrorist threat, turned its attention to the politicians, deeming them corrupt. The military, without significant popular opposition, started its slow coup in 1973, taking over the country.

Peru

From 1980, the Peruvian democracy faced a severe violent threat from guerrilla groups. In addition, its economic crisis was prolonged and severe. Peru's military had a history of intervention, although it willingly gave up power in 1980. The guerrilla groups severely disrupted the already weak political community as leaders and commoners were killed.

Election boycotts were brutally enforced by the main guerrilla group, Sendero Luminoso. Hundreds of local officials, candidates and grassroots leaders were assassinated. The typical Peruvian state response to the violence before Fujimori was incoherent and inconsistent. One fairly constant component of the counterinsurgency plans was a reliance on repressive means to combat the violence. States of emergency, extrajudicial executions and torture were commonly used. Moreover, democratic governance was replaced by military control in these zones. Many citizens, especially those living in zones under a state of emergency, faced threats from both guerrilla groups and state forces. The military became more and more directly involved in the counterinsurgency efforts. Disgusted by the inability of previous civilian leaders to react to the many problems facing the state, the military backed the actions of democratically elected Fujimori, who, with the support of the military, dissolved Congress and the judiciary in his 1992 *autogolpe*.

Spain

The new Spanish democracy faced a well-organized violent threat. However, the state did not respond to the terrorist threat in an indiscriminate, repressive manner. The military was not placed in charge of a 'war against subversion'. Instead, the state declared amnesties, released prisoners, reinstated political liberties and granted regional autonomy. The majority of Spaniards defended their democracy during and after the coup attempt in February 1981.

Hypothesis one

Terrorist violence threatens democratic stability by undermining both rudimentary purposes of the state, security and integration. As the purposes of the state are unfulfilled, citizen confidence in the state declines. As citizen confidence decreases, democratic instability increases.

Uruguay

Uruguay was fairly peaceful until the late 1960s. An average of ten or fewer incidents occurred yearly until 1968. Despite

Figure 4.1 Uruguay: total incidents of terrorist violence, 1963–73

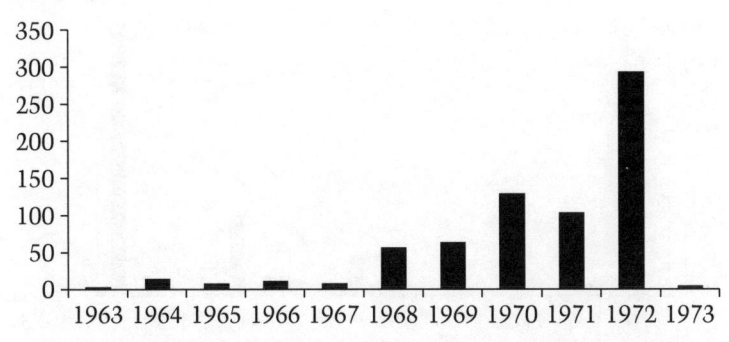

Source: Republica Oriental del Uruguay Junta de Comandantes en Jefe, *La Subversion* (Montevideo: Las Fuerzas Armadas al Pueblo Oriental, 1978).

Uruguay's well-established democracy, the Tupamaros emerged. In Uruguay, terrorist violence can be measured by tallying the number of bombings, assassinations, robberies, instances of forced propaganda, armed attacks and kidnappings.

In 1968, the number of incidents increased tenfold. The amount of violence continued to increase until the election year of 1971. During this year, the major group, the Tupamaros, had declared a unilateral cease-fire to participate in the presidential elections, favouring the Frente Amplio. After the 1971 elections and the inauguration of President Bordaberry, the Tupamaros launched more attacks. The year 1972 showed an increase of over 300 per cent in violent incidents. The eruption of violence was short-lived, however. The following year, only two incidents were reported (figure 4.1).

Figure 4.2 breaks down the incidents into the type of action involved. Overall, bombings were most common, followed by robberies. Armed attacks and assassinations occurred, but were less frequent than other means. The spreading of propaganda by creating captive audiences was a common, bloodless action of the Tupamaros. The vigorous fundraising by kidnapping and robbery is also apparent. The peak of kidnappings occurred in 1971. There were more robberies in 1972.

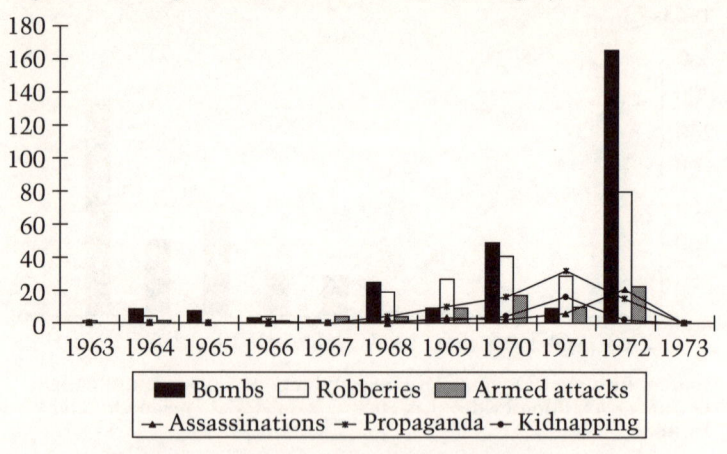

Figure 4.2 Uruguay: terrorist incidents by category, 1963–73

■ Bombs ☐ Robberies ■ Armed attacks
─▲─ Assassinations ─■─ Propaganda ─●─ Kidnapping

Note: In this chart, bombs are counted one per location, and unspecified pluralities are counted as two. Robberies are armed assaults with the gain of some material as the aim of the action (this includes money, supplies, automobiles, evidence, etc.). Propaganda is material publicly released by subversive groups. This includes numerous incidents of the Tupamaros holding a captive audience to make announcements. Armed assaults are armed attacks by seditious groups on the military, the police or other people affiliated with the government. Assassinations are deaths of people caused by seditious action. (Note: if an armed assault resulted in a death, it is counted both as an assassination and as an armed assault.)

Source: Republica Oriental del Uruguay Junta de Comandantes en Jefe, *La Subversion* (Montevideo: Las Fuerzas Armadas al Pueblo Oriental, 1978).

Figure 4.3 shows how explosive the growth in terrorist violence was in 1972. The first half of the year saw prolific action by the Tupamaros and by others. Although the year had over three times as many incidents as 1971, most of them occurred in the first half of the year. To Uruguayans, it appeared that there were more than six times the incidents than the year before.

On 14 April 1972 the Tupamaros started a new offensive against the armed forces. After Bordaberry assumed the presidency, the Tupamaros kidnapped a policeman named Nelson Bardesio. Bardesio confessed to the Tupamaros that he had participated in an extreme right anti-Tupamaro group, although he claimed he had been forced to participate. He produced evidence for his claims that the Tupamaros

Figure 4.3 Uruguay: monthly terrorist incidents by category, 1972

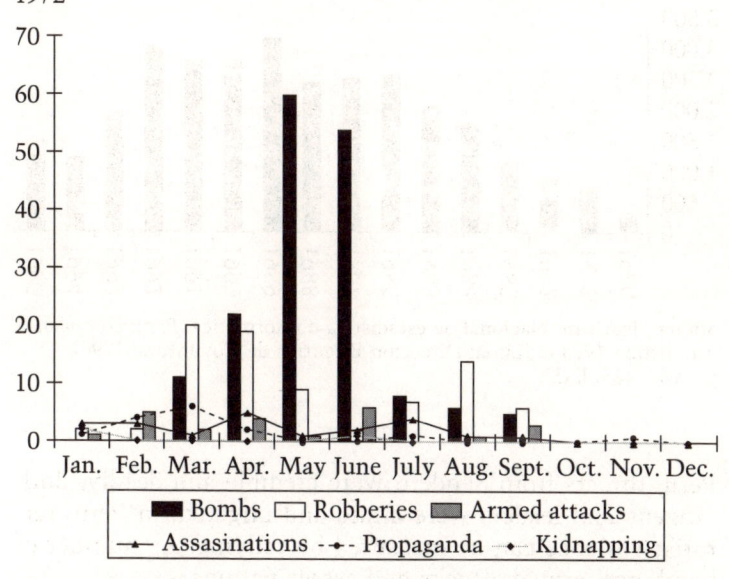

[Bar chart showing monthly terrorist incidents with categories: Bombs, Robberies, Armed attacks, Assasinations, Propaganda, Kidnapping]

Source: Republica Oriental del Uruguay Junta de Comandantes en Jefe, *La Subversion* (Montevideo: Las Fuerzas Armadas al Pueblo Oriental, 1978).

forwarded to the press. Shortly after, the Tupamaros issued a communiqué condemning to death officials who had participated in the anti-Tupamaro commando group, Caza Tupamaros. Four were assassinated within hours of the announcement. In May, there was a significant increase in the number of bombings, from twenty-two in April to sixty in May. However, this frantic pace of increases in violence did not last. After the military's takeover of the fight against subversion, rapid gains were made in quelling the terrorist violent activity. As of September 1972, for all practical purposes, the threat from the terrorist groups had ended.

Peru

The amplitude of the threat of guerrilla groups[1] to Peruvian democracy exceeded that of the other countries examined in this study. Violent rebellion greatly increased despite the return to democratic governance in 1980. In the case of

Figure 4.4 Peru: terrorist violent incidents, 1980–95

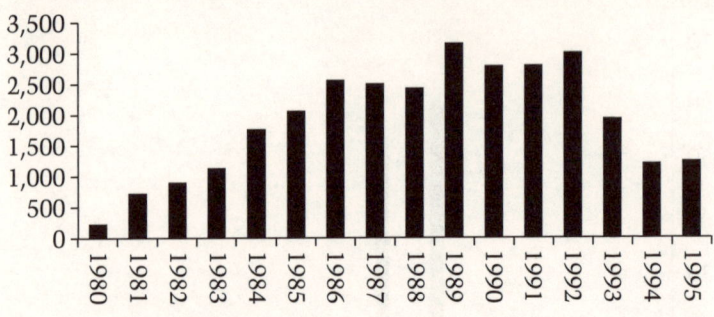

Source: Instituto Nacional de estadistica e informatica, *Peru: compendio estadístico 1995–6* (Lima: Dirección Ejecutiva de Coyuntura, 1996), pp. 959, 435; INEI.

Peru, threats from Sendero were credible and deadly. Both citizens and leaders were afraid and targeted. In Peru, terrorist violence can be measured by tallying the number of bombings, armed attacks and assassinations.

From the restoration of democracy in 1980 to the *autogolpe* of Fujimori in 1992, the number of terrorist violent incidents increased tenfold. During the last three years of democracy, the level of violence stabilized, but at an alarmingly high level. The most striking increase of violence occurred during Belaúnde's presidency of 1980–85. The frequency of incidents increased 936 per cent. During García's term (1985–90) violence increased by an additional 135 per cent. In the two constitutional years of Fujimori's rule (1990–92) violence increased an additional 8 per cent (figure 4.4).

Table 4.1 provides a breakdown of the victims of terrorist violence for 1991. The top row designates the group blamed for the death. The first column contains categories of the victims. It is interesting to note that Sendero killed more members of the MRTA than did the military in 1991. However, Sendero attacked and killed people from all parts of society. Its strategy was that if you were not a supporter, then you were an enemy. Peasants, residents, MRTA members, ronderos (members of armed peasant groups) and members of the military were all frequently targeted by Sendero. The MRTA tended to target members of the police, the

Table 4.1 Peru: victims and those responsible, 1991

	Sendero Luminoso	MRTA	Other subversives	Unidentified
Professional	46	0	0	7
Businessmen	54	4	0	11
Workers	58	8	1	17
Peasants	420	0	0	27
Ronderos	172	0	0	2
Residents	227	13	0	51
Students	26	0	0	16
Authorities	44	2	0	3
Foreigners	6	0	0	0
Police	92	37	0	12
Military	121	40	0	16
Sendero Luminoso	26	34	9	10
MRTA	366	1	0	5
Comando Rodrigo Franco	0	0	0	0
Narco-traffickers	0	0	0	0
Total	1314	139	10	177

Source: Comisión Especial de Investigación y Estudio sobre la Violencia y Alternativas de Pacificación, *Violencia y Pacificación en 1991* (Lima: Senado de la República, 1992), pp. 185–99.

military and Sendero, although it did target civilians as well.[2]

Sendero also asserted its power by depriving Lima and Peruvian industry of electricity. This type of attack had grave consequences for the economic activity of the country. A total of 1,409 electrical towers were toppled from 1980–91, with a peak of 276 towers toppled in 1989. The Senate Commission of National Pacification estimated that the total cost was $19,440,984,000 from mid May 1980 to December 1991.[3]

The influence of the terrorist violent groups, Sendero and the MRTA, can also be measured by the rankings of their respective leaders, Abimael Gúzman of Sendero and Victor Polay of the MRTA as powerful Peruvians. Gúzman emerged on the survey of Peruvian power in 1982, in twenty-eighth place. Since 1983, however, he has been consistently rated in the top ten. For example, in 1991 Gúzman ranked fourth. Polay did not appear on the list until 1989. In that year, he ranked twenty-fifth. In 1990 he ranked seventeenth, and tenth in 1991.[4] In 1992, Gúzman ranked third and Polay twenty-fourth.[5] In that year, only Fujimori and one of his top ministers ranked higher than Gúzman. Gúzman evidently was considered a very powerful man as a result of his leadership of Sendero.

Spain

It is interesting to note that the main terrorist groups emerged while the authoritarian Franco still ruled. Despite the origin of these groups under Franco's non-democratic regime, the new democracy inherited the challenge of responding to their threats. As democratic consolidation progressed, it continued to be challenged by violent groups. Terrorist violence can be measured by the number of bombings, armed attacks and assassinations.

The violence in Spain was significant. Six hundred and ten people died as a result of terrorism between 1976 and 1986. Approximately half of those killed were either affiliated with the professional military or with the police. Almost 90 per cent of the police and professional military fatalities were caused by ETA. In the same ten years, 289 civilians and non-professional military personnel were killed. (Spain has a mandatory military service for young men. Non-professional military personnel include young men serving their compulsory service.) Of the civilian and non-professional military casualties, 58.5 per cent were caused by ETA. Of all those killed, ETA was responsible for almost 75 per cent of the deaths.[6] ETA's activity increased yearly until 1980. The data of the number of attacks similarly show a peak in 1980. In that year, ETA and the extreme right engaged in record numbers of attacks. The activity of GRAPO peaked in 1979. After 1980, the activity was reduced by approximately half (figure 4.5). The number of kidnappings by ETA follows a similar pattern, with a peak of kidnappings occurring in 1979. By 1981, the activity had dropped by about half (figure 4.6).

In response to ETA, violent groups emerged from the right. There is some disparity in accounts tallying the number of people killed by the extreme right. In figure 4.7, different accounts of the numbers killed by the extreme right are represented. These groups included Antiterrorísmo

TERRORIST VIOLENCE 87

Figure 4.5 Spain: number of attacks with victims, 1968–86

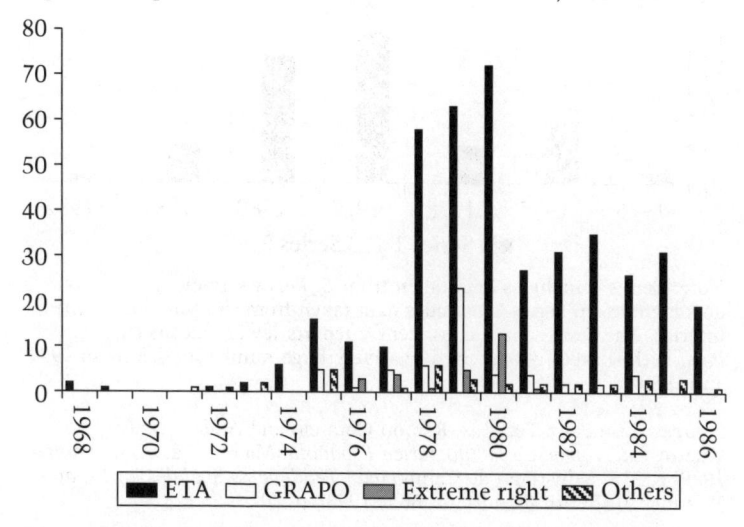

■ ETA ☐ GRAPO ▨ Extreme right ▩ Others

Source: Salustiano del Campo (ed.), *Tendencias Sociales en España Volumen II* (Bilbao: Fundacion BBV, 1993), p. 70. Reproduced by permission of the publisher.

Figure 4.6 Spain: number of kidnappings by ETA, 1976–86

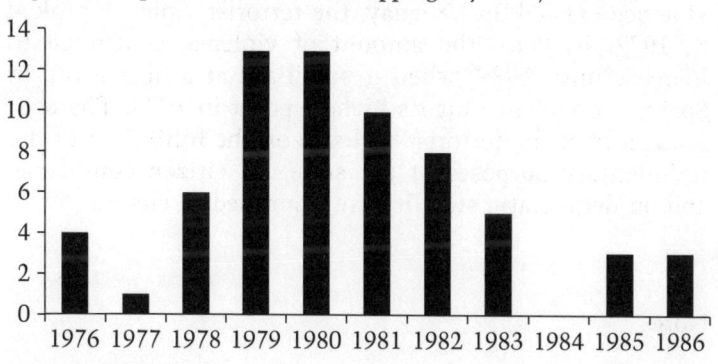

Source: Spanish Ministry of the Interior, http://www.mir.es/oris/infoeta/esp/p12-esp.htm

ETA, Alianza Apostólica Anticomunista (AAA) and the Acción Nacional España. These groups targeted suspected members of ETA in Spain and France. Sometimes leftist activists were targeted. For example, in 1977 the AAA killed four lawyers who represented illegal workers' organizations.[7]

Figure 4.7 Spain: deaths attributed to the extreme right, 1976–82

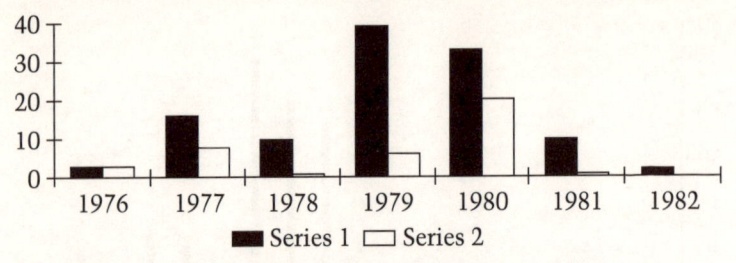

Note: Series 1 includes data taken from *El Pais's* servicio de documentacion. Series 2 includes data taken from the Ministry of the Interior. The state source consistently reports fewer victims than *El Pais*. Both sources document a relatively large number of deaths in 1979 and 1980.

Sources: José Feliz Tezanos, Ramón Cotarelo and Andrés De Blas Guerro. *La Transición Democrática Española* (Madrid: Editorial Sistema, 1989) p. 215; Salustiano de Campo (ed.) *Tendencias Sociales en España Volumen II* (Bilbao: Fundacion BBV, 1993), p. 70.

Summary

In all three countries, a significant amount of terrorist violence existed. In Uruguay, the terrorist violence peaked in 1972. In Peru, the amount of violence continued to increase until 1989, when it stabilized at a high level. In Spain, the violence hit its highest point in 1980. The consequences of the terrorist violence on the fulfilment of the rudimentary purposes of the state, on citizen confidence and on democratic stability are examined in chapter 6.

Notes

1 Edward Muller, Henry Dietz and Steven Finkel examine the reasons for participation in the insurgent groups in Peru. They find that alienation from the political system is the most relevant to explain participation. Edward Muller, Henry Dietz and Steven Finkel, 'Discontent and the Unexpected Utility of Rebellion: The Case of Peru', *American Political Science Review*, Vol. 85, No. 4, December 1991, pp. 1261–83.

2 Comisión Especial de Investigación y Estudio sobre la Violencia y Alternativas de Pacificación, *Violencia y Pacificación en 1991* (Lima: Senado de la República, 1992), pp. 185–99. The Commission acknowledged some of the difficulties involved in its study, especially in terms

of methodological issues. It lists the lack of adequate information in parts of the country, the anonymous character of much of the violence, the fear of many people to denounce abuses, the clandestine and mimetic nature of the seditious action, the cover-up of the actions of government forces and the lack of an adequate census as problematic (p. 17).

3 Comisión Especial de Investigación y Estudio sobre la Violencia y Alternativas de Pacificación, 1992, pp. 70–72.
4 FBIS LAT 91 180, pp. 32–6.
5 FBIS LAT 92 179, p. 38.
6 *El Pais*, 4 May 1986, p. 30. See also Aguero, 1995, p. 143.
7 Peter Janke, *Guerrilla and Terrorist Organizations* (New York: MacMillan, 1981), pp. 76–86.

5
State repression and violence

This chapter examines state repression and violence in the context of democratic stability. To fully understand the consequences of terrorism, both the terrorism and the state response to it must be examined. It is theorized that state repression and violence, like terrorism, undermine the rudimentary purposes of the state. Consequently, declines in citizen confidence in the state and an increase in democratic stability are expected.

Hypothesis two

State repression and violence also undermine the rudimentary purposes of the state, integration and security. Decreases in citizen confidence should follow a decrease in the fulfilment of the rudimentary purposes. Finally, as citizen confidence in the state decreases, increases in democratic instability should be identifiable.

Uruguay

In Uruguay, repressive state action can be measured by policies that indiscriminately suspend individual liberties, such as freedom of speech and association, freedom from arbitrary arrest or imprisonment, and freedom from invasion of the home and the forced drafting of workers. State violence can be measured by incidents of torture and extra-judicial executions.

How did Uruguay respond to Tupamaro violence? One statistic is very informative of state priorities. From 1968–73 education spending went from 24 per cent of the budget to only 16 per cent of the budget. At the same time, military spending rose from 13.9 to 26.2 per cent of the budget.[1] When faced with guerrilla groups and economic unrest, the Uruguayan state turned to indiscriminate, repressive means. Instead of due process for suspected criminals, the state invoked security measures that suspended the individual rights of all citizens. The police began to torture those in its custody. Striking workers were drafted. The media were censored. The military was put in charge of anti-terrorist operations and the prisons.

Repressive state actions and policies

When Jorge Pacheco Areco became president after the death of President Oscar Gestido on 6 December 1967, Pacheco was faced with severe national problems: deep economic trouble, strikes, student unrest and violent rebellion. Pacheco responded by ruling by executive decree and suspending rights. Within a week of taking office, he banned six small leftist parties for their alleged support of armed conflict. These actions were taken despite the lack of a legal statute allowing the executive branch to close newspapers or to outlaw political associations.[2] The five parties banned by executive resolution 1788/967 were the Socialist Party, the Uruguayan Anarchist Federation, the Oriental Revolutionary Movement, Movimiento de Acción Proletario Unitario and the *Movimiento de Izquierda Revolucionario*.[3] Also in response to worker and student unrest, President Pacheco declared the establishment of prompt security measures (medidas prontas de seguridad, or MPS) on 13 June 1968.[4] These security measures were implemented many times prior to the dissolution of the National Assembly.

President Pacheco also introduced another repressive policy. To prevent workers from striking, he militarized the workers, forcibly drafting them into service. Consequently, the workers could be court martialled for striking. In July 1968, Pacheco drafted 15,000 striking workers from the National Telephone Company; 11,500 from the National

Fuel, Alcohol and Cement Administration; 1,600 from the State Telecommunications Agency; and 4,000 from the State Sanitation Department.[5] Faced with more labour unrest, Pacheco militarized the police force on 7 July 1969. Later, in response to a bank strike, he militarized the workers and ordered them back to work.[6] In general, 1969 was not a good year for labour. During that year, hundreds of labour leaders were arrested and allegedly beaten. In response to the repression, in July 1969 the labour union CNT (National Confederation of Workers) was operating clandestinely.[7]

Pacheco also responded forcibly to student protest. In August 1968, police raided the central university and the Colleges of Agriculture, Architecture, Fine Arts and Medicine. On 14 August 1968 a student, Liber Arce, was killed in a student protest. Two more were killed on 20 September and forty were wounded.[8] In general, Pacheco did not hesitate to use his powers, constitutional or otherwise, to suppress unrest.

Starting in late 1967, the closure of news agencies became a common occurrence in Uruguay. Pacheco's government also instituted press censorship on 24 September 1968. The InterAmerican Press Society declared that in 1968, 1969 and 1970 freedom of the press did not exist. For example, the words 'Tupamaros', 'seditious' and 'subversive' were banned. The censorship of private mail was allowed.[9] Starting in November 1970, newspapers were only able to publish items and pictures of the Tupamaros provided by the state.[10] From 1967 to 1972, thirty-six papers and radio stations were temporarily closed and ten were permanently closed.[11] Censorship, practically previously unknown in Uruguay, was thorough and pervasive beginning with Pacheco. Pacheco also moved beyond standard censorship in controlling the press by instituting news blackouts. On 12 April 1971, he decreed that only state-supplied news about guerrilla activities could be reported. This was expanded on 11 August 1971 to include labour strikes, union meetings and decisions, and anything else the state considered subversive. A few days later, on 16 August 1971, another decree was issued prohibiting any printed material dealing with armed protest or with an origin in 'nondemocratic', 'totalitarian' or 'subversive' countries. On 4 September 1971, Pacheco temporarily closed all opposition newspapers after the assassination of two national guardsmen.[12]

After 1970, the police and armed forces conducted numerous house searches. For example, in August 1970 the police searched approximately 20,000 houses, attempting to uncover Tupamaro hideouts and rescue kidnapped victims. Often these searches occurred at night and without proper warrants. Instead of finding Tupamaros, these searches 'created great resentment among Montevideo's population'.[13]

In June 1971, Interior Minister Santiago de Brum Carbajal declared the country to be in a state of war. He also announced that a registry to track every Uruguayan residence, occupation and place of work was almost complete. He said it was necessary to know ' "what every Uruguayan was doing all the time" '.[14] On 9 September 1971, after the jailbreak of 106 Tupamaros, Pacheco reassigned jurisdiction of the prisons to the military. On the same day he placed the military in charge of the anti-Tupamaro campaign.

President Pacheco also suspended the right of habeas corpus. On 25 October 1971 the Uruguayan Supreme Court challenged the legality of the decree. The court ruled that the 'recourse to habeas corpus is the indispensable remedy that keeps the security measures from losing their existence of that same Rule of Law, in moments of unexpected disturbance'.[15] In spite of the court challenge, Pacheco continued with the policy. The president replied that habeas corpus no longer applied under MPS or prompt security measures.

The universities were also affected by the repression. In December 1972, the system of public education lost its long-held autonomy and was placed under the authority of the National Council on Education (CONAE). According to article 25 of the Law of General Education, CONAE 'is authorized to apply or see to the application, individual or collective, restrictive disciplinary and eliminatory measures, including transfer, change to open scheduling or whatever measure is considered appropriate to the gravity of the situation'. It also allowed prison terms for professors who 'attack the sovereignty of the state'.[16] In addition, the law required that all meetings be authorized. The law was followed by protests.

The recourse to repressive state actions that became habitual under President Pacheco was continued by President Bordaberry. A state of internal war was declared in April 1972. It was imposed 'for the sole purpose of authorizing the measures necessary to suppress the activities of individuals or groups that in any way conspire against the nation, in the terms set forth in the constitution'.[17] That same month and despite opposition in the National Assembly, Bordaberry gained passage of his 'Law of State Security'. The new law institutionalized many of the decrees that Bordaberry and Pacheco had instituted in their attempts to curb subversion. It increased penalties to thirty years in jail for revolutionary activity, to eighteen years for association with a subversive group, and to two years for journalists who committed 'press crimes'.

Security measures, suspension of liberties and the militarization of society became common. From October 1965 to June 1973, there were twenty suspensions of individual liberties and impositions of MPS. In addition, a state of internal war was declared three times: on 15 April 1972, extended on 12 May 1972 and again extended on 30 June 1972. On 10 July 1972, military courts were established for civilians.[18] The stern policies continued in 1972 and resulted in the elimination of Tupamaro activity. For example, in June 1972 the 'people's jail' of the Tupamaros was discovered. In July 1972, civil rights were suspended for another ninety days and the state of internal war was extended.[19] Law 14068 also placed civilians under military control.[20] The events of the month of July 1972 included massive and indiscriminate arrests of leftist politicians and supporters. Estimates of those detained range from 1,600 to 4,000 for the month.[21] By the end of 1972, over 5,000 people had been arrested by the military and the Tupamaro organization was virtually destroyed.[22]

Were these repressive policies legal? Some of Pacheco's actions had a basis in Uruguayan law. According to the constitution, article 29 allows the judiciary to interfere with the press and impose a penalty of a three to twelve month imprisonment. However, there is no statute allowing the suppression of a newspaper.[23] The MPS were to be used in times of extraordinary internal disturbance.[24] However, they were applied in ways that were not originally intended. According to *Violations of Human Rights in Uruguay (1972–1976)*, 'in principle, the basis for instituting these measures was the fight against subversion, but they were applied in a much broader sense. Thus striking workers and employees were put into military service; churches, hospitals, high schools, and schools of the university were raided'.[25]

Uruguayan state violence

The use of state violence began in 1970. The police and the military began to use torture, extrajudicial executions and other unconstitutional means in police activities. Originally, the Uruguayan National Police was responsible for combating the Tupamaros. Specifically, the Information and Intelligence Directorate, composed of eight departments, and the Metropolitan Guard, a paramilitary organization headed by army officers, were in charge. The Tupamaros accused the Metropolitan Guard of mistreating, torturing and killing guerrillas who had surrendered. The beginning of the violent state policy is marked by the resignation of the head of the Department of Intelligence and Liaison, Alejandro Otero, over the introduction of state violence in police work in January 1970. Porzecanski reports that Otero was replaced

> Since his superior officers reportedly were impatient for more arrests and disagreed with his practice of being 'soft' on captured guerrillas. On the other hand, Mr. Otero was supposedly upset by his superiors' lack of support for detailed and patient police laboratory work as well as by the introduction and extensive application of torture.[26]

After his dismissal, Otero reported to the *Jornal de Brasil* that the wave of Tupamaro violence was a result of repressive methods.[27] Evidence of torture was corroborated. In addition, in July 1970 it was alleged that some detained Tupamaros were executed even though they had surrendered to police.[28] In June 1970, dissident Colorado Senator Vasconcellos headed a commission of inquiry, which unanimously concluded that 'inhuman torture, including electric shocks, cigarette burns and psychological pressure, was used by police as a "normal, frequent, and habitual" matter on Tupamaros, common criminals and innocents alike'. The committee called for further inquiry.[29]

The military was placed in charge of the effort to end the violence of the Tupamaros in 1971. After the initiation of the Tupamaro campaign of assassinations in April 1972, the Tupamaros discovered that the military had used the cease-fire to organize an effective counter-campaign. The military killed nineteen within four days in clashes with the Tupamaros. Under a state of internal war, the armed forces were free to engage in a counterinsurgency war, 'without regard for judicial accountability or individual rights'.[30] By 2 June, thirty Tupamaros, soldiers, policemen and innocents had been killed and more had been wounded. More than five hundred suspected Tupamaro members and collaborators were held by the military. This counterinsurgency policy included the use of truth drugs and torture in the interrogation of those arrested, including leftist politicians and their supporters.[31]

In addition to violence carried out by official state institutions, other groups emerged and operated with the approval of officials. These groups were formed to counter the leftist groups, such as the Tupamaros. The Juventud Uruguaya de Pie (JUP) and Comando Caza Tupamaros were allegedly established with the blessing of the Ministry of the Interior and other law enforcement officials. In the spring and summer of 1971, JUP began a series of disturbances in Montevideo high schools. JUP members beat leftist teenagers who were accused of collaborating with the Tupamaros. As a result, one-third of Montevideo high schools had to be closed because of the violent clashes between students. JUP also harassed the families of captured Tupamaros and others who had been released. Comando Caza Tupamaros killed at least two suspected Tupamaros. Nelson Bardesio, who began as the driver for CIA officer Cantrell, became part of a secret team under the control of the Minister of the Interior. This team, composed of three traffic police and two police institute members, was sent to Argentina's Information Service, the SIDE. This group was later implicated in the bombing of the houses of lawyers and teachers sympathetic to the Tupamaros.[32] Other senior officials have also been implicated in right-wing death squads. In July 1970, a senior official in the Pacheco administration was rumoured to have said 'They too have families', implying extrajudicial reprisals.[33] In addition, there were other violent groups with ties to the state, such as the Defensa Armada Nacionalista, Comando Armando Leses, Movimiento Armado Nacional Oriental (MANO), Brigadas Nacionales and a Brazilian-style death squad.[34] Many of the counterguerrillas targeted members and supporters of Frente Amplio

Figure 5.1 Uruguay: state violence, spring and summer 1973

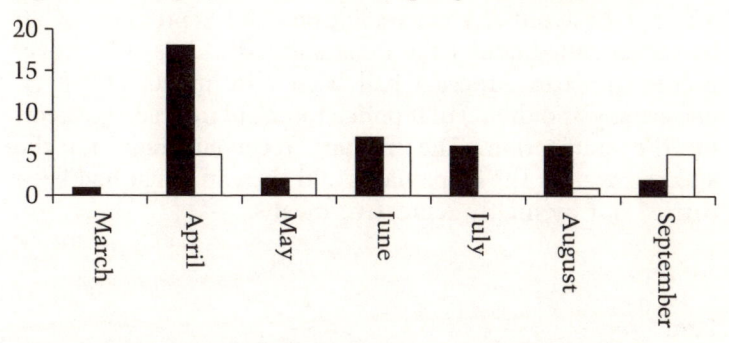

Notes: The number killed is represented by the black bar and the number wounded is represented by the white bar. Deaths include people killed as a result of operations carried out by the joint forces, or assumed to have been, and prison deaths. Servicio Paz y Justicia: Uruguay, 1986, p. 337. An additional three deaths were attributed to the government between October and June. The figures for arrests, confiscations, hideouts discovered, wounded and wanted come from *Siete*, pp. 88, 357. 'During 1970–71 at least 15 innocent people were accidentally killed by policemen or soldiers while engaged in searches, arrests, and patrol operations'. Porzencanski, 1973, p. 61.

Sources: Servicio Paz y Justicia: Uruguay, *Nunca Más: Human Rights Violations, 1972–1985* (Philadelphia: Temple University Press, 1986), p. 337; Uruguay Ministro del Interior, *Siete Meses de la Lucha Antisubversiva* (Montevideo: Ministro del Interior), pp. 88, 357.

and the traditional left.[35] The violence became prevalent such that it created the fear of 'an expanding civil war situation'.[36]

As the number of terrorist actions decreased, state anti-subversive actions increased. July, August and September of 1972 were marked by the increasing eradication of the seditious movements by the military and the increase in actions by state groups (figure 5.1). According to the standard of eradicating the Tupamaros, the military was very successful. From 28 November 1972 to 15 February 1973 a total of 2,228 cases were tried in the military courts with only 55 cases remaining and 321 outstanding arrests.[37] In fact, the military campaign was so successful that Bordaberry also found himself in trouble rhetorically. At the same time that he was lobbying for an extension of the suspension of individual liberties, he attempted to take credit for the elimination of the Tupamaros, the threat upon which the suspension of liberties was justified. Later Colonel Bolentini announced the discovery of new terrorist movements, in an attempt to avoid any contradiction.[38] By September, what had been called one of the most successful guerrilla movements in Latin America had been eliminated. However, democracy and the regular police force did not receive credit for the eradication. The military received credit for the success against the Tupamaros and the campaign had been carried out by highly repressive means.

Peru

> The great virtuality, not virtue, of Sendero, was to touch the skin of our institutionalization and immediately provoke a vomit of bitterness that generated an official terrorism more cruel, more harsh and more morally forbidden than the insurrection.
> Javier Valle Riestra, Diputado and Senator, APRA[39]

The Peruvian state's policy towards violent groups was inconsistent but it persistently included repressive and violent elements. During the terms of Belaúnde and García, it could be said that a guiding policy was absent. Instead, these governments largely abdicated responsibility for the containment of terrorism to the military. The only policy or oversight given to the military was a directive to eliminate terrorism. A mixture of states of emergency, military control over civilian areas, forced participation in armed peasant groups and some incentives for cooperating with the state against terrorists was used to combat the violent groups. Under President García, paramilitary groups with ties to the governing APRA party emerged.

In Peru, repressive state action can be measured by policies that indiscriminately suspended individual liberties, such as freedom of speech, of association, freedom from arbitrary arrest or imprisonment, freedom from invasion of the home and freedom from military control of civilians. State violence can be measured by allegations of torture, extrajudicial executions and forced disappearances.

Peruvian state repressive policies

All three democratically elected presidents pursued repressive policies. The first democratically elected president since the military coup in 1968, President Fernando Belaúnde, was largely unaware of the threat posed by Sendero. At first, he relied on the ill-equipped 'Sinchis', a special police battalion, to combat Sendero. As the threat continued to grow, Belaúnde resorted to involving the military and using his constitutional powers to fight terrorism. Article 231 of the Peruvian constitution of 1979 recognizes two levels of states of exception: a state of emergency and a state of siege. Both states of exception involve the suspension of liberties. The constitution allows a state of emergency when there are 'disturbances of peace and internal order, catastrophes or grave circumstances affecting the life of the nation'.[40] A state of emergency lasts sixty days.[41] It allows security forces to enter houses and make arrests without warrants. Freedom of movement and the right to assemble are also suspended. Americas Watch notes that although the accused's right to know the charges against him and his accusers are not legally suspended in these states of exception, in practice they were.[42] In December 1982, Belaúnde formally involved the military. Invoking articles 231 and 276 of the 1979 constitution,[43] he placed the military in control of the counterinsurgency campaign. Belaúnde also transferred control of areas under a state of emergency to political military commanders, reducing the power of civilian authorities in those areas.[44]

Belaúnde declared a state of emergency fifty-six times during his presidency. Of those, forty-six were related to Sendero, with the remaining ten used as a response to social or labour unrest. Laws of counterinsurgency were written and re-written in the 1980s to allow the police and military more control of the counterinsurgency efforts. Belaúnde also decreed Anti-Terrorist Law 46, which allowed police to hold suspects for fifteen days without court interference and also dictated stiff penalties for terrorists and their accessories.[45] Under this law, many opposition political activists, peasant leaders and labour officials were prosecuted.[46] In 1983, the executive attempted to define terrorism as treason, so that it would meet constitutional standards for capital punishment.[47]

Alan García, the leader of APRA, was elected president in 1985. In the beginning of his administration, García tried to change the state's policy. He forcibly retired some military commanders who were implicated in human rights violations. In addition, he announced a limited amnesty and the establishment of a peace commission. However, by February 1986 Lima was under a curfew and a state of emergency due to the escalation of bombings. García attempted another amnesty aimed at the MRTA, but the group responded by assassinating a police sergeant. García, in response, mobilized the army and sent counterinsurgency troops into the area. He continued with more repressive policies. One year later, in 1987, the García administration amended Law 24,700, which had established procedures for the investigation, prosecution and trial of alleged terrorists. The changes limited the ability of provincial prosecutors and human rights organizations to intervene in cases. A new law (No. 25,031) granted police control of investigations and expanded allowable circumstances of an *incommunicado* detention.[48] García continued Belaúnde's practice of imposing states of emergency and increasing military involvement. There was little judicial presence in these areas.[49]

Fujimori was elected president in 1990. Upon taking office he began to expand and consolidate the state's policies with the cooperation of the military. For the first time since the return to democracy in 1980, Fujimori appointed a general as Minister of the Interior. In Decree Law 171-90, Fujimori granted all military members in emergency zones protection from civilian charges. Military courts would handle all charges. The decree also guaranteed their anonymity.[50] As the policies became more coherent, opposition to them increased. These acts were repealed in February 1991 by Congress.[51] In November 1991, after receiving greater power from Congress, Fujimori decreed 120 laws, ranging from land reform to an expansion of the power of the armed forces. One law allowed civilians to be drafted and their property expropriated to assist the fight against subversion.[52] The decrees expanded the power of the military in areas not under a state of emergency. The law also restructured the SIN and the National Mobilization and Defence System.

In general, there was a constant increase in areas under a state of emergency in Peru. In 1980, at the beginning of the restoration of democracy, no provinces were under a state of emergency. By 1984, 18 per cent of provinces were under a state of emergency. In addition, the entire country was under a state of emergency in 1983 from 30 May to 9 September, and in 1984 from 20 March to 3 September and from 27 November to 30 November. By 1990, 63 per cent of the provinces were under a state of emergency. After 1990, the number fell to approximately 43 per cent for 1991 and 1992.[53] However, under Fujimori, even though there was a decrease in the percentage of provinces under a state of emergency, the broad powers given to the military gave the institution the ability to operate freely in areas not under a state of emergency.

Critics complained that Fujimori only further militarized the state's response to terrorism.[54] The opposition in the Senate, in December 1991, released a statement that the presidency was in effect vacant because the chief executive was morally incapable.[55] Manuel Dammert, sociologist and Senator of the Revolutionary Communist Party, described Peruvian democracy in February 1992: 'Y lo que tenemos ahora es un régimen autoritario del cual esperamos que no sea un régimen cívico militar e inconstitucional'.[56] In February 1992, Congress reconvened and rescinded many of Fujimori's decrees.[57] For example, it passed Law 25397 to restrict the legislative power of the president.[58] Congress also stipulated that states of exception should specify the territory included, the time of exception and which constitutional rights would be suspended.[59] Congress was preparing to fully examine the counterinsurgency strategy at the next session, which was to begin on 6 April 1992, when Fujimori committed his *autogolpe*.

Peruvian state violence

In Peru, state violence had numerous sources. Some sources were official branches of the state. The military used violent means to achieve its goals. In addition, the state set up armed groups of civilians, called *rondas*, to defend against terrorist violent groups. In addition to these 'official' groups, there were covert state-sponsored violent groups.

The military, placed in control of the fight against terrorist violence in December 1982, gained new powers in July 1984, when Belaúnde placed it in control of the entire country's counterinsurgency policy. Military action was no longer limited to areas under a state of emergency.[60] The state gave the military one objective: 'to defeat Sendero, to make it disappear'.[61] Massive human rights violations followed.[62] President García did not establish any more oversight than

Belaúnde. In spite of his rhetorical commitment to human rights, he too tolerated military violence. His commitment to human rights was viewed as hypocritical after a June 1986 Sendero prison mutiny in which García gave the military permission to do whatever was necessary to retake the prisons. Over 250 prisoners died in the shelling of one prison and another hundred were shot and killed after surrendering to the authorities.[63] According to Americas Watch, the repressive policies of García were ineffective at curbing the violence. In 1987, the organization determined that the invocation of the state of emergency was ineffective and harmful: 'Unfortunately, the imposition of a state of emergency also has tended to correspond to an increase in human rights abuses'.[64]

In Peru, state forces kill many people under the pretext that they are subversives. Raúl González cites a widely accepted belief that the military and police forces execute all who belong to Sendero. According to González, the army and intelligence services require 90 per cent certainty of an individual's complicity in guerrilla groups before execution, while the marine infantry requires only 5 per cent probability to pull the trigger.[65]

Another source of state violence were the *rondas campesinas*. These peasant groups were armed by the state[66] and were mainly of two types.[67] The first type of *ronda* was a civil defence committee that was organized in the emergency zones. Membership of this group was not voluntary. Refusal to participate resulted in suspicion of being a subversive. These *rondas* were under military jurisdiction. The military used both coercion and rewards for villagers to participate in the *rondas*. Orin Starn reports a meeting of *ronda* leaders in which the military leaders provided tools, medicine, guns, trucks and food as rewards for cooperation.[68] Sometimes participation was effective. Many local residents learned that by volunteering for a *ronda*, it was possible to ameliorate military repression and to repel Sendero.

The second type of *ronda* was a civil defence patrol. These groups participated with the military in operations against Sendero and the MRTA.[69] Instead of living scattered about the countryside, the political/military commander would transplant them into 'strategic hamlets'. Some have charged that these patrols had a 'licence to kill'. *QueHacer* reports that a doctor from an international organization, who travelled the Peruvian countryside on a vaccination campaign, felt more threatened in areas controlled by the committees of civil defence than in those controlled by Sendero.[70] Indeed, many reports of disappearances and executions have been reported in areas with these committees.[71] In addition to threatening other citizens, the creation of the *rondas campesinas* had other effects. According to Americas Watch, it was a 'tactic that converted civilians into targets for insurgent reprisals'.[72]

In 1989, García added the *rondas* as a new component to the counterinsurgency policy. Fujimori also placed more emphasis on the *rondas*. They were expanded, armed and empowered. Fujimori had armed 526 peasant communities by the end of 1992.[73] More than ten thousand shotguns were distributed to the *rondas*. By 1993, almost every village had a *ronda*.[74]

In addition to the military and *rondas campesinas*, state violence took the form of groups with unofficial ties to the state. Many of these groups emerged during the presidency of García. García seemed to encourage violence. For example, at an APRA youth rally in 1988, he stated that he admired the dedication of the Senderistas.[75] He also condoned some violence within the party. For example, in 1987 Rodrigo Franco, a friend of García, was assassinated by Sendero.[76] After this assassination, García called human rights groups 'accomplices of subversion' and alluded to the need for APRA's right to protect itself. Shortly after, the group Comando Rodrigo Franco (CRF) began its attacks on leftist politicians and supporters. The military did not pursue the CRF.[77] Javier Valle Riestra, a high-ranking APRA senator, admitted '"of course everyone knew that the party had búfalos" [APRA-affiliated violent groups that first gained notoriety in the 1940s[78]] but maintained that the party had a right to protect itself'.[79] The spread of violence to state-led violence increased the threats to the political community.

Table 5.1 characterizes the victims of state violence in 1991 and ascribes responsibility of for their deaths. The military killed the most people, over 1,000 in 1991, targeting mostly alleged members of the MRTA and Sendero. The police killed almost 350 people, mostly alleged terrorists, but also including 33 noncombatants. Local organizations

Table 5.1 Peru: state violence with categories of victims and those responsible, 1991

	Rondas	Local organizations	Police	Military	Unidentified
Professional	0	0	2	0	7
Businessmen	0	0	1	2	11
Workers	0	0	3	2	17
Peasants	0	3	12	14	27
Ronderos	0	0	0	0	2
Residents	0	3	11	2	51
Students	1	1	4	0	16
Authorities	0	0	0	0	3
Foreigners	0	0	0	0	0
Police	0	0	0	13	12
Military	0	0	1	0	16
Sendero Luminoso	84	23	248	720	10
MRTA	0	0	42	296	5
CRF	0	0	0	0	0
Narco-traf	0	0	22	0	0
Total	85	30	346	1049	177

Source: Comisión Especial de Investigación y Estudio sobre la Violencia y Alternativas de Pacificación, *Violencia y Pacificación en 1991* (Lima: Senado de la República, 1992), pp. 195–9.

and *rondas* killed 115 in that year. The Senate Commission stated that the numbers of MRTA and Sendero deaths are probably underreported because of the hesitance, due to fear of reprisal, of family members to report deaths to the state. Overall, the 1991 Senate report estimated that its figures could reasonably be increased by 10 per cent.

In addition to the confirmed dead, many citizens were reported missing (figure 5.2). Although people reported as missing occasionally reappear alive, the majority are presumed dead and are never found. It should be noted that tallies of the disappeared vary considerably according to the source used. For example, in 1991 the Asociación pro Derechos Humanos (APRODEH) reported 208 disappearances, the Comisión Episcopal de Acción Social 62, the Nacional de Derechos Humanos (CNDDHH) 287, the Comisión de Derechos Humanos (COMISEDH) 199, and the Centro de Estudios y Acción para la Paz 43. The Senate Commission stated that it believed an additional two to three thousand should be added to the tally of the disappeared.[80]

Figure 5.2 Peru: number of 'disappeared', 1982–91

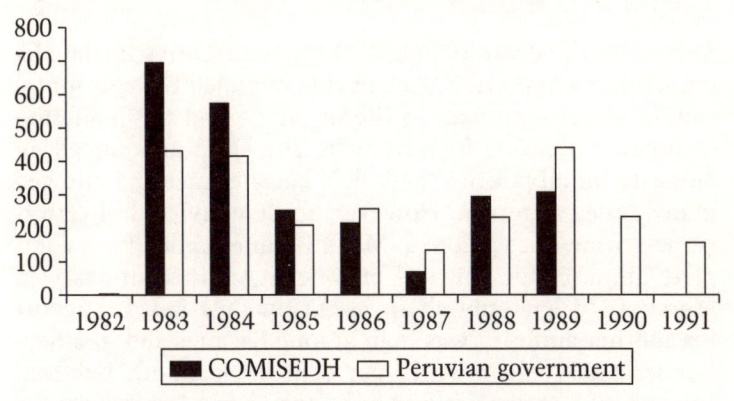

[Bar chart showing COMISEDH and Peruvian government figures for disappeared persons from 1982 to 1991]

Sources: Comisión de Derechos Humanos (COMISEDH), quoted in Americas Watch *Peru Under Fire* (New Haven: Yale, 1992), p. 19; Peruvian Ministry of Exterior Relations, Comisión Especial de Investigación y Estudio sobre la Violencia y Alternativas de Pacificación, *Violencia y Pacificación en 1991* (Lima: Senado de la República, 1992), p. 96.

Spain

Spain, unlike Peru and Uruguay, did not engage in widely applied indiscriminate or excessive force to combat its terrorist threat. In general, democratic Spain reacted to the terrorism within its own constitutional bounds. This commitment to the law and due process helped to maintain a steady support for Spanish democracy, even among opposition political parties.

Violence caused significant disturbance in Spain. People were afraid. However, the state attempted to remove the incentives to join violent groups. Compared with the Franco regime, the citizens had full political liberties. In addition, the previous restrictions on regional languages and cultures were abolished. For example, under Franco Basque cultural activity was severely limited and the language outlawed.[81] Eventually the violence became less frequent, especially after 1980. The state's attempts at reinforcing the political community seemed to be working.

Spanish state reaction

Soon after the death of Franco, King Juan Carlos initiated a national reconciliation. Part of this included the commutation of death sentences to life in prison and the reduction of other sentences. In July 1976, the state announced an amnesty for all political and ideological crimes and allowed many exiles to return. However, those convicted of terrorist acts were not pardoned. Many Basques called for a complete amnesty for political prisoners. Another amnesty in March 1977 left only about twenty people jailed. Support for another amnesty was high among Basques and in a September 1977 poll, only 12 per cent of Spaniards believed the previous amnesties had been excessive. Another 16 per cent thought they were sufficient. However, a third of Spaniards and almost one half of Basques thought that it was not enough.[82] Finally, in October 1977 the state freed the remaining prisoners, on the condition that they left the country.[83] In 1984, the Spanish state began to offer another form of amnesty called 'social reintegration' to ETA members who were ready to publicly renounce future acts of violence. Incarcerated ETA members and exiled ETA members were allowed to participate.[84]

In 1977 another tough issue was tackled: regional separatist demands. The new constitution allowed two procedures for each region in Spain to gain the status of an autonomous community within Spain. The historical communities of Galicia, Catalonia and the Basque country were offered fast routes to autonomy, while the other regions were allowed a slower route to autonomy.[85] In addition, the autonomy agreement for the Basque country granted the region more autonomy than ever before. The 1979 statute 'estatuto de Guernica' delegated to the Basque community the administration of justice, some control over economic policy and the creation of a Basque public television channel. The statute also established the Basque language as a joint official language, established a Basque government and gave the community the option of later joining with Navarre.[86] The control over economic policy included restoration of the 1876 economic agreements. These agreements allow the Basque government to collect taxes, but only requires it to give the national state about one-third of the proceeds. In 1981, the new Basque police force of 500 started traffic duties, while the old Civil Guard (Guardia Civil) maintained control of security. By 1999, the new force, called Ertzaintza, had grown to more than 7,000 agents.[87] The new force helped to abate the tension that had previously existed between the forces of the national police and Guardia Civil and the general Basque public. For example, in the last half of 1977 police broke up 30 demonstrations, killing 3 and wounding 87 in the process.[88]

Political liberties were also restored by the new democracy. By the end of 1976, the King had abolished Franco's special courts for trying terrorists.[89] In 1978, press censorship was greatly reduced from the policies created under Franco.[90] Spain's was generally considered a free press by 1979.[91] Overall, the state did not implement indiscriminate repression, although charges of torture are occasionally raised, most often in the Basque region. However, the Spanish state has cooperated with human rights organizations such as Amnesty International.[92] In 1983, the Spanish Human Rights Association received 120 complaints of torture or mistreatment. Of those, 30 cases were actively investigated. The conclusion of Amnesty International was that the incidents were the results of individual transgressions, as opposed to an officially sponsored policy.[93]

The state did institute some anti-terrorist legislation. In 1978, Law 21/1978 was passed, giving the police new powers of arrest and detention. Suspects could be held for up to seventy-two hours without charge. Judicial oversight of this practice was also established, but rarely invoked. The police could also intercept the mail and telephone messages of suspected terrorists. This law was supplemented by Law 56/1978, 'Special Measures toward Crimes of Terrorism Committed by Armed Groups Act', which allowed detention of up to ten days and the holding of suspects *incommunicado*. Also, the decree law 'On the Protection of Citizen Security' was instituted in January 1979; this increased penalties for terrorist crimes, restricted the rights of prisoners to seek provisional release from prison and criminalized statements that could be interpreted as defending terrorist acts or groups.[94] A 1980 law passed by the National Assembly allowed an extension of preventive detention, the searching of homes without a warrant, and the violation of privacy of mail and telephone communications. This suspension of rights could be applied to people suspected of complicity in or participation in terrorist acts. Preventive detention and observation had to be ordered by a magistrate. Searches were conducted, arrests were made, and ETA infiltrated by new police forces. A new anti-terrorist police force of fifty men based in Bilbao, led by Roberto Conesa, was formed in 1978. In February 1980, two counter-terrorist police forces were formed: the 120-member Special Operations Group dealt with urban terrorism and the 450-member Rural Antiterrorist Groups of the Guardia Civil operated in other areas. These forces were supplemented by 12,000 regular Guardia Civil troops and 6,000 national police. The increase in arrests resulting from these forces undoubtedly created resentment in the Basque country.[95] In 1980, the number of arrests increased to 2,140 from only 561 in 1979. Previously the peak of arrests had occurred in 1975, the year of Franco's death, with over 4,600 arrests. By 1983, the number had dropped to under 1,200 a year.[96] In May 1981, a new law called the 'Law for the Defence of the Constitution' was passed. The definition of terrorism now included non-violent efforts to secure independence from the Spanish nation. The state also had the power to close media that communicated any apologia for terrorism.[97]

After the coup attempt in 1981, further legislation was passed, generally intensifying Spanish anti-terrorism policy. In May 1983, a new security initiative called Operation Zen was instituted in the Basque region. The Civil Guard was given extra training to introduce them to the special circumstances of the Basque region; a public affairs initiative was launched to engender cooperation between the public and the police; more cooperation was established between the Civil Guard and the Basque police; and, finally, judges were allowed to shut down associations and publications that advocated terrorism.[98] The Basque government, however, refused to cooperate with the Spanish state in implementing the plan. In 1984, a new law, Law 8/1984, was passed that reaffirmed many earlier police powers included in prior laws. In addition, judges were now allowed to ban political parties and groups headed by convicted terrorists and to order the detention of suspected terrorists for up to two and a half years. Not surprisingly, Basque political leaders resisted the law. For example, HB leader Miguel Castells described it as a 'Nazi law more regressive than the Francoists in many respects'. Spain's highest court deemed part of the law unconstitutional and, in December 1987, the Spanish state repealed the remainder.[99]

Spanish state violence

Despite the efforts of the state in restoring liberties, declaring amnesties and granting autonomy, the actions of the state were not entirely nonviolent. The police and Civil Guard killed many in violent clashes. For example, between February 1976 and December 1979 forty people were killed in demonstrations in the Basque provinces by police 'in spite of efforts at "re-education"'.[100] In March 1981, in response to a flood of ETA attacks and the attempted military coup, the state deployed army and navy troops to the Basque provinces for the first time since the return to democracy.[101] From 1976 to 1979, eighty people were killed by the police or Civil Guard. In 1980, six were killed. In 1981, sixteen were killed. In 1982, the number fell to seven.[102]

In addition, a clandestine group, the Anti-Terrorist Groups of Liberation (GAL), with ties to the state, became active in 1983, killing suspected terrorists. GAL used illegal means, including assassination and kidnapping, to fight terrorism. In the early 1980s, GAL assassinated at least twenty-six alleged members of ETA. GAL was also active abroad and is attributed with the deaths of twenty ETA members in France.[103] In fact, in the summer of 1998, José Luis Barrionuevo, former Minister of Security (Interior) from 1982–88, and eleven others were found guilty of kidnapping and murdering suspected terrorists. Most of the deaths occurred in France or very near the border. It has since transpired that one-third to one-half of the victims were innocent.[104] However, the actions of GAL were not widely known until the 1990s. Because of the relatively small number of dead, the ten to fifteen year delay until the actions became known and the location of the occurrences, the Spanish state did not lose citizen support before the events became known. Many scholars partly attribute the loss of the socialists in the 1990s to the emergence of evidence linking the Spanish government to GAL. However, overall, in spite of the deaths, GAL and the March 1981 military deployment, the Spanish state did not appear to be pursuing an indiscriminate repressive state response.

Summary

Whereas in the first stage of analysis, all three countries were faced with a similar violent challenge, this second stage of analysis uncovers an important difference. Both Uruguay and Peru responded to the terrorist violence with extensive state violence and indiscriminate repression. Spain, on the contrary, did not implement either policy. It is expected that this difference will account for the consolidation of Spanish democracy and the demise of Uruguayan and Peruvian democracies, discussed in chapter 6.

Notes

1 Weinstein, 1988, p. 44.
2 Porzencanski, 1973, p. 57.
3 Inter-Church Committee on Human Rights in Latin America, *Violations of Human Rights in Uruguay (1972–1976)* (Toronto: Inter-Church Committee on Human Rights in Latin America, 1978), p. 2.
4 MPS emergency powers are granted to the president by the constitution in article 168, 'in case of serious and unforeseen events, foreign attack or internal upheavals'; Labrousse, 1970, p. 53. However, the executive must consult parliament within twenty-four hours. Jellinek and Ledesma, 1979, Part 1; see also Porzencanski, 1973, p. 57.
5 Inter-Church Committee on Human Rights in Latin America, 1978, p. 3. According to article 27 of law 9943, a state of emergency entitles the president to break trade unions: 'Under a state of emergency the citizens may be placed under martial law and jurisdiction ... so that services indisputable to the life of the country may be maintained'. See also Labrousse, 1970, p. 56.
6 Porzencanski, 1973, p. 57. This strike took place from 26 July–15 October 1969.
7 Weinstein, 1988, p. 46.
8 Labrousse, 1970, p. 63.
9 Servicio Paz y Justicia: Uruguay, 1986, p. 11.
10 Labrousse, 1970, p. 54.
11 Porzencanski, 1973, pp. 58, 64.
12 Porzencanski, 1973, pp. 62–3.

13 Porzencanski, 1973, p. 56.
14 *Generals and Tupamaros*, p. 26.
15 Servicio Paz y Justicia: Uruguay, 1986, p. 17.
16 Inter-Church Committee on Human Rights in Latin America, 1978, p. 19.
17 Decree 277/972, Inter-Church Committee on Human Rights in Latin America, 1978, p. 11.
18 The preceding list was compiled with data from Inter-Church Committee on Human Rights in Latin America, 1978, and Republica Oriental del Uruguay Junta de Comandantes en Jefe, 1977, Tomo 1.
19 *Generals and Tupamaros*, pp. 44–6.
20 Inter-Church Committee on Human Rights in Latin America, 1978, p. 17.
21 *Generals and Tupamaros*, p. 47.
22 Porzencanski, 1973, pp. 62–8.
23 Labrousse, 1970, p. 53.
24 US Government, 1990, p. 40.
25 Inter-Church Committee on Human Rights in Latin America, 1978, p. 5.
26 Porzencanski, 1973, pp. 53–5.
27 *Generals and Tupamaros*, p. 17.
28 *Generals and Tupamaros*, pp. 13, 24.
29 *Generals and Tupamaros*, pp. 10–12.
30 Porzencanski, 1973, pp. 61–8.
31 *Generals and Tupamaros*, p. 47.
32 A. J. Langguth, *Hidden Terrors* (New York: Pantheon Books, 1978), p. 246.
33 *Generals and Tupamaros*, p. 15.
34 Porzencanski, 1973, p. 61.
35 Kaufman, 1979, p. 38.
36 Kaufman, 1979, p. 38.
37 Inter-Church Committee on Human Rights in Latin America, 1978, p. 21.
38 *Generals and Tupamaros*, p. 70.
39 Chang-Rodríguez, 1987, p. 164.
40 Americas Watch, *A Certain Passivity: Failing to Curb Human Rights Abuses in Peru* (New Haven: Yale University Press, 1987), p. 5.
41 Comisión Especial de Investigación y Estudio sobre la Violencia y Alternativas de Pacificación en el Perú, *Violencia y Pacificación* (Lima: Senado de la República, 1989), p. 298.
42 Americas Watch, 1992, p. 6.
43 Article 276 of the Peruvian constitution gives the armed forces the fundamental aim of protecting the independence, sovereignty and territorial integrity of the republic. Under article 231, they may assume control of the country. Comisión Especial de Investigación y Estudio sobre la Violencia y Alternativas de Pacificación, 1992, p. 27.

44 Mauceri, 1991, pp. 90–1.
45 Werlich, 1984, p. 81.
46 Americas Watch, 1992, p. 7.
47 Javier Diez Canseco, *Democracia, militarización y derechos humanos en el Perú 1980–1984* (Lima: APRODEH, Servicios Populares, Edition 2a ed, 1985), p. 48.
48 Americas Watch, 1992, p. 22.
49 Americas Watch, 1992, p. 22.
50 'Impundid official', *Caretas*, No. 1141, 7 January 1991, p. 31.
51 Americas Watch, 1992, p. 27.
52 Mauceri, 1991, p. 100.
53 David Scott Palmer, 'The Revolutionary Terrorism of Peru's Shining Path', in Crenshaw (ed.), 1991, Table 7.7, p. 299.
54 Amnesty International, *Peru: Human Rights During the Government of Alberto Fujimori* (New York: Amnesty International, 1992), pp. 7–8.
55 Escalante and Vidal, 1993, p. 50.
56 'What we have now is an authoritarian regime that we hope will not become a civil military regime or unconstitutional'. My translation. González, 1993, p. 59.
57 Cameron, 1995, p. 149.
58 Cameron, 1995, p. 149.
59 Escalante and Vidal, 1993, p. 78.
60 *Equis X*, No. 400 'FFAA asumen control', 23–30 July 1984, pp. 16–18.
61 Raúl González 'Y ahora qué, especial sobre Sendero', *QueHacer*, No. 30, August 1984, p. 9.
62 Mauceri, 1991, p. 91.
63 Bourque and Warren, 1989, pp. 18–24.
64 Americas Watch, 1987, p. 24.
65 González, 1984, p. 15.
66 Mauceri, 1991, p. 101.
67 These *rondas* should not be confused with an earlier type of Peruvian *ronda*. In Peru, there are numerous types of ronda. For a complete discussion of *rondas*, see Raúl González, 'Campesions, Ronderos y Guerra Antisubversiva', *QueHacer*, No. 46, April/May 1987, p. 72 and Orin Starn, 'Noches de ronda', *QueHacer*, No. 69, Jan./Feb. 1991, pp. 76–92.
68 Orin Starn, 'To Revolt Against the Revolution: War and Resistance in Peru's Andes', *Cultural Anthropology*, Vol. 10, No. 4, Nov. 1995, p. 562.
69 González, 1987, p. 78.
70 'Politica antisubversiva: Algun Cambio?' *QueHacer*, No. 58, April–May 1989, p. 29.
71 'Politica antisubversiva: Algun Cambio?', p. 29.
72 Americas Watch, 1992, p. 9.
73 Daniel Masterson, 'In the Shining Path of Mariategui, Mao Zedong or Presidente Gonzalo? Peru's Sendero Luminoso in Historical

Perspective', *Journal of Third World Studies*, Spring 1994, Vol. 11, No. 1, p. 169.
74 Starn, 1995, p. 553.
75 Carol Graham, *Peru's APRA* (Boulder: L. Rienner Publishers, 1992), pp. 132–9.
76 Bourque and Warren, 1989, p. 17.
77 Mauceri, 1991, p. 97.
78 Bourque and Warren, 1989, p. 11.
79 Graham, 1992, p. 164.
80 Comisión Especial de Investigación y Estudio sobre la Violencia y Alternativas de Pacificación, 1992, p. 102.
81 Shub and Carr, 1985, p. 122.
82 Centro de Investigaciones Sociológicas, 'Encuesta y Sondeos del Centro de Investigaciones Sociológicas', *Revista Española de la Opinion Publica* (Madrid: Instituto de la Opinion Publica, 1977), Vol. 50, p. 266.
83 Janke, 1980, p. 10. See also Clark, 1979, p. 299.
84 Moxon-Browne and Janke, 1988, p. 167.
85 Arango, 1995, p. 139.
86 Juan Díez Medrano, *Divided Nations: Class, Politics, and Nationalism in the Basque Country and Catalonia* (Ithaca: Cornell University Press, 1995), p. 146.
87 Spanish Ministry of the Interior, <http:www.mir.es/oris/infoeta/esp/p06-esp.htm>.
88 Clark, 1990, p. 39. See also Arteche, 1982.
89 Clark, 1990, p. 38.
90 Department of State, *Report Submitted to the Committee on International Relations. U.S. House of Representatives and Committee on Foreign Relations* (Washington, DC: Government Printing Office, 1978), p. 310.
91 Department of State, *Report Submitted to the Committee on International Relations. U.S. House of Representatives and Committee on Foreign Relations* (Washington, DC: Government Printing Office, 1979), p. 659.
92 Department of State, *Report Submitted to the Committee on International Relations. U.S. House of Representatives and Committee on Foreign Relations* (Washington, DC: Government Printing Office, 1980), p. 875.
93 Department of State, *Report Submitted to the Committee on International Relations. U.S. House of Representatives and Committee on Foreign Relations* (Washington, DC: Government Printing Office, 1983), p. 1089.
94 Clark, 1990, p. 41.
95 Clark, 1990, pp. 42–3.
96 Francisco J. Llera, José M. Mata and Cynthia L. Irvin, 'ETA: From Secret Army to Social Movement – the Post Franco Schism of the Basque National Movement', *Terrorism and Political Violence*, Vol. 5, No. 3, Autumn 1993, pp. 106–34.
97 Clark, 1990, p. 49.

98 Moxon-Browne and Janke, 1988, pp. 165–6.
99 Clark, 1990, p. 65.
100 Carr and Fusi, 1981, p. 237.
101 Lancaster and Prevost, 1985, p. 77.
102 Tezanos *et al.*, 1989, p. 215.
103 Alonso and Reinares, 1993, p. 39.
104 Clark, 1990, ch. 2.

6
Testing of hypotheses one and two

Introduction: the hypotheses

Terrorist violence threatens democratic stability by undermining both rudimentary purposes of the state, security and integration. As the purposes of the state are unfulfilled, citizen confidence in the state declines. As citizen confidence decreases, democratic instability increases.

State repression and violence also undermine the rudimentary purposes of the state, integration and security. Decreases in citizen confidence should follow a decrease in the fulfilment of the rudimentary purposes. Finally, as citizen confidence in the state decreases, increases in democratic instability should be identifiable.

According to these hypotheses, the cases of Uruguay and Peru, countries that suffered both increasingly high levels of terrorist violence and state repressive policies and violence, should offer evidence of a lack of fulfilment of the rudimentary purposes of the state and decreased citizen confidence. In addition, as these measures decline, it is expected that there should be an increase in democratic instability. In the case of Spain, a country that faced terrorist violence but not extensive state repressive policies or state violence, some declines in measures of security due to terrorist violence are expected but not from the state reaction.

Rudimentary purpose of the state: security

Security can be measured in different ways in different countries. Security can be indicated by the number of people killed by terrorist and state violence. It can also be indicated by public opinion data concerning violence and violent groups. In each country, different data are available. However, the different measures represent indicators of the same rudimentary purpose of the state: security.

Uruguayan security

How did the state and terrorist violence affect the fulfilment of security in Uruguay? Four measures of the rudimentary purpose of the state, security, can be used. Public opinion data provide the first three measures. Specifically, data about fear, disorder and the Tupamaros are available. Finally, the death toll due to violence also serves as an indicator of a failure to maintain security.

Clear evidence exists documenting concern about terrorist violence. Concern about the disorder was evident as early as 1968. Gallup Uruguay, in a random selection of Uruguayan adults over the age of eighteen, asked the respondents to describe the current social situation. This measure is not perfect, since disorder is not defined and includes an evaluation of sources other than terrorism, such as labour disputes. Nonetheless, Uruguayans perceived an increase in disorder as the incidents of terrorist violence increased from six incidents in 1967 to fifty-six in 1968 and sixty-three in 1969. In October 1968, 46 per cent thought there was major disorder and 35 per cent thought there was minor disorder. By June 1969, 54 per cent thought there was major disorder and 37 per cent thought there was minor disorder. Uruguayans believed their social situation to be more disorderly in 1969 than in 1968. There was a 13 per cent increase in the number of terrorist actions in the same period. Uruguayans found the late 1960s to be particularly turbulent for a society that had previously been peaceful.[1]

The main group responsible for most of the terrorist violence, the Tupamaros, was viewed as dangerous by the citizens, reflecting a concern for security. Gallup asked some specific questions about the Tupamaros in the late

1960s and early 1970s. With an increase in the frequency of violence in 1969, the group was increasingly viewed as dangerous. The respondents were asked to fill in the blank to the question, 'How would you describe the [Tupamaros]? ... It [The Tupamaros] is an organization that is——'. In 1969, almost half (48 per cent) of the respondents believed the Tupamaros to be highly dangerous, up from 40 per cent in 1968. Only 10 per cent believed them to be harmless, down from 18 per cent in 1968. These numbers are significant as they show that the threat was realized even before the higher levels of violence were reached in 1972.[2]

Another measure of security is the number killed by terrorist actions. Although the method of choice for the terrorist groups was not assassination, on occasion assassination was used. The political killings began in 1969, with three killed. In the following year, only two were killed, followed by six in 1971. A relative eruption of political killings occurred in 1972, when twenty-one people were killed. In 1973, there were no political killings by the terrorist groups.[3]

Adding to the insecurity caused by the Tupamaros was violence from groups originating from the far right. For example, MANO was formed in July 1970. MANO threatened to 'terminate five "useless lives" for every policeman, soldier or other citizen killed by left wing terrorists. The "useless lives" would be selected from a list of known left-wingers and common criminals'.[4] Not only were those targeted by the Tupamaros afraid, but also many on the legal left who were targeted by far right groups.

One of the scholars who studied Uruguay at this time, Howard Handelman, conducted polling and interviews of industrial leaders. Handelman concluded that industrial leaders feared for their safety in the early 1970s. They were the targets of Tupamaro bombings and kidnappings. These industrial leaders increased their ties to the state and to the military.[5]

The effects of state violence are harder to document due to a lack of data. In spite of this, it is probable that the suspension of individual liberties, including habeas corpus and the practise of torture in interrogations, resulted in some citizens viewing the state as a threat to their security. Moreover, with the appearance of clandestine violent state-sanctioned groups such as JUP and the Comando Caza Tupamaro, it seems reasonable to infer damage to security due to state repression and violence.

Peruvian security

How did the state and terrorist violence affect the fulfilment of the rudimentary purpose of the state, security, in Peru? Evidence of a decrease in the fulfilment of security can be measured in public opinion data and in the death toll. Through an examination of public opinion, the main concerns of the citizens can be tracked. Not surprisingly, the people viewed violence as a severe problem. Public opinion data also document fear of both state and terrorist groups. Finally, the death toll confirms that the citizens' perception of insecurity was based on a bloody reality.

According to public opinion data, the violence of Sendero, the MRTA and other terrorist groups was viewed as threatening. The National Questionnaire about Violence, commissioned by the Bernales Senate Commission in 1988, reported that 64.3 per cent of the people viewed terrorist violence as the predominant type of violence in the country; 12.6 per cent chose delinquency, 7.5 per cent drug trafficking, 6.9 per cent police or military, and 4.8 per cent domestic violence.[6] The population clearly viewed the terrorist violence as more of a threat than police or military violence in 1988.

In general, terrorism was consistently ranked among the most critical problems of Peru. Table 6.1 charts the perception of inflation, unemployment, terrorism and nutrition. Respondents were asked: 'In your opinion, what are the three principal problems facing the country?' The table includes the top four problems placed most frequently in the top three. January 1988 showed the highest concern about terrorism. However, in April 1992, the month of the coup, terrorism was still considered one of the most severe problems facing the nation, with 49 per cent of those questioned choosing it. Unemployment, nutrition and inflation followed as severe problems. The violence was perceived to be so severe that some considered the country to be in a state of civil war. In a poll conducted on 25 July 1989, 56 per cent of Peruvians feared that their country was on the brink of a civil war and that, in some parts of the country, subversive forces were in control. Nineteen per cent of the people believed that a civil war already existed.[7] The

Table 6.1 Peru: four principal problems

	Inflation	Terrorism	Unemployment	Nutrition
January 1988	51	67	32	22
April 1989	61	59	49	23
February 1990	59	62	58	46
October 1990	46	35	50	34
January 1991	27	53	31	36
July 1991	34	43	34	41
October 1991	–	43	31	35
April 1992	14	49	39	16

Note: Figures are the percentage of respondents that named the category as one of the top three problems facing Peru.

Sources: APOYO, *Informe de Opinion*, January 1991; APOYO, *Informe de Opinion*, July 1991; APOYO, *Informe de Opinion*, October 1991; APOYO, *Informe de Opinion*, April 1992; Foreign Broadcast Information Service.

importance of violence as a concern to the Peruvians is even more impressive given the context of the prolonged and severe economic crisis that Peru was facing.

The violence instilled a sense of fear in the vast majority of the population. The 1988 Bernales Commission documents the fear of terrorist groups. It reported that 72.6 per cent of Peruvians admitted that the terrorist acts had made them afraid, 15 per cent said they were somewhat afraid and only 6.5 per cent said the acts had not succeeded in frightening them.[8] Three years later, in January 1991, a majority of respondents reported being afraid. *Perú Económico* reported an APOYO survey of Lima residents on terrorism. Of those questioned, 78 per cent admitted that terrorist attacks and blackouts had created an environment of fear and anxiety.[9]

In addition, the citizens were not only afraid of terrorist groups, such as Sendero; they were afraid of state forces. APOYO asked: 'What does a policeman inspire – security or fear?' The National Police inspired more fear than security in three out of four surveys (figure 6.1). Moreover, beginning in July 1991, there was a steady decline in the amount of security that the National Police inspired. By October, approximately two-thirds of those questioned replied that the police made them feel fearful instead of secure.

The general fear that three out of four Peruvians felt reflected the bloody reality of Peruvian life. Thousands of

Figure 6.1 Peru: view of what the National Police inspire

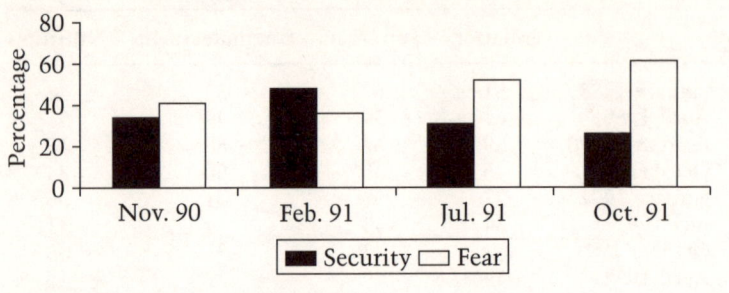

[Bar chart showing Security and Fear percentages for Nov. 90, Feb. 91, Jul. 91, Oct. 91]

Source: FBIS LAT 91 211, pp. 40–1.

Figure 6.2 Peru: deaths due to state violence and terrorism, 1980–92

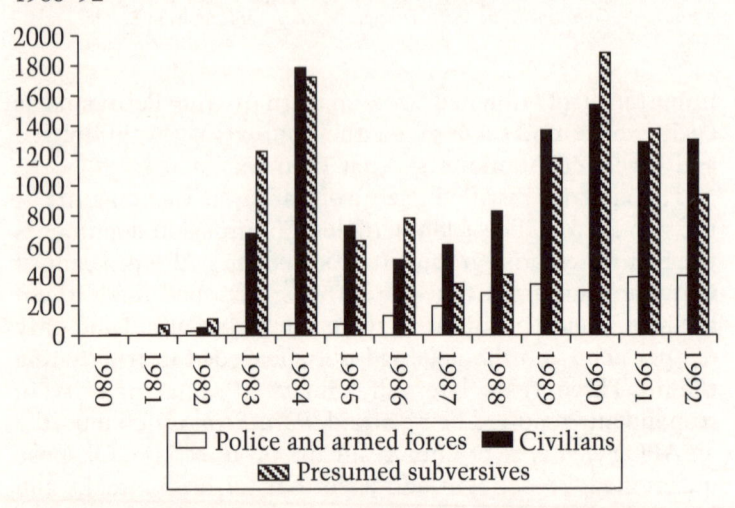

[Bar chart showing Police and armed forces, Civilians, and Presumed subversives deaths from 1980 to 1992]

Source: David Scott Palmer, 'The Revolutionary Terrorism of Peru's Shining Path', in Martha Crenshaw (ed.), *Terrorism in Context* (University Park: Pennsylvania University Press, 1995), Table 7.1, p. 271. Reproduced by permission of the publisher.

noncombatant civilians had been killed by both state and terrorist groups (figure 6.2). Hundreds of officials had been assassinated. Many of the deaths in 1983 and 1984 were due to the actions of the military in emergency zones. Peruvian scholar Carlos Iván Degregori called Belaúnde's policy of those two years 'genocidal' for the peasants in the emergency zones, and according to Starn,

General Noel's counteroffensive of 1983–4 displayed the most brutal and imperial side of the military. Torture, rape and murder of suspected rebels remained a mainstay of the counter-insurgency in subsequent years, leaving Peru with the world's highest number of 'disappeared' from 1988 to 1991.[10]

The increasing numbers of dead starting in 1989 reflect the recovery of Sendero from the June 1986 prison massacre and their advancement into their phase of 'strategic equilibrium' where Sendero tried to match the strength of the state.

Peruvians from all parts of the ideological and economic spectrums were victims of violence. In an examination of the total death toll, it can be seen that civilians and alleged subversives make up the overwhelming majority of victims. However, some groups have questioned the number of subversive deaths, believing many of the dead who were labelled subversive actually to be noncombatant citizens. Of the 24,250 killed from 1980 to July 1992, approximately 1 per cent were drug traffickers, 42 per cent civilians, 49 per cent alleged subversives and 8 per cent security forces.[11] Noncombatant civilians have paid a high price for the conflict, with more than ten thousand deaths in twelve years. This conflict was also economically costly. In the fifteen years from 1980–95, economic losses due to the violence were estimated to total approximately $25 billion dollars.[12]

Both state and terrorist violence threatened the security of citizens. Raúl González describes a frightening situation in Ayacucho:

> Nadie sabe dónde está seguro, nadie: ni el policía que espera en caulquier momento un ataque ni el habitante que teme, si no la detención, el prepotente registro de su domicilio por una policía que busca terroristas y que cree que todos son senderistas.[13]

Sendero and other terrorist groups targeted victims. State human rights violations threatened the safety of citizens. Forced participation in *rondas* transformed citizens into targets. In Peru, it seemed difficult not to be perceived as the enemy of either the terrorist or the state.

Spanish security

How did the terrorist violence affect the fulfilment of the rudimentary purpose of the state, security, in Spain? Available evidence of the Spanish case is limited to data

Table 6.2 Spain: top problems facing the country, 1977–86

	Dec. 77	Nov. 78	June 79	Mar. 80	July 80	Feb. 81	July 82	April 84	July 86
Unemployment	66	91	88	84	88	91	88	91	85
Crime			72	35	33	30	23	38	63
Drug trafficking									53
Terrorism	32*	51*	72*	49	60	61	68	63	28
Cost of living	70	82	72	40	40	35	39	30	19

Sources: Gallup, Spain, IG-600/085; Gallup, Spain, IG-600/129; Gallup, Spain, IG-600/067; Gallup, Spain, IG-600/081; Gallup, Spain, IG-600/147; FBIS; *El Pais*.

documenting the top problems facing the nation and death tolls from violence. Unfortunately, specific questions documenting fear are unavailable.

During the transition to democracy, two main problems dominated public opinion: economic troubles and public order. A series of Gallup polls traced the public concern for different problems (table 6.2). In 1977, inflation and public order consistently ranked among the highest concerns. The numbers for the problem of public order were broken down according to party affiliation for the December data. Not surprisingly, members of the conservative AP and the centre right UCD were more concerned about order. Over half of the members of the AP, 57 per cent, were most concerned with order. Forty-four per cent of the UCD were most concerned about order. Order remained important for other party members also. Over 20 per cent of those affiliated with the regional and leftist parties listed it as a top problem.[14] In 1978 and 1979, public order and economic issues were the first two concerns but, starting in 1979, more than 70 per cent of those questioned chose order as a top problem. The increase in concern about public order corresponds to the increase in deaths due to terrorist violence, which increased from 28 in 1977 to 85 in 1978 and to 108 in 1979. A follow-up poll in March 1980 by Gallup found that unemployment and terrorism were the top concerns for the year.[15] Concern about terrorism continued to increase as the number of deaths increased that year. Concern for terrorism remained high through to 1985.

The responses for 1977 to 1979, marked with an asterisk in table 6.2, instead of asking about terrorism, asked about

Figure 6.3 Spain: deaths and those responsible, 1968–86

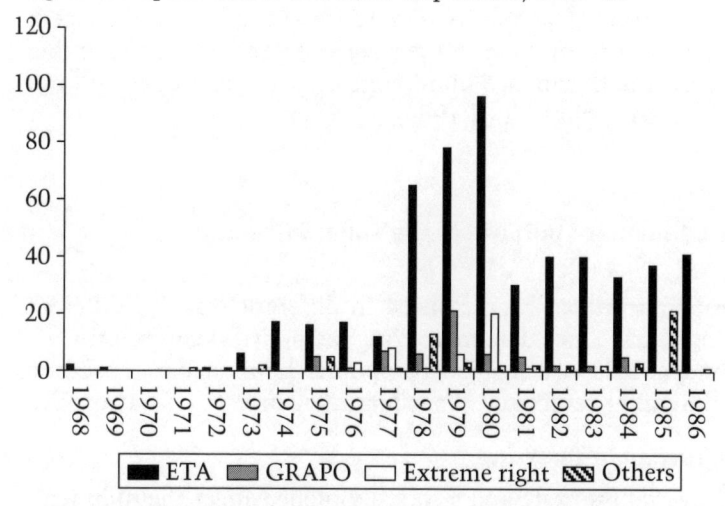

■ ETA ▨ GRAPO □ Extreme right ▩ Others

Source: Salustiano del Campo (ed.), *Tendencies Sociales en España Volumen II* (Bilbao: Fundacion BBV, 1993), p. 70. Reproduced by permission of the publisher.

public order. Economic troubles and terrorism dominate citizen concerns throughout the first years of the democracy. Concern about terrorism peaked in July 1982. By July 1986, only 28 per cent listed it within the top three problems facing the nation.

Finally, the death toll from terrorist violence measures the fulfilment of state security. The bloodiest year was 1980 (figure 6.3). In that year 91 people were killed by ETA alone, with 124 people being killed in all. Two years earlier, in 1978, 85 people were killed. The number of deaths from terrorist violence dropped after 1980 and began to stabilize at a lower level. By 1981, the number of dead had dropped to a quarter of the number of victims of the year before.

A relationship between the number of dead and the amount of concern about terrorism or public order can be seen. Unfortunately, the wording of the question changed from 'public order' to 'terrorism' during the critical year of 1980. However, we can still establish that as the number of deaths increased from 1977 to 1979, the percentage of people choosing public order as a main problem increased from

32 to 72 per cent. Similarly, as violence increased in 1980, the percentage of people listing terrorism as a main concern increased from 49 to 60 per cent. After 1981, the number of deaths declined. Public concern with terrorism did not begin to decline until 1984, however.

Rudimentary purpose of the state: integration

Integration can be measured in different ways in different countries. Since data measuring the political community are unavailable, we instead use public opinion data based on individual responses. Anecdotal evidence is also available.

Uruguayan integration

How did the state and terrorist violence affect the rudimentary purpose of the state, integration, in Uruguay? Specific questions of tolerance towards citizens of opposing views are unavailable. However, anecdotal evidence about levels of tolerance is available. In addition, evidence from secondary sources is available. Integration can be indicated by whether or not tolerance for those with differing views is expressed.

The anecdotal evidence is compelling. The reaction to state policies appeared to undermine integration. For example, in June 1970 Generals Borda and Francese, as police chief and Minister of the Interior, insisted that the state decree that attacks against military establishments or personnel would be tried by court marshal. Penalties for 'spreading subversive ideas and undermining public order' were also greatly increased. The punishment for those who 'aid, organize, direct or participate in association tending to arouse hate or violent class struggle, or upset the political and social order of the state, as well as those who diffuse ideas of this kind' would be up to fifteen years' imprisonment.[16] This broadly defined law did not make an exception of the Communist Party. The communists objected to the law, noting that it would possibly implicate them, given their belief in the class struggle as a law of history. More anecdotal evidence is available. For instance, after an incident at a communist club in April 1972 in which seven people were killed, one officer involved in the incident commented, 'so long as my comrades are being killed [four officials were shot dead by the Tupamaros three days earlier on 14 April] I am not making fancy distinctions between leftists'.[17] This statement definitely indicates a lack of tolerance for citizens who ascribed to a leftist view of politics.

In addition to anecdotal evidence, my expectations about the consequences of terrorist and state violence are supported by the work of other scholars in the existing literature. Charles Gillespie, in his study of the eventual redemocratization of Uruguay based on interviews with the country's leading politicians and businessmen, concludes that the Tupamaros 'had a corrosive effect on the Uruguayan political system, eroding tolerance for opponents and creating a polarized ideological climate. Traditional politicians became more and more convinced that guerrillas represented a threat to democracy'.[18] Howard Handelman, in a study conducted in the late 1970s based on interviews with leading businessmen, concluded that there was a 'conspiratorial view of the left which failed to distinguish between differing (and often hostile) leftist factions or divisions within the labor movement'. Of three hundred people surveyed,[19] one half believed the labour strife and guerrilla movement to be part of a leftist conspiracy. Ultimately, Handelman believed that this conflict and decrease in tolerance led to instability. A majority of the 'industrial elite felt that the dissolution of Congress and the elimination of democratic processes in 1973 was necessary for the nation's political and economic survival ... Questions regarding unions and labor relations prior to 1973 often elicited highly emotional, at times hysterical responses'.[20] Carina Perelli, in her study of the Uruguayan military in the 1970s, concludes that the attitude of the business class was shared by others. Within the circle of politicians, the same distrust and intolerance of opposing views became prevalent. According to Perelli,

> To make things worse, the new breed of Leftist politicians was not particularly accommodating. Opposition was understood as adversarial politics, which meant, among other things, that the rules of courtesy stemming from the feeling of belonging to the same 'club' or political class no longer applied. This, in turn, made it more and more difficult to maintain the old division between private vices and public virtues, even as a pretense ...

Confrontational politics, hostility, and polarization began to dominate the political arena, reducing the possibilities of dialogue and negotiation to nil. Little by little the more polarized sectors of society started to equate difference and diversity with enmity. The breakdown of consensus had an immediate paralyzing effect on state bureaucracies heavily dependent on the guarantees given by the political and party systems.[21]

The long tradition of cooperation among politicians seems to have disappeared. The limited available evidence suggests that the violence of the Tupamaros did undermine integration. However, the evidence also suggests that state action also undermined integration by polarizing the political community and reducing tolerance. The fear and mistrust led to a situation in the spring of 1972, according to Langguth, in which 'families were reduced to whispering to each other in their own homes. Everyone was taken for being a spy'.[22]

Peruvian integration

How did the state and terrorist violence affect the rudimentary purpose of the state, integration, in Peru? Historically, the political community in Peru was weak even before the outbreak of violence. For instance, when asked about the possibility of national integration, Senator Enrique Bernales replied that

> Va a ser muy difícil, porque los estigmas del pasado, de las divisions étnicas y culturales son muy fuertes y muy profundos. Este es un país racista. El *apartheid* no está escrito en leyes, pero funciona en la vida cotidiana y eso no sé cuánto tiempo tomará cambiarlo.[23]

It is expected that the stresses of state and terrorist violence further undermined integration. Decreasing levels of integration can be measured by examining different indicators. In Peru, integration can be measured by examining electoral and public opinion data. Elections were interrupted, as candidates were assassinated and election boycotts enforced by Sendero violence. Tolerance for opposing viewpoints decreased. Many young people reported being suspected of being terrorists. Finally, many citizens declined to cooperate with the state's antisubversive campaign.

Integration can also be indicated by measures of participation. Electoral participation was hindered due to the violence.

In an already poorly performing state, death threats from Sendero drove many from office and prevented others from replacing them. For example, at the end of 1984 224 council members and 104 mayors had resigned because of death threats.[24] In 1988, dozens of mayors resigned because of lack of protection from death threats.[25] In 1989, 10 governors and lieutenant-governors, 6 engineers and officials of development projects, 7 judicial officials and 19 other state officials were killed. Between January and October, 46 mayors were killed and 263 received death threats. Sendero's attacks had the effect of leaving 123 out of 435 districts without registered candidates in that year's elections.[26] From 1986 to August 1989, 99 mayors and 350 town councillors either resigned or abandoned their posts, and 17 mayors and 2 town councillors were killed.[27] The result of this intimidation was less state presence. For example, in August 1989 80 districts and 4 provinces had no municipal authority due to the assassination of 92 public officials.[28] In addition, many more local officials resigned due to threats. For example, in the department of Huánuco, more than 70 officials resigned.[29] Although these data could be reasonably viewed as an indicator of security, they are a more salient indicator of integration. Death threats and assassinations of community leaders and officials are an extreme example of the undermining of integration by preventing political participation.

In addition to creating vacancies in official offices, Sendero also influenced the ability of many citizens to vote. Voting is universal and mandatory in Peru, with the exception of active-duty military personnel and police, who are barred from voting.[30] In spite of mandatory voting, many people did not participate in elections. Not all abstentions, nulls and blank votes can be attributed to Sendero's boycotts of elections, but the forced boycotts and the threatened retaliation against voting did affect many areas. Nationally, votes varied from 7 to 19 per cent null votes, from 3 to 6 per cent blank and from 16 to 30 per cent absenteeism.[31] At the department level, there were wild variations. In areas with a strong Sendero presence, such as in Ayacucho, elections were strongly affected. For example, in the 1983 municipal elections, 75 per cent of eligible voters either abstained or cast blank votes. Of the votes cast, 56 per cent were blank or spoiled.[32] In addition, elections could not be held in the four rural Ayacucho provinces of Cangallo, Victor Fajardo, La Mar and Huanta in 1983. In the 1989 municipal elections in Ayacucho, absentee rates approached 56 per cent, with null and blank votes totalling 73 per cent.[33] In the areas under a state of emergency, many elections were annulled because of low turnout or too many invalid votes.[34] In addition to problems with excessive blank and null votes or absenteeism, some districts did not have candidates to fill the open positions because of Sendero intimidation. For example, of all districts holding elections in 1991, 123 districts, or 25 per cent, did not have candidates to fill the positions open for election.[35]

In addition to electoral disturbances, the violence affected tolerance for people of opposing views and increased suspicion of others. Sendero's threat was recognized by those on the legal left. Many on the left rejected the violence of Sendero. For example, an *Equis X* editorial states, 'la izquierda socialista tiene que optar, sincera y conscientemente por la democracia representativa, y rechazar el camino de la violencia, de la cual ella resultaría sin duda la primera víctima'.[36] José María Salcedo, in *QueHacer*, commented that Sendero was the principal enemy of the left and that the left had the most to lose because of Sendero: 'Más temprano que tarde, una repression militarizada no podría coexistir con los espacios democráticos. Esto, que es algo que no le importa a "Sendero," sí resulta vital para la izquierda'.[37] The legal left feared that they would pay for the actions of Sendero in the form of repression and intolerance.

In addition to a lack of tolerance, many Peruvians reported being suspected of being terrorists by other Peruvians and by the state authorities. *QueHacer* reported that young people, especially students, reported being harassed and suspected of being terrorists. According to one student, 'los estudiantes universitarios somos sospechosos de ser terroristas... todos y especialmente los que estamos en universitarios estatales'.[38] Peruvians living in areas with a Sendero presence were assumed to be Senderistas. For example, a general in charge of one emergency zone stated of the success of Sendero's attacks, '"Es possible gracias al apoyo que muchas veces le prestan los habitantes" y porque "pueden confundirse con mucha facilidad con los lugareños"'.[39] Moreover, people who fled the violence-plagued interior were assumed to be Senderistas either spreading violence to new areas or fleeing prosecution. In general, Peru became very dangerous for everyone. For instance, Enrique Mayer characterizes contemporary Peru as a country in which 'security employees, narco-traffickers, arms dealers, grave robbers, and police all operate underground. Terrorists dress up as police, while police don Sendero guise to carry out acts of unauthorized violence. Is it any wonder that no one can trust anyone in Peru?'[40]

The undermining of integration is also indicated by the unwillingness of Peruvian citizens to cooperate with the state to apprehend known terrorists. In spite of the broad fear that the terrorist violence inspired, the state could not rely on citizens' collaboration to fight the subversion. When asked whether or not they would collaborate with the state against terrorism, 30.2 per cent of respondents said they would collaborate, 48.7 per cent said they would not and 18.7 per cent did not know what they would do.[41] More specifically, when asked what they would do if they witnessed a terrorist act, 41.1 per cent would 'forget it', 10.0 per cent would report it without reservation, 39.5 per cent would report it with reservation, 4.8 per cent would intervene and 3.7 per cent did not know (0.9 per cent 'other').[42] Unfortunately, the poll did not ask for reasons for the lack of cooperation. However, the hesitation could be due to a fear of reprisal, a lack of faith in the ability of the state to respond, or perhaps even a lack of sympathy and support for the state itself, among other plausible reasons. Given the number of civilians, judges, mayors and other collaborators who were killed by Sendero, a fear of reprisal would be understandable. Considering the low citizen confidence in the state, it is not surprising that many Peruvians would be hesitant to risk their lives to cooperate, even if they did not support Sendero or other groups.

Sendero's intimidation of citizens impeded participation and functioning of the state. Officials and candidates were threatened and killed by Sendero. In addition, Sendero violently encouraged citizens either to abstain or to cast blank votes in elections. Moreover, it is plausible to infer that the repressive state response of invocations of states of emergency and the placement of areas under military control, with the suspension of individual liberties, further undermined integration. Many citizens, students and refugees reported the reaction of others, citizens and officials, who suspected them of being terrorists.

Spanish integration

How did the violence affect the rudimentary purpose of the state, integration, in Spain? Unfortunately, specific questions about violence are unavailable. No questions were asked as to whether citizens' participation was affected or whether their feelings towards other citizens changed. However, a deduction that civic friendship is harder to maintain or to create during instability would not be hard to imagine. Certainly, the killings of 289 civilians and non-professional military personnel did not bolster feelings of a community of equals and peers. However, there is evidence of the state acting to improve integration by resolving long-standing disagreements about regional autonomy. It is plausible that the state's efforts may have ameliorated some of the negative consequences of terrorist violence on integration.

To many regional groups, resentment against the central state was the legacy of the Franco regime. Although the restrictions against regional language and culture disappeared under the new democratic state, some of the distrust remained. Many citizens felt persecuted and discriminated against because of their regional origin. However, these feelings of discrimination appear to be fading over time. The worst dispersion of the community was ameliorated by the new democracy. In fact, the state acted to improve integration by conceding to regionalist demands.

Feelings of regional patriotism were especially high in Catalonia and in the Basque country. In a 1979 study, half of the Basque natives identified themselves as only Basque. An additional 15 per cent identified themselves as more Basque than Spanish. Only 24 per cent felt as Spanish as they were Basque. In Catalonia, 20 per cent of the Catalan natives identified themselves as only Catalan. An additional 16 per cent identified themselves as more Catalan than Spanish. Forty-two per cent felt as Spanish as Catalan. The citizens in these regions demanded autonomous status.[43]

Almost immediately, the new democracy acted to reconcile regional demands. In 1977, the regional Catalan Generalitat, the former self-government of Catalonia, was restored and steps were taken to accommodate Basque autonomy.[44] The new constitution of 1978 included an autonomous community clause. Catalonia and the Basque country moved first to apply and the autonomy statute was approved on 18 December 1979.[45] Many more regions acted to gain autonomy. In spite of the enthusiastic response of some regions, many on the right were strongly opposed to regional autonomy, which they viewed as an attack against national unity. Even regions not historically recognized were granted autonomy. By the end of February 1982, seventeen regions had approved a statute of autonomy.[46]

In many of the regions, a majority of citizens felt discriminated against by other Spaniards. For example, the Basques complained that they paid more in taxes than they received in benefits from the state. Under Franco, this was often the case. For example, in 1968 Basques supplied 14 per cent of tax revenues but received only 6 per cent of expenditure.[47] This trend continued in the early 1970s, when the state financed new industrial research centres. Of the total, 10 per cent were in Catalonia, 70 per cent were in Madrid and none were in the Basque country. In another example, in 1974 educational expenditures were much lower for Basque students, at 1,371 and 1,755 pesetas per student in the provinces of Guipúzcoa and Vizcaya, compared with 2,501 pesetas per student nationally.[48] Feelings of discrimination can be documented in limited public opinion data. Data are available for only two years, 1979 and 1988. In two of the three major historical regions, Galicia and the Basque land, feelings of discrimination were significantly lower in 1982, down from 61 to 30 per cent in Galicia and from 51 to 36 per cent in the Basque country. In Catalonia the numbers were slightly higher, up to 26 per cent from 24 per cent.[49] The state's actions appeared to have improved integration in at least the regions of Galicia and the Basque country.

Purposes of the state: summary

In Uruguay and Peru, countries with both state and terrorist violence, a decrease in integration and security is expected to follow increases in terrorist violence. Decreases in integration and security should follow the implementation of repressive policies and state violence. In Spain, however, only the negative consequences of terrorist violence on integration and security are expected to result. Since the Spanish state did not respond in a repressive or violent manner, further decreases in integration and security that cannot be accounted for by the terrorist violence are not expected.

Uruguay

Data measuring the purposes of the state in Uruguay are scare. However, they do suggest that both security and integration were undermined in this period by both terrorist violence and the state's response to it. Congruent with hypothesis one, as the activity of the Tupamaros increased, decreases in security are evident. This was indicated by an increasing proportion of Uruguayans who described their country as disorderly and who described the Tupamaros as a dangerous group. In addition, there is evidence that many industrialists, frequent targets of the Tupamaros, were fearful. Similarly, a decrease in integration can also be seen in the secondary literature supporting a general decline in tolerance. The evidence is also consistent with hypothesis two. Some evidence is available to support the notion that state violence also undermines security. For example, many on the legal left were frightened. They were targeted by violent groups, some of which were associated with state officials. It is also plausible to infer that the indiscriminate arrests, torture in interrogation and suspension of liberties reduced the security of those suspected by the authorities of being involved in subversive activities. Evidence for a decrease of integration caused by state policies can be seen in the incident in which the Communist Party charged that the new laws designed to punish public support of subversion would also implicate those on the legal left who believed in class struggle.

Peru

The available data measuring the purposes of the state in Peru suggest that both security and integration were undermined in this period by terrorist violence and the state's repressive and violent response. Hypothesis one is supported by the evidence. A decrease in security is indicated by the death toll and public opinion data substantiating that the violence of Sendero and other terrorist groups caused fear in almost 80 per cent of the population. Decreases in integration can be measured by the electoral disturbances and lack of tolerance. Officials and candidates were assassinated. Many political positions were unfilled due to lack of candidates. The pressure from Sendero to enforce electoral boycotts was effective as abstentions and blank votes were predominant in many areas.

Hypothesis two is also supported by the evidence. A decrease in security is also attributable to state actions. One instrument of the state responsible for the violence, the National Police, inspired more fear than security in a majority of citizens. This signifies that the security of citizens was being undermined by the state as well as by the terrorist groups. Decreases in integration due to state violence and repression are shown by the stated fear of lack of tolerance for those on the legal left and by the suspicion of being Senderistas reported by students and residents of areas plagued by Sendero activities.

Spain

In Spain, the data are consistent with hypothesis one. Although public opinion data are limited, concern for terrorist violence was evident. No conclusions can be drawn in terms of integration due to the terrorist violence. In terms of hypothesis two, there is evidence that state actions actually improved feelings of integration for two historically alienated communities, the Basque country and Galicia.

Citizen confidence

Citizen confidence can be measured in different ways in different countries. In general, we are looking for measurements of citizen confidence in the state and its institutions. Not all countries had similar data and some countries had only limited data. In Uruguay and Peru, declines in citizen confidence due to both terrorist and state violence are expected. In Spain, decline in citizen confidence, due to terrorist violence, is expected.

Uruguayan confidence in the state

> We were getting tired of it ... The police nearly always lost to the Tupamaros, and the jails couldn't hold them even when they were captured.[50]
>
> José Romer, a waiter in Montevideo

Public opinion data allow us to examine the reaction of Uruguayan citizens to terrorist violence, to the state's policies and to state violence. Citizen confidence can be measured by public opinion data of the general mood of the country, electoral support for traditional parties, the emergence of non-traditional presidential candidates and public opinion data of satisfaction with the state and its policies. The indicators show a thorough dissatisfaction with the state that continues to worsen even after the end of Tupamaro violence.

Some public opinion data are available assessing the general situation of the country. In general, Uruguayans did not positively assess the state of their country in the late 1960s. Respondents were asked to describe the situation of the country. In the years 1967–69, consistently over half the population listed the situation of the country as poor or very poor. Only 6–7 per cent of those questioned replied that the country was in a very good or good situation.[51] Another question probed the depth of the pessimism. An excellent measure of the general situation in Uruguay is the desire to emigrate. In 1968, only 55 per cent of the population preferred to stay in Uruguay, while 33 per cent expressed a desire to emigrate. Just one year later, only 39 per cent preferred to stay in Uruguay, while 42 per cent stated they would emigrate if they could.[52] Moreover, many Uruguayans followed through with their desire to emigrate. Although comprehensive emigration statistics are unavailable, anecdotal evidence is available. For example, there were a large number of absentee ballots in the 1971 election. Of a total of 700,000 Montevidean ballots, 150,000 people voted as an absentee from abroad.[53]

More specific data are available assessing citizen satisfaction with the state and its policies. Broad dissatisfaction with state policies towards the disorder is evident. Generally, the evaluation of the state continues to worsen even after the end of Tupamaro violence. One state branch received higher ratings of satisfaction as those of the state worsened: the military.

The disillusionment with the National Assembly's performance is evident as early as 1968. One of the early state strategies for dealing with both labour unrest and terrorist actions was the MPS. However, this strategy was not popular among Uruguayans. In August 1968, a question probing the public's opinion about the MPS and other restrictions revealed that only 33 per cent believed the MPS to be helpful, 58 per cent believed they were not helpful and 9 per cent were unsure.[54] The respondents were asked whether or not the National Assembly should lift the MPS. A strong majority, 62 per cent, said lift them, only 29 per cent said allow them to remain and 9 per cent were unsure.[55] Then, respondents were asked why the National Assembly would not lift the MPS. More than one-third, 39 per cent, chose the irresponsibility of the National Assembly, 30 per cent chose political reasons and only 5 per cent chose the situation of the country. Only one out of twenty Uruguayans believed that the situation of the country merited the continuation of the MPS. A small minority, 3 per cent, feared that the National Assembly would be dismissed if the MPS were lifted.

Some more questions about the MPS were asked in late 1971. Although individuals were more likely to view the MPS as beneficial the older they were, no age group reported a majority positive view of the measure. Only 29 per cent of those aged 18-32, 40 per cent of those aged 33-47 and 44 per cent of those over 48 viewed the measures as beneficial. Among all age groups there was a majority view that the measures were not beneficial. Seventy-one per cent of those aged 18-32, 60 per cent of those aged 33-47 and 56 per cent of those over 48 viewed the measures as not beneficial. Three years later, there was still a strong rejection of the MPS. A large majority of Uruguayan citizens viewed the MPS as harmful.

Some polls assessed public reaction to other repressive policies and actions in 1968. A prohibition on public gatherings was rejected by almost half of respondents, 47 per cent, while 40 per cent supported the measure. In another question, people were asked if they supported the detention of people without judicial intervention. Of those questioned,

69 per cent disagreed and only 11 per cent approved. In the same year, after the clashes between police and university students on 14 August that resulted in the death of one student, respondents were asked: 'Who is responsible for the death of Liber Arce [the student killed]?' Almost half, 46 per cent, of respondents blamed the police and the state, 11 per cent blamed the students, 13 per cent blamed Liber Arce himself, 0.5 per cent blamed the communists and 0.5 per cent blamed the university authorities. Twenty-nine per cent did not know whom to blame.[56] The repressive response of the state to the troubles was rejected by a large majority of citizens.

Until 1971, the main agent of the state to respond to the disorder was the police. The unrest at this time was a mixture of both seditious activity and labour protest. In August 1968, respondents were asked to rate the attitude/position of the armed forces and the police during recent events. As early as August 1968, the armed forces, at 48 per cent of those believing that their attitude was correct, were twice as popular as the police, with only 26 per cent, and received half the negative rating, with 24 per cent believing that their attitude was incorrect compared with 46 per cent for the police.[57] *Cuadernos de Marcha* in late 1971 followed up on an earlier question, asking whether or not the police posture and attitude was correct. In response to this question, a slight majority (53 per cent) of those over thirty-three supported the police. However, a strong majority (64 per cent) of younger citizens did not approve of the police posture. This reflects the greater suspicion of young Uruguayans for participating in illegal activity. Overall, the police were viewed more negatively than before.[58]

The record of Uruguayan presidential voting also demonstrates a growing frustration with the two main political parties. This serves as a rough indicator of the public's displeasure with the main politicians and policies. The share of the vote for the traditional party significantly declined in the 1970s. The leftist coalition group the Frente Amplio had 30.1 per cent of the electoral support in Montevideo by 1971. The combination of the vote for the Blanco and Colorado parties had shrunk from 83 per cent in 1966 to 69 per cent in 1971. The interior vote is typically more conservative than the vote in Montevideo. In the interior, non-traditional parties had only 10 per cent support.[59] By 1971, electoral results showed a three-way split in Montevideo for the Colorados, the Blancos and Frente Amplio. Only the interior vote saved the traditional parties from defeat.[60]

In addition to looking at the electoral success of non-traditional parties, disillusionment with traditional candidates can be seen by the sudden appearance of military men as political candidates. In 1966, Colorado Oscar Gestido, a sixty-five-year-old retired air force general was elected to the presidency.[61] Later other generals served as ministers. The appointment of military men was also seen as a strategy of military appeasement. General Antonio Francese served as Minister of Defence from 1967–70, under President Pacheco. In May 1970, Francese became Minister of the Interior and General César Borda became Chief of Police. Rumours reported by *Latin America* alleged that

> only by the appointment of military men to these two key posts, it was said, were the army and the police persuaded to give up the idea of a bloody revenge on the best known left-wing figures in the country in reprisal for the killing of police inspector Héctor Morán Charquero by the Tupamaros on 13 April.[62]

Later, in January 1971, Pacheco replaced Francese as Minister of the Interior with General Rafael Milans. Colonel Julio Vigorito was appointed Undersecretary of the Ministry. General Borda then became Minister of Defence.[63] President Bordaberry continued the trend with Defence Minister General Enrique Magnani. The trend grew to include generals as presidential candidates in the 1971 elections: General Seregni for the Frente Amplio, General Aguerrondo for the Blanco Party and General J. Ribas for the Colorado Party. The candidacy of General Aguerrondo for the Blancos is especially important since his political ambitions were usually reported within the context of speculation of possible coup attempts. However, at the time of the election he had supposedly been persuaded to think in terms of a Peruvian-style programme of reform.[64]

The increasing frequency of military officers serving as ministers and running for office seems to reflect a growing confidence in the military as opposed to the rest of the state. The credibility of the state continued to fall in 1971. In one study, only 13 per cent of Montevideans thought that the National Assembly was acting well and only 23 per cent said the president was acting well. The military received the highest rating, with 41 per cent approval.[65] Lack of citizen confidence hit critical levels during the first severe confrontation between the state and the military in February 1973. An Instituto de Opinión Pública poll recorded that 89 per cent of Uruguayan citizens believed that the state bureaucracy was corrupt, 60 per cent agreed with military proposals for reform, 60 per cent believed a coup was immanent, and 88 per cent believed that state corruption should be dealt with severely.[66] It appears that democracy, in practice anyway, and the leading politicians of the time had lost the support of the people. The evidence suggests that, by 1973, the rejection of the state had progressed to a rejection of democracy, in the sense of an Aristotelian constitution. These negative trends continued even though the threat from the Tupamaros had ended. The Uruguayan people who had rejected the state's repressive policies were not only rejecting the state, but ultimately democracy.[67]

Peruvian confidence in the state

Citizen confidence in the Peruvian state can be measured in five ways. Two broad indicators are available. First, an increasing dissatisfaction with the main political parties and a growing preference for new and independent parties indicate a lack of confidence in the leading politicians. In addition, public opinion data concerning desires to emigrate indicate a low level of citizen confidence in the state. More specifically, presidential popularity polls indicate a level of satisfaction with particular leaders, with implications for their parties. Questions of confidence and performance of institutions can measure citizen confidence and approval of state performance. Finally, public opinion data assessing support for reform plans also reflect the level of support for these institutions.

Electoral results indicate a growing dissatisfaction with the traditional parties. The traditional parties in Peru began to lose broad public support as early as 1985 with the emergence of United Left (IU) candidate Barrantes. In that year APRA candidate Alan García received 47 per cent and Barrantes 22 per cent of the vote. However, Barrantes declined to participate in the runoff since he doubted he would win and he feared an outbreak of violence between APRA and IU militants.[68] By 1989, independent candidates had started to win. For example, in the 1989 municipal elections Ricardo Belmont Cassinelli, founder of the independent Workers' Movement (Movimiento Obras) won the mayoral election in Lima in November 1989 and again in 1993. According to Wilson Jaime Barreto, 'the triumph of Ricardo Belmon... indicated that the electorate was searching for new options, and as a consequence, rejecting the old parties and old politicians'.[69] There was a general increase in the popularity of the independents and a turning away from the traditional parties that began to increase dramatically after the 1986 municipal elections. Since 1980, support for independent parties had varied from 3 to 8 per cent. In the general elections of 1985 and the municipal elections of 1986, the conservative parties AP and the Popular Christian Party (PPC) did not gain many votes. To maintain support in the 1990 elections, they formed a coalition party, Frente Democrático (FREDEMO). By 1990, the independents had secured the vote of a third of the population and the independent candidate, Alberto Fujimori, won the presidential election in the runoff. The share of the votes for the independents had increased from just 3 per cent in 1985 to 62.5 per cent in the second-round presidential election.[70] A majority of voters had repudiated the traditional parties and politicians.

Another general indicator of low citizen confidence in the state's ability to solve national problems is the percentage of Peruvians who would like to emigrate. The available evidence about the willingness to emigrate reflects a deep pessimism about the direction and future of the country. In July 1988, 52 per cent of those polled said they would emigrate if they could. By May 1991, that number had peaked at 71 per cent wishing to emigrate. Not until the presidency of Fujimori did the numbers begin to decline, reaching 56 per cent in May 1992 and 46 per cent in May 1996.[71] When asked why they wished to emigrate, in October 1989, 55 per cent chose the reason that there are more possibilities to develop/flourish abroad, 33 per cent chose the economic crisis and 9 per cent blamed the violence. The numbers did not begin to decline until after Fujimori's election. Another drop occurred one month after the *autogolpe*, from 62 to

56 per cent, indicating the confidence gained by the election of Fujimori.

Public opinion tracking presidential popularity is also informative of the level of citizen confidence in the state. Of all the democratically elected presidents in Peru from 1980–92, only Fujimori maintained reasonably high and constant approval ratings throughout most of his first two terms as president. Considering that Fujimori is an independent, this reflects a thorough dissatisfaction with the traditional parties and perhaps even reflects on democracy as practised in Peru. President Belaúnde began his term with a 67 per cent approval rating. However, for more than the last two years of his presidency, from April 1983 until the 1985 presidential elections, his approval rating was consistently lower than 25 per cent, with disapproval ratings ranging from 60–70 per cent.[72] Belaúnde's successor, García, started his term with extremely high ratings, at 96 per cent.[73] However, his popularity plummeted in October 1988. During 1989 and 1990, his approval ratings did not exceed 15 per cent.[74] Although the polls indicated that the majority of Peruvians blamed the state officials for the nation's problems, approximately 66 per cent of respondents believed that García should finish his term. However, García's popularity continued to decline. The percentage of Lima residents who rejected the president in 1988 rose from 71 per cent in October to 74 per cent in December. Only 21 per cent approved of García's administration, down from 24 per cent in October. However, at this time 71 per cent of the respondents did not believe a coup would solve the crisis.[75]

This pattern of optimism followed by high dissatisfaction was broken with the election of Alberto Fujimori. Fujimori did have a few low points in his popularity, especially during the summer of 1991 with approval ratings of between 25 and 35 per cent, but he later recovered to his original high levels of approval. By December 1991, his approval rating was measured at 69 per cent by the polling firm DATUM and at 60 per cent by APOYO.[76] In March 1991, at the beginning of a summer of low popularity, the displeasure with Fujimori had also spread to members of his government and party. Vice-President Carlos García indicated that he would not oppose the removal of Fujimori as head of state. However, even at the lowest point in

Fujimori's popularity, he was viewed more positively than Alan García. In an APOYO poll conducted in Lima between 25 and 26 of July 1991, during a point of Fujimori's lowest popularity, when asked who had a better administration 41 per cent believed Fujimori had done a better job than García. Only 23 per cent believed that García did a better job than Fujimori. Some of the respondents, 28 per cent, believed that neither administration was good.[77] After December 1991, Fujimori's approval ratings continued to improve. The December poll came after his successful handling of a border conflict with Ecuador.[78]

Public opinion data from the late 1980s and early 1990s reveal a deep dissatisfaction with the performance of most state institutions. For example, in 1988 only 10 per cent believed the government was doing a good job, about half thought government performance was average, about 30 per cent thought the government did a poor job and about 10 per cent were undecided.[79] As Peru moved into the 1990s the evaluation of the state worsened. Only President Fujimori, the Catholic Church and the military maintained positive evaluations.

The state was not judged to be efficient or effective in its attempts to quell the violence.[80] Moreover, perhaps because of the paramilitary groups and the repressive response to the terrorist threat, the state was not perceived by the population as pursuing peace. In the 1988 National Questionnaire about Violence, when asked which institutions worked for national pacification, the state was not mentioned often. When asked to identify organizations that worked for peace, 58.1 per cent identified the Catholic Church, 18.2 per cent identified the Commissions of Human Rights, 3.0 per cent identified the police and only 4.5 per cent identified the state.[81]

In 1991, only President Fujimori and the military received favourable ratings. While Fujimori's popularity continued to increase after the summer of 1991, other institutions lost more citizen confidence. *Debate*'s annual survey of power in Peru, in May 1991, included a questionnaire about institutional rankings. Less than one year before the coup, the legislative branch was viewed as doing a poor or very poor job by 92 per cent of those questioned. The judiciary fared only slightly better, with 82 per cent responding that it was functioning poorly. The police force received a 74 per cent negative rating. Only four institutions had a majority of those questioned rate them as average, good or very good in terms of their performance: the executive branch (82 per cent), the armed forces (60 per cent), the Catholic Church (74 per cent) and the press (66 per cent).[82] This dissatisfaction is corroborated by later polls. In July 1991, in an Imasen poll conducted in Lima, 88.5 per cent of respondents believed that the political parties did not fulfil their functions that year.[83] In the same month, Congress's disapproval rating reached 80.8 per cent and was still high at 71.3 per cent in August.[84] Not only were Congress and the political parties held in low esteem, but the populace seemed to view them as insignificant. In 1991, 40 per cent of the population could not identify a single leader of the opposition.[85] Also in 1991, the political parties received a low approval rating of 13 per cent.[86]

Other studies conducted by APOYO underline the dissatisfaction. In an October 1991 poll conducted in Lima, respondents were asked which institutions they trusted. Only the Church (85 per cent trust, 11 per cent distrust), the media (55 per cent trust, 32 per cent distrust) and the armed forces (47 per cent trust, 42 per cent distrust) generated more trust than distrust. Congress had an overwhelmingly negative rating of 72 per cent distrust and 19 per cent trusting. The judicial branch fared only slightly better, with 22 per cent trusting it and 68 per cent distrusting it.[87] A separate APOYO poll conducted on 26 October 1991 asked respondents, 'Should the national police be dismantled?' Fifty-one per cent agreed, 40 per cent disagreed and 9 per cent did not respond. On the contrary, the executive branch was rated as average or good by 83 per cent of the people. The armed forces were positively rated by 60 per cent of the population. Those were the only groups evaluated positively.[88] A series of studies conducted by APOYO corroborated the increasing rejection of institutions (table 6.3). One month before the coup, only the armed forces, the Catholic Church, the media and the president had high confidence ratings. Political parties and the judiciary were rated favourably by less than 15 per cent of the population. The confidence rating of Fujimori, the armed forces and the police increased after the *autogolpe*.

Table 6.3 Peru: average or good rating of institutions, 1990–92

Institution	Sept. 1990	Mar. 1991	Sept. 1991	Mar. 1992	Sept. 1992
Council of Ministers	52	25	24	27	37
Armed forces	58	53	47	54	57
Church	81	83	85	80	81
Media	60	48	55	57	58
Political parties	21	13	13	12	13
Judiciary	23	16	22	14	28
National Police	47	31	33	20	48
President	57	29	26	42	54

Sources: APOYO, *Informe de Opinion*, October 1991; APOYO, *Informe de Opinion*, August 1993; FBIS LAT; 91–180, p. 36.

By late 1991, citizen dissatisfaction with the state seemed to be progressing into a rejection of democracy as it existed in Peru at the time. Fujimori took advantage of the lack of popularity of the other institutions to push through reforms and ultimately to seize power. Public opinion data seem to suggest a growing confidence in Fujimori, independent of his office, and in the military. For example, Fujimori's reform plans for Congress and the judiciary were well supported. In a December 1991 poll, Fujimori's proposal to renew one-third of Congress at two year intervals was approved by 80 per cent of those questioned. His proposed reorganization of the judiciary was approved by 89 per cent and the reorganization of the comptroller's office received 69 per cent approval. Fujimori's motives for his reform were viewed positively by a strong majority of citizens. When the respondents were asked why Fujimori criticized Congress, 47 per cent believed Fujimori wanted to make it work harder, 27 per cent believed he wanted to make the Congress more efficient, 7 per cent believed in a smoke screen theory, 6 per cent believed Fujimori wanted to dissolve Congress, and 4 per cent believed he wanted to legislate through decree. Overall, Fujimori's confrontations with Congress and the judicial branch were approved by 72 per cent of those questioned.[89]

Spanish confidence in the state

Citizen confidence in the Spanish state can be measured in different ways. First, data are available outlining what sort of response to violence Spaniards wanted the state to make. The actual actions of the state can be compared with these wishes. Second, data evaluating the general mood and direction of the country are available. Finally, public opinion data of satisfaction with different governments according to policy area are available.

Public opinion data analysing citizen evaluation of state policy towards terrorism are available. Few Spaniards desired a repressive response to the terrorism. The state basically followed those demands. At the beginning of the transition to democracy in March and April 1977, Spaniards were asked how they thought the state should react to the claims of the regions and the terrorist threats. A strong majority, 78 per cent, agreed with the following statement: 'In Spain, the most important thing is to maintain the order and the peace'. Interestingly, only 22 per cent supported a more firm police response to the disorder, agreeing with the statement that 'the police should be more firm to avoid public disorder'. Spaniards wanted peace, but did not want a heavy-handed police response to achieve it. Moreover, a majority of Spaniards supported total regional autonomy: 55 per cent agreed with the statement 'The different regions should have total autonomy'.[90]

In an earlier study in December 1976, respondents were asked how the state should respond to terrorist kidnappings. From these early data, it appears that Spaniards were unwilling to sacrifice liberties for more order. On the contrary, almost one-third of respondents preferred a widening of political liberties, agreeing with either the statement that the state should 'negotiate and widen political liberties' or 'stay firm and widen political liberties'. Eleven per cent were in favour of negotiation and ultimately freedom for terrorists in exchange for prisoners. Thirty-six per cent agreed that the state should 'stay firm to avoid future kidnappings'.[91] This same principle can be seen three years later, under even more prevalent terrorism. In 1979, 55 per cent of Spaniards preferred that the state maintain order within the law. The willingness to accept terrorist demands or to negotiate was low at 2 per cent and 16 per cent, respectively. However, there was much more support for negotiation among the regional left, at 67 per cent compared with 16 per cent nationally. Support for a harsher reaction was low. Overall only 20 per cent favoured making a 'war on terrorism'. Most of the support came from the AP (34 per cent) and the extreme right (48 per cent). Similarly, only 7 per cent favoured a return to military rule. Over one out of four (27 per cent) on the extreme right favoured this response.[92]

In September 1979, Spaniards were asked to predict the future performance of their democracy. Citizens were optimistic about the country. Forty-two per cent of those questioned believed that the country's problems would be solved, 26 per cent believed they would continually get worse and 33 per cent believed they would stay the same.[93] A separate study conducted in September 1980 asked citizens to assess the performance of the new democracy up to that point. The results were mixed. Only 23 per cent of respondents believed that the country had progressed better than expected. Thirty-six per cent stated that things had gone worse than expected.[94] A different study conducted two months later probed anticipated state performance in particular areas. The numbers for November 1980 reveal a low level of satisfaction and pessimism for the future. Beliefs about the direction of prices were strongly negative, with only 9 per cent believing things would get better and 55 per cent believing they would worsen. Results were slightly better in regard to unemployment, but still pessimistic; only 19 per cent believed unemployment would improve, 24 per cent predicted it would remain the same and 37 per cent believed the situation would get worse. The response about terrorism was split (20 per cent better, 27 per cent the same and 29 per cent worse), but with a leaning towards a more pessimistic view.[95]

Two years later, the level of optimism had increased as levels of satisfaction improved. In October 1982 the response in regard to terrorism was much improved. Now only 11 per cent believed it would get worse and 40 per cent believed it would improve. In terms of unemployment, 30 per cent thought the situation would improve, 26 per cent believed it would stay the same and 23 per cent thought it would get worse. Views of prices remained negative. Only 15 per cent thought they would improve, 28 per cent thought they would stay the same and 30 per cent thought they would get worse.[96]

In 1980, people were asked to evaluate whether or not the following problems had improved or become worse since Spanish democratization. In 1980, many important indicators of state performance were highly negative. On the following issues, more respondents believed that things had changed for the worse than for the better: unemployment (3 per cent for the better and 89 per cent for the worse), delinquency (2 per cent for the better and 81 per cent for the worse), the economic situation (12 per cent for the better and 72 per cent for the worse), security and public order (11 per cent for the better and 63 per cent for the worse), labour conflicts (22 per cent for the better and 47 per cent for the worse), corruption (7 per cent for the better and 63 per cent for the worse), and the principle of authority (22 per cent for the better and 31 per cent for the worse). In spite of the severity of the terrorism and economic crisis in 1980, the state received high marks in areas that affected integration. Interestingly, citizen liberties (53 per cent for the better and 27 per cent for the worse), regional autonomy (48 per cent for the better and 20 per cent for the worse) and information (61 per cent for the better and 12 per cent for the worse) all received significantly higher marks of improvement. Regardless of the effectiveness of the state's policies towards the economic crisis and terrorism, it appears that state action or inaction did not exacerbate the strains on security or integration caused by other crises. In fact, the policies seemed to compensate somewhat for the negative effects of the terrorist violence on security and integration.

In another Gallup survey, citizens were asked to indicate their level of satisfaction with different governments according to policy area on a scale of one to ten, with one representing the lowest level of satisfaction and ten representing the highest. In general, the level of satisfaction increased as time progressed. In 1978, the average score was 4.46. In 1980, the average score was 4.49. By 1984, the average had increased to 4.81. Franco received his highest ratings in law and order and in living standards. In fact, his 1980 rating of 5.15 was the highest received in that category. By 1984 the

PSOE government outscored the memory of Franco 4.7 to 4.31 for level of citizen confidence. The socialists received the highest rating for social equity and living standards. In all categories, the PSOE received the highest ratings. The most popular figure in Spain was the King. The next best figure was the Pope. Of the politicians, González and Suárez fared best.[97] With time, Spaniards evaluated the state in a more positive manner in every category.

Citizen confidence: summary

Uruguay

In Uruguay, citizen confidence levels decreased as the amount of terrorist violence increased. In the years 1967 to 1969, many citizens evaluated the general situation of the country as poor. In addition, there was evidence of many Uruguayans wishing to emigrate and anecdotal evidence of many who carried through on their desire. There was a growing repudiation of the traditional parties, culminating in the 1971 presidential elections. However, after the elimination of Tupamaro violence in September 1972, citizen confidence continued to decrease, suggesting that the state response to the violence was also a factor. Specifically, the poll conducted in February 1973 documents the highest rejection of the state. This lack of citizen confidence remains even after the demise of terrorist violence. The evidence is congruent with both hypotheses.

Peru

Citizen confidence levels in most Peruvian institutions, except the executive, the Catholic Church and the armed forces, continued to worsen until the *autogolpe* in 1992. As terrorist violence increased and then stabilized at a high level, citizen confidence decreased. As repressive policies were pursued and state violence introduced, citizen confidence levels decreased. Separation of the causation is difficult since both the terrorist and state violence persisted in the same time period. Nonetheless, the evidence is clear that approval ratings of the state and its institutions, with the noted exceptions, continued declining until the *autogolpe* of Fujimori. In addition to poor approval ratings, a strong majority of citizens expressed a distrust of Congress, the judiciary and the National Police. Only Fujimori, the military, the Catholic Church and the media received good approval ratings. In addition, Fujimori had broad support for his drastic reform proposals, signifying a rejection of the existing institutions. The lack of citizen confidence in the state appeared to progress to a rejection of democracy as practised in Peru before April 1992.

Uruguay and Peru

In both the Uruguayan and Peruvian cases, low levels of citizen confidence in the state progressed to a general dissatisfaction with democracy as practised in those countries. At the same time, the armed forces in both countries had managed to disassociate their institutions from the failed policies of the state, in spite of being involved in the implementation of those policies. The degeneration of democracy was progressing with the approval of the majority of citizens. Consistent with an Aristotelian approach that examines citizen support and stability in terms of the purposes of the state, as the purposes of the state are not met by the state more opportunities for sedition arise. Citizen support for alternative regimes, in the sense of an Aristotelian constitution, becomes more probable. As the lack of citizen confidence in the state progresses to a lack of confidence in the state, not just limited to a lack of confidence in particular governments, then support for an alternative, in hope of gaining a more practicable constitutional form or regime, becomes likely. The evidence suggests that the Peru of 1992 and the Uruguay of 1973 had exhausted the possibilities of improvement within a democratic form. Hopes for improvement thus moved from an internal reform to a fundamental change of constitutional form.

Spain

An evaluation of the Spanish experience meets the expectation that the differences in security, integration and citizen confidence derive from the fact that the Spanish state did not violently and repressively react to the terrorist violence.

Table 6.4 Spain: summary table of terrorist attacks and impression of terrorism

	Number of attacks with victims		Response to terrorism	Response to public order
1980	91			
		better	20	23
		worse	27	30
		same	29	24
1982	35			
		better	40	36
		worse	25	30
		same	11	9

Sources: Juan Linz (ed.), *Un presente para el futuro* (Madrid: Instituto de Estudios Economicos, 1985), pp. 37–9; Salustiano del Campo (ed.), *Tendencias Sociales en España Volumen II* (Bilbao: Fundacion BBV), 1993, p. 70.

The evidence of citizen confidence supports hypothesis one in the sense that, as incidents of terrorist violence increase, there is a decrease in citizen confidence. Until 1982, there was a persistent pessimism about the state's ability to ameliorate terrorism. The difference in the level of satisfaction looking towards the future in regard to terrorism and public order from 1980 to 1982 is consistent with hypothesis one (table 6.4). The levels of citizen confidence and measures of terrorist violence seem to be related in a manner consistent with hypothesis one. During the years 1979 and 1980, terrorist violence peaked. However, by 1982 violence had decreased by approximately two-thirds. This decrease in terrorist violence was followed by an increase in citizen confidence in the state.

In regard to the second hypothesis, we do not have an indiscriminate, violent and repressive state response. Interestingly, during 1980, a low point in satisfaction with the new democracy referred to as the *desencanto* or period or disenchantment, the state received positive marks in areas that are related to integration. Specifically, the state's performance in terms of an improved political situation, the quality of political leadership, citizen liberties, regional autonomy and freedom of information was viewed positively by most Spaniards. The state maintained support in spite of overwhelmingly negative evaluations in regard to unemployment, the economic situation in general, security and public order, corruption, labour conflicts and the principle of authority. These data are consistent with hypotheses one and two, since the effects of terrorist violence can be seen, while the negative consequences of a violent and repressive state response are absent.

Democratic stability

In each of the three cases, it is easiest to measure democratic stability by looking at its opposite, democratic instability. Democratic instability can be indicated by successful coups. It can also be measured by other indicators, depending on the information available in each country. In Uruguay and Peru, declines in democratic stability due to both terrorist and state violence are expected. In Spain, some instability due to terrorist violence is expected, but not as much as in Uruguay and Peru, due to the lack of Spanish state violence.

Uruguayan Stability

In addition to the final breakdown of Uruguayan democracy in June 1973, democratic stability can be measured by looking for signs of instability. In any constitution, broad support for seditious groups is an indication of instability. This can be measured by public opinion data inquiring about support for groups. Another indicator of instability is electoral irregularities. This can be measured by looking for charges of electoral fraud and violence in the elections. Public opinion data concerning choice of regime and perception of risk of instability to the existing constitution can also indicate instability. Public statements encouraging military intervention and calling for the resignation of the president indicate instability. A supportive public reaction to the coup also demonstrates democratic instability.

Although the Tupamaro violence was rejected by a majority of Uruguayans, a minority of citizens admitted supporting the aims of the Tupamaros. *Marcha* reported consistent minority support, at least indirectly, for the Tupamaros. In June 1971, 41 per cent believed that the Tupamaros were at least partially justified in their actions. This number shrank to 36 per cent in September, with 49 per cent of the respondents denying them reasonable justification.[98] However, the Tupamaros still had much support. This support was corroborated by a similar poll conducted one year later, in July 1972. A Gallup poll revealed that 20 per cent of the public were Tupamaro sympathizers.[99]

Another indicator of democratic instability became apparent in the 1971 presidential elections. Instead of the typically peaceful elections, the campaigns were marked by violence. However, this violence did not originate from the Tupamaros. A frequent target of attacks was General Liber Seregni, the sole presidential candidate for the Frente Amplio.[100] For example, on 7 November 1971 Seregni was stabbed in the chest by a youth member of a far-right group. Another time, a boy was killed by a bullet intended for Seregni. These incidents were the first attacks made on an Uruguayan presidential candidate in thirty years.[101]

The 1971 election results were also hotly contested. In the end, Juan Bordaberry was announced winner, in spite of documented charges of electoral fraud.[102] A public opinion poll asked: 'Recently there have been a lot of protests about the elections. In your judgment, were these elections as clean as any, or was there fraud?'[103] Only the victorious party, the Colorados, had a majority response (72 per cent) affirming the fairness of the elections. Almost half of those affiliated with the Blanco party (48 per cent) and three-quarters (72 per cent) of those affiliated with the Frente Amplio believed fraud occurred. The credibility of the Bordaberry government was questioned and fewer than half of Uruguayans believed the elections to be honest.

Public opinion polls conducted in 1971 investigated citizen perceptions of a risk to the democratic system. In late 1971, citizens were asked whether or not the democratic system was at risk. In almost every age group, a majority believed that the democratic system was either at risk or had already been damaged. Of those aged 18–32, 68 per cent agreed. In the middle age group of 33–47, 60 per cent agreed. Of those aged 48 or over, 55 per cent agreed.[104] Unfortunately, the question did not follow up with attribution of blame for the damage to the democratic system.

In spite of the belief that democracy was at risk in Uruguay, the general preference among Uruguayans for democracy remained strong. When asked what form of regime or constitution they preferred, in January 1971, 73 per cent of respondents chose democracy. In October 1971, 79 per cent chose democracy. However, it is striking that approximately one in eight citizens (16 per cent in January 1971 and 13 per cent in October) admitted a preference for a 'strong and orderly military state' in a country with seventy years of stable democratic rule.[105]

In addition, public statements were made encouraging sedition. Seditious statements came from across the political spectrum. An early statement was made on 9 June 1969. Eugenio Baroffio, the Managing Director of *El Diario*, signed an editorial asking for a coup: 'because the parliament [National Assembly], by constitution, cannot be dissolved, which would allow an appeal to the electorate, the executive power must free itself from constitutional norms'.[106] Calls to sedition were also made from the left. Even the Frente Amplio's 1971 presidential candidate, General Seregni, said after the contested elections:

> Hemos enfrentado las elecciones más sucias que recuerda nuestra memoria: ... Nos quieren acostumbrar a comportarnos como un rebaño, pero el pueblo oriental no nació para la mansedumbre! Esto implica lucha, implica resistencia popular organizada. Lucha y resistencia que serán más duras que ayer.[107]

A statement encouraging popular resistance by a popular leader definitely indicates instability. Seditious calls were also made by the extreme right. In April 1972, *Azul y Blanco*, an ultra rightist publication that is considered to be the voice of *golpista*, or pro-coup, members of the military, ran an editorial entitled 'Govern or Resign'. It advocated eliminating legislative and judicial branches of the state.

In addition to public calls for military intervention, President Bordaberry faced calls for his resignation from many sectors. Both presidential candidates who Bordaberry faced in the 1971 election called for his resignation. On 9 February 1973, General Liber Seregni, candidate for the Frente Amplio, stated:

El gobierno, el señor Bordaberry, no solo no ha sabido sorregir el desorden, sino que ha contribuído a agravarlo. El gobierno se ha convertido en el mayor agente de desorden que sufre la patria, opone entre sí a los orientales, que impede una verdadera concordia entre los patriotas de verdad. El señor Presidente no ha tenido la capacidad ni la voluntad de corregir la situación que vive la patria, y ha tratado de ocultar su inepititud reprimiendo toda manifestación del descontento popular ... Por todas estas rezones, entendemos que el señor Presidente debería renunciar.[108]

A main leader of the other major political party, the Blancos, Wilson Aldunate Ferreira, stated on 30 March 1973 in *Marcha*:

Yo creo que todo esto es consecuencia directa de la debilidad del Poder Ejecutivo ... Uruguay necesita un Poder Ejecutivo fuerte a través de una amplicación de su base política y fundamentalmente del señor Bordaberry en la primera magistratura?[109]

Instead of opposing factions joining to defend the president, Bordaberry was attacked by some as others courted military action.

Another indicator of democratic stability is the reaction of citizens to attacks against the state. By using the concept of the purposes of the state, it can be understood why so few citizens supported Uruguayan democracy and why there was support for the military action that began in February 1973. Citizens from across the political spectrum supported the idea of further military involvement. Factions within the military were still active, and different groups of Uruguayans supported the idea of military intervention, expecting different outcomes. Unfortunately, public opinion data during the slow coup are scarce. Other than one poll in February 1973, no data are available. When the army and air force rebelled in February, Bordaberry made an emotional plea to the people to support the state. The paper *Opinion Nacionalista* reported that 'Cuando hizo un Llamado emocionado, respondieron 20 ó 25 niñas vestidas de voladitos que fueron a pararse en la vereda en frenta. Pero el pueblo no estuvo'.[110] In a February poll, 60 per cent agreed with military proposals.[111] Support for military intervention also included some leftists. A 11 February 1973 editorial called 'Proposed Objectives of the Armed Forces' in the communist-leaning newspaper *El Popular*, stated, 'estamos de acuerdo en lo esencial con las medidas expestas por las FFAA como salidas inmediatas para la situación que vive la República y por cierto no incompatibles con la ideología de la clase obrera'.[112] Its support for the intervention was stated again in June. In that month, at the same time that most politicians in the National Assembly were coming together to resist military demands, a general strike was organized by the communist-led labour union, the Confederación Nacional de Trabajadores,[113] five days before the coup. Those leading the strike called for increased wages 'in the spirit of army communiqués four and seven', in addition to calling for the resignation of Bordaberry.[114] After the coup, other than the pre-planned strike, the public reaction was calm.

Peruvian stability

In Peru, in addition to the *autogolpe* of April 1992, there are other indicators of democratic instability. For example, publicly acknowledged support for seditious groups is an indication of instability. This can be measured by public opinion data inquiring about support or justification for seditious groups. Public opinion data concerning choice of constitution or regime and perception of risk of instability to the existing constitution can also indicate instability. Finally, calls for military intervention also indicate democratic instability.

One indication of democratic instability is support for seditious groups. Two studies track empathy for terrorist acts. In the 1988 National Questionnaire about Violence, a rejection of terrorist means prevailed. Only 9.9 per cent understood the terrorist acts, 73 per cent rejected them, 12.0 per cent were indifferent to them and 1.0 per cent reacted otherwise.[115] Two years later, the results were almost identical when Peruvians were asked how they felt about terrorist acts: 72 per cent replied they were repulsed, 11 per cent were indifferent and 9 per cent were empathetic. Among Peruvians in the lowest economic stratum there was slightly more support of and indifference to terrorist acts: 14 per cent were indifferent to terrorist attacks and 12 per cent were empathetic.[116] In spite of a frustration with democracy as practised in Peru, a majority of citizens rejected violent protest. Three years later, most citizens still did not condone subversion. In June 1991, the bloodiest month in terms of death toll casualties in ten years, APOYO conducted a poll to assess subversion. Overall, only 17 per cent believed that subversion was justified, 78 per cent did not. APOYO used a stratification of A–D. Stratum A included about 5 per cent of the population of Lima, including mostly the upper class. In this category, 78 per cent did not believe subversion was justified. Stratum B included 24 per cent of metropolitan Lima, including professionals, merchants and the upper middle class. In this category, 96 per cent believed that subversion was not justified. Stratum C included 39 per cent of metropolitan Lima, including wage earners, workers in the private sector and merchants in the informal sector of the economy. In this group, 78 per cent believed subversion was not justified. Stratum D included 33 per cent of the metropolitan population, including public sector employees, the unemployed and poor merchants in the underground economy. Justification for subversive actions increased among the lower socioeconomic stratums of the respondents. Among those in the lowest socioeconomic strata, over one in five thought terrorism was justified. This constant minority support for terrorism is an indication of democratic instability. Even in the lowest category, however, 66 per cent of those questioned rejected subversion.[117]

Another indicator of democratic instability can be found in public opinion data of desired regime type. Many Peruvians were frustrated with democracy as practised in Peru. The first democratically elected president since the 1980 return to democracy, Fernando Belaúnde, was not considered very democratic by a majority of Peruvians. When asked to evaluate his administration in 1987, 58 per cent of those questioned stated that it was only 'a little' or 'not at all' democratic.[118] Although the affirmation of democracy in Peru increased from 1982 until June of 1986, support began to falter afterwards. As the gap between the popularity of Fujimori and the armed forces, on the one hand, and the popularity of the rest of the institutions on the other, increased, support for democracy declined. As the actions of Sendero and other groups spread throughout the country, and as the state implemented a violent and repressive response, the affirmation of democracy declined. A sixteen-point decline occurred from 1988 to 1989. In this time period, there was a significant increase in the incidents of subversive actions and deaths due to the MRTA, Sendero and paramilitary groups. At the same time the percentage of provinces under a state of emergency increased from 30 to 50 per cent.

We have public opinion data from three sources. Datum, APOYO and a Peruvian scholar, Eduardo Ballón, conducted polling during this time (table 6.5). In 1989, we see a dramatic drop in the support for democracy, down to only 61 per cent. This is evident in both Ballón's data and APOYO's study. By 1991, a significant number of citizens, 30 per cent of those questioned, admitted a preference for military rule, reflecting a significant and persistent disillusionment with democracy. In addition, some civilian sectors of society expressed support for a coup. For example, prominent banker Francisco Pardo Mesones suggested that García be removed from power in 1988.[119] Support for military rule peaked in March 1991. As Fujimori became more popular, support for democracy increased and those believing that a coup was probable fell from 41 per cent to 31 per cent. With Fujimori's approval ratings as high as they were in 1992, few people believed a coup was immanent.

Public opinion about the *autogolpe*

Fujimori's *autogolpe* was very popular among Peruvians. It was supported by 80 per cent of the population.[120] In a Peruvian public opinion poll, 12 per cent of Lima residents thought Fujimori's measures to create a new constitution, dissolve Congress and reorganize the judiciary were excellent, 14 per cent thought they were very good and 41 per cent thought they were good. Only 9 per cent thought they were bad, 2 per cent thought they were very bad and 3 per cent considered them terrible. Overall, 83 per cent of those surveyed supported the changes.[121] Interestingly, few people thought that Fujimori's actions were an attack against democracy. After the coup, only 25.8 per cent of the respondents in the popular sector of Lima considered the coup an attack against democracy.[122] In fact, in an APOYO survey on 13 April it was discovered that 50 per cent of those polled believed the post-coup Fujimori rule to be democratic,

Table 6.5 Peru: choice of regime, 1982–92

	Democratic (%)	Military/ by coup (%)	Marxist/ socialist by revolution (%)	Coup probable (%)	Coup improbable (%)
February 1982D	66	11	16		
January 1984D	72	9	13		
June 1986D	88	3	6		
April 1987B	86	7	10		
1988B	77				
March 1988D	75	7	13		
April 1988A	77	9	4		
April 1988D	81				
September 1988A				44	51
1989B	61				
March 1989A	61	14	8	23	65
March 1990A	78	13	5	27	47
June 1990A	76	15	4	38	48
September 1990A	70	17	6	33	57
March 1991A	59	30	6	41	47
September 1991A	65	22	6	31	57
March 1992A	73	16	2	30	63

Source: Dates with an 'A' after the year come from *Informe de Opinion*, APOYO March 1992. Data with a 'D' after the year are from Datum polls. Question: 'Which of these types of government do you consider to be the most adequate for a country such as ours?' (400 < n < 800), Table 4, Cynthia McClintock, 'The Prospects for Democratic Consolidation in a "Least Likely" Case: Peru', *Comparative Politics*, Vol. 21, No. 2, January 1989, p. 140. Data with a 'B' after the year are from Eduardo Ballón's work in Pablo González Casanova and Marcos Roitman Rosenmann (eds), *La Democracia en América Latina: actualidad y perspectivas* (Mexico D.F.: La Jornada, 1995), p. 276.

with only 30 per cent thinking it was a dictatorship.[123] The rest of the population approved of Fujimori's actions on the grounds that he acted to improve the country. When asked if they approved that the armed forces controlled the country,

60 per cent approved of military control for a time, 18 per cent approved of permanent control and 22 per cent disapproved of military control.[124] In a May 1992 APOYO study, the poll found overwhelming support, 73 per cent, for the use of military courts to try alleged terrorists. Fujimori's proposal for the death penalty for some terrorists was approved by 64 per cent. In sum, Peruvians supported Fujimori's *autogolpe* precisely because they thought that he would improve the state.

Spanish stability

In Spain, democratic stability can be indicated in numerous ways. General public opinion data are available. Overall, perceptions of the state and levels of optimism are probed. These general questions allow an examination of levels of satisfaction with democracy in general. Finally, although the attempted coup in 1981 may be considered by some to be an obvious sign of instability, the strong public rejection of that attempt indicates an underlying stability.

Throughout the difficulties of the transition, Spain's democracy gained in support. According to Peter McDonough, Samuel Barnes and Antonio López Pina's study of system support, the citizen's view of the state improved from 1978 to 1984.[125] The numbers of those who trusted the state increased from 27 per cent in 1978 to 41 per cent in 1984. More Spaniards believed that the state was for the many in 1984 (58 per cent, up from 35 per cent in 1978) as opposed to for the few (42 per cent, down from 65 per cent in 1978) as the democracy consolidated in those six years. A separate study corroborates the increasing satisfaction with democracy during the same period. The respondents were asked to indicate their level of satisfaction on a scale of one to ten, with one representing the lowest level of satisfaction and ten representing the highest. The idea of democracy, alone, fared better than democracy under any particular government.[126] It should be noted that these numbers are rebounding from what has been called the '*desencanto*' or disillusionment of the early 1980s. This disillusionment, according to José Ramón Montero, was caused by the 'high expectations raised during the first stages of the transition from authoritarian rule'.[127]

In spite of the ongoing problems, both economic and violent, the citizens maintained a strong support for democracy; indeed, the idea of democracy continued to gain popularity. Three studies are available to document the increase in support for democracy. First, a study which began before the death of Franco and continued until 1982, shows a growing support for democracy as a constitutional form. In 1966, when Franco was still alive, only 35 per cent agreed that 'it is better that officials, elected by the people, decide'. Eleven per cent agreed that it was 'better that a distinguished man decide for us'. In 1974, one year before his death, a majority of 60 per cent preferred democracy. Immediately after Franco's death, support for an authoritarian rule was highest, with 24 per cent. However, as the transition progressed democratic principles enjoyed a stable, strong majority. Care should be taken with the interpretation of the 1966 and 1974 data, since more respondents may have felt pressured not to answer or to choose the 'distinguished man' option. By May 1976, only 8 per cent agreed that one man should decide and 78 per cent chose elected officials. These numbers remained stable until 1982.

A second study covers 1980 to 1985. In 1980, respondents were asked to agree or disagree with the statement that 'democracy is preferable to any other form [of government]'. In 1980, only 49 per cent agreed. By 1984, 69 per cent did and in 1985, 70 per cent.[128] This improvement in support for democracy is corroborated by data from 1983–86. Respondents were asked if they were satisfied with democracy. By November 1986, 57 per cent of Spaniards believed democracy functioned very well or well enough, compared with 47 per cent in December 1983.[129] All three studies, although different measures of democratic stability, generally indicate a growing support for democracy.

As the popularity of democracy increased, the fear of a coup subsided. When asked in November 1983, 'Do you believe that in Spain today there exists the possibility of a new attempted coup?' 42 per cent said yes. Only 30 per cent believed that a new coup was possible in 1986. Those most confident that there would be no further coup attempts were the socialists (PSOE) at 59 per cent and the nationalists at 61 per cent.[130] Nonetheless, 30 per cent of all respondents still believed that a coup was possible.

Public opinion after the coup attempt

Many politicians blamed terrorism for the attempted coup. Conservative Manuel Fraga stated, 'if things simply went on as before, there would be a new attempt to seize power because the causes which led to the attempted coup – terrorism and the absence of proper communications between politicians and the military and between the military and the king – would remain'. Surprisingly, even ETA-pm accepted that terrorist violence was partially to blame. ETA-pm instead embraced a negotiated solution instead of more violence.[131] The conspirators themselves blamed terrorism. At the end of the attempted coup, Tejero described the army and Civil Guard members who participated in the attempted coup:

> No admiten las autonomies separatistas y quieren una España descentralizada, pero no rota. No admiten la impunidad de los asesinos terroristas, contra los que es preciso aplicar todo el rigor de la ley. No pueden aceptar una situación en la que el prestigio de España disminuye día a día; no admiten la inseguridad ciudadana que nos impide vivir en paz.[132]

Terrorism and the granting of autonomy to regions, in the view of some in the military, precipitated the crisis. However, the Spanish citizens did not support the coup attempt, in spite of Spain's troubles.

Democratic stability was indicated by the actions of the Spanish citizens in reaction to the attempted coup. Days after the attempted coup on 27 February 1981 large demonstrations broke out in major cities in favour of democracy. In Madrid, the demonstration was led by diverse political leaders, from Manual Fraga of the AP to socialist leader Felipe González and communist leader Santiago Carrillo.[133] Approximately 1.4 million people participated in the Madrid march in support of democracy.[134] This anti-coup sentiment was corroborated by the polls. In a post-coup survey, 76 per cent were against the coup and only 4 per cent admitted being in favour of it. In addition, 47 per cent stated that they would personally defend democracy.[135] Another survey conducted two days after the failed coup showed that only 9 per cent of those questioned supported the coup attempt.[136] A repeat survey in October 1982, after news of another plot, demonstrated that less than 5 per cent of the population would support a coup attempt.[137]

Democratic stability: summary

Uruguay

In Uruguay, democratic instability followed terrorist and state violence. The violence of the Tupamaros and other seditious groups created an atmosphere of hostility, paranoia and fear in the political community, undermining both security and integration. The repressive state response aggravated both the rudimentary purposes of the state. The censorship, suspicion of the opposition, repression and politicization weakened the integration of the political community and also created fear and distrust. The violent and contested elections, public assessment of the risk to democracy, a small but persistent preference for a strong and orderly state, and the disparate calls for sedition, all reflect democratic instability. The democratic instability until the end of the Tupamaro violence in 1972 is difficult to separate from the instability due to the state violence. However, the calls for the resignation of the president, the calls for military intervention, the public opinion poll of February 1973 and the public reaction to the dissolution of democracy in June 1973 cannot be attributed to the terrorist violence. Despite the end of terrorist violence, state violence and repression continued. The severe democratic instability of 1973 occurred after the end of the terrorist violence.

After the beginning of the slow coup in February 1973, 60 per cent of respondents in a survey approved of the military proposals for political involvement and the same number expected a full coup. This continued decrease cannot be accounted for by the previous amounts of terrorist violence. Moreover, specific evidence of citizen rejection of state repressive policies is available. Uruguayans supported the final dissolution of the National Assembly in June in hopes of obtaining a more practicable constitutional form.

This conclusion is corroborated by evidence gathered by Charles Gillespie. Gillespie conducted interviews in 1984, attempting to map the deterioration of Uruguayan democracy. He asked politicians to rank factors causing the democratic breakdown. The question used was: 'In 1973, Uruguay experienced a crisis that led to a new system of government. Contradictory explanations have been given for this process ... What importance would you assign the following statements (ranking them from most important to least important)?'[138] As we would expect, overall, violence (47 per cent) and the military (49 per cent) were marked as the most or second important factor causing breakdown. Gillespie's research also corroborates the broad lack of support for the state, by examining perceived loyalty to democracy according to parties and factions. The question was: 'In the crisis of a democracy political parties may be judged by their behavior as loyal to the rules of the democratic game, whether they are in office or in the opposition; semi-loyal when they are only sometimes loyal; or disloyal (anti-system parties). Thinking about parties and their factions from 1968 to 1973, if "1" represents an unimpeachably loyal democratic conduct, and "10" one totally anti-democratic, where would you place the following?' It is interesting to note that no faction gave themselves a perfectly democratic score of 1. The Colorado party gave themselves the most anti-democratic rating, with a 3.5, followed by the Frente Amplio, 3.1, and the Blanco party, 2.2. This communicates that many politicians were courting subversives, either of the left or the right.[139] Gillespie's data also corroborate the dual responsibility of both the state and the terrorist violent groups. Gillespie asked: 'In your opinion, which groups were principally responsible for the disorder and violence which the country faced 1968–1973?' The state (59 per cent), the extreme left (81 per cent) and the extreme right (51 per cent) received most of the blame. Only 34 per cent blamed the police and the military. Gillespie's later public opinion research significantly corroborates my hypotheses.[140]

Peru

Violence in Peru had a devastating effect on democratic stability. The violence of Sendero, the MRTA and other groups created widespread fear. The state was unable to protect citizens or even judges from the violence. In addition, this violence harmed the integration and functioning of the community. In many areas of the violence, participation in politics or even voting was dangerous. In addition, citizens suspected each other of being members of either Sendero or the MRTA or a member of one of the death squads. The state's response to the violence was repressive.

In a country in which much of the poputation has limited contact with the state, much of that contact was violent. The repression of the state resulted in more resentment towards state institutions. The state's policy also reflected a greater suspicion and harassment of its citizens. Finally, the military, long in charge of the counterinsurgency strategy, along with the general population, lost faith in the traditional parties and institutions. Many Peruvians did not view the democratically elected presidents as democratic. Moreover, state institutions demonstrated an extreme inability to meet the challenges facing the nation. The governments of Belaúnde and García undermined both security and integration of the political community, all without improving the effectiveness of the institutions. The terrorist and state violence in Peru undermined democratic stability. The democratic instability is demonstrated by some public support for terrorist groups, a decline in support for democracy and calls for military intervention. The instability culminated in Fujimori's *autogolpe* of April 1992. For the average Peruvian, the situation was sufficiently desperate that they supported the only institution and man who appeared capable of doing something: the armed forces and Fujimori. Only the military, the Catholic Church and Fujimori maintained support. Under the pretext of the Congress and the judiciary's gross inability to function, the military and Peruvians supported Fujimori in his 1992 *autogolpe* with the hopes that it would be a more practicable solution for Peru.

Spain

Despite grave challenges, Spanish democracy retained the support of its citizens. However, public opinion data demonstrate that citizens were not rating state performance very well in terms of inflation, unemployment, order or terrorism. Indeed, violence was prevalent and the economy suffered. Why, then, did the citizens support democracy? The use of the purposes of the state allows an understanding of upon what basis citizens support a state with poor performance in key issues. Instead of focusing on state performance in economic issues or order, it looks to how the state responds to these challenges and how that response affects the political community. The new Spanish democracy improved integration of the community by attempting to reconcile demands for regional autonomy with national unity. How did the state actions affect the political community and the purposes of the state? In general, the state opted for a legal response and accommodation of regional demands. In prosecuting only the perpetrators of violence, as opposed to indiscriminate repression, the state furthered, instead of harmed, reciprocal justice. In other words, the state tried to return evil for evil and good for good. By not pursuing a policy of repression and suspension of individual liberties, the state did not further harm the political community. The state restored freedoms and eliminated repression. Citizens were free to participate, to deliberate and to act politically, without restrictions on their participation. This state response encouraged a political community based upon civic friendship as opposed to one plagued by enmity. Although the attacks by ETA, GRAPO and others continued to threaten security and integration, the state did not worsen the situation by introducing its own indiscriminate violence. It appears that the citizens took this into account when evaluating democracy. In spite of negative performance evaluations in regard to economic and order-related issues, Spaniards still supported democracy. Improvement in areas of citizen liberties, autonomy and information seemed to matter more. Measures of democratic stability overall showed an increase from the beginning of the transition to democracy until the end of the study in 1986. Although the attempted coup of February 1981, attributed to terrorist violence by the involved elites, demonstrates some threat to democracy, the bold affirmation of democracy by Spanish citizens reflects an underlying democratic stability in Spain.

Notes

1 Informe Gallup 1970, *Futuro Inmediato y Previsible del Uruguay* (Montevideo: Gallup Uruguay, 1970), p. 12; see also Gallup Uruguay OP 130/131. The size of the study was between 750 and 900 respondents.
2 Informe Gallup, 1970, p. 13. See also Gallup Uruguay 107, ex. 19.
3 The data are compiled from Republica Oriental del Uruguay Junta de Comandantes en Jefe, Tomo 1, 1977.
4 *Generals and Tupamaros*, p. 15.

5 Howard Handelman, 'Labor–Industrial Conflict and the Collapse of Uruguayan Democracy', *Journal of Interamerican Studies and World Affairs*, Vol. 23, No. 4, November 1981, pp. 377–9.
6 'Violencia y pacificación: un informe que debe ser escuchado', *QueHacer*, August/September 1988, p. 19.
7 FBIS LAT 89-143, p. 40.
8 Comisión Especial de Investigación y Estudio sobre la Violencia y Alternativas de Pacificación en el Perú, 1989, p. 372.
9 FBIS LAT 91 047, p. 44.
10 Starn, 1995, p. 562.
11 General Secretariat, Organization of American States *Report on the Situation of Human Rights in Peru* (Washington, DC: OAS, 1992), p. 2.
12 Manuel Castillo Ochoa, 'Fujimori and the Business Class', *NACLA*, Vol. XXX, No. 1, July/August 1996, p. 26.
13 'No one knows where it is safe, no one: neither the police who expect an attack at any time, nor the citizen, who fears if not the detention, the exceptional authority used in the search of his house by the police who are looking for terrorists and who believe that all are terrorists'. My translation. Raúl González, 'Ayacucho: por los caminos de Sendero', *QueHacer*, No. 19, Oct. 1982, p. 41.
14 Gallup, 16:41. Respondents were asked: 'You have a card with a list of problems that affect the country in general. Please tell me the three that you consider the most important. If there is something not on the list, you may express it in two words'.
15 Gallup, published 4 May 1980; IG 600/081, IG 600/085.
16 *Generals and Tupamaros*, p. 12.
17 *Generals and Tupamaros*, p. 43.
18 Gillespie, 1991, p. 32.
19 Handelman also interviewed 100 of Uruguay's industrial, commercial and agricultural leaders.
20 Handelman, 1981, pp. 377–9.
21 Perelli, 1993, p. 31.
22 Langguth, 1978, p. 297.
23 'It will be very difficult, because of the past stigma and because of the deep and strong ethnic and cultural divisions. This is a racist country. The apartheid doesn't exist in the laws, but it functions in everyday life and I don't know how much time it will take to combat it'. González, 1993, p. 41.
24 Mauceri, 1991, p. 97.
25 Graham, 1992, p. 166.
26 Americas Watch, 1992, p. 65.
27 John Crabtree, *Peru Under Garcia* (Pittsburg: University of Pittsburg Press, 1992), p. 194.
28 Sandra Woy-Hazleton and William A. Hazleton, 'Sendero Luminos and the Future of Peruvian Democracy', *Third World Quarterly*, Vol. 12, No. 2, 1990, p. 29.
29 'Alcaldes muertos', *Caretas*, No. 1062, 19 June 1989, p. 33.

30 US Senate, *Committee Report of Human Rights Practices 1991* (Washington, DC: US Government Printing Office, 1992), p. 718.
31 Fernando Tuesta Soldevilla, *Perú Político en Cifras* (Lima: Fundacion, 1994), pp. 142–201.
32 Palmer, 1986, p. 129.
33 Soldevilla, 1994, p. 163.
34 Woy-Hazleton and Hazleton, 1990, p. 31.
35 US Senate, 1992, p. 718.
36 'The socialist left has to sincerely and consciously opt for representative democracy and reject the road of violence, which would lead to the left being the first victim'. My translation. *Equis X*, 'Guerrillas Ayacucho' No. 204, 12–14 August 1980, p. 11.
37 'Sooner rather than later, militarized repression will be unable to coexist with democratic spaces. This is something which would not affect Sendero, but which is vital to the left'. *QueHacer*, 'Sendero: ¿conciencia de la inzquierda?', No. 16, April 1982, p. 20.
38 'We university students are suspected of being terrorists, all of us, especially those who attend state universities'. My translation. 'Los jóvenes dicen: "somos sospechosos de ser terroristas"', *QueHacer*, No. 24, September 1983, pp. 28–31.
39 'It is possible thanks to the support which the inhabitants many times lend . . . [and because] many times they can easily blend in with the villagers'. My translation. González, 1982, p. 41.
40 Enrique Mayer, 'Patterns of Violence in the Andes', *Latin American Research Review*, Vol. 29, No. 2, 1994, p. 153.
41 The National Questionnaire about Violence, 'Violencia y pacificación: un informe que debe ser escuchado', *QueHacer*, August/September 1988, p. 22.
42 The National Questionnaire about Violence, 1988, p. 25.
43 Medrano, 1995, p. 175.
44 Edward Malefakis, 'Spain and its Francoist Heritage', in John Herz (ed.), *From Dictatorship to Democracy* (Westport: Greenwood Press, 1982), p. 227.
45 Robert Clark, 'The Basques, Madrid, and Regional Autonomy: Conflicting Perspectives between Center and Periphery in Spain', in William D. Phillips, Jr and Carla Rahn Phillips (eds), *Marginated Groups in Spanish and Portuguese History* (Minneapolis: Society for Spanish and Portuguese Historical Studies, 1989), p. 225. For more recent discussions of the evolution of the autonomous communities in Spain, see Rafael Banon and Manuel Tamayo, 'The Transformation of the Central Administration in Spanish Intergovernmental Relations', *Publius*, Vol. 27, No. 4, Autumn 1997, p. 85; Luis Moreno, 'Federalization and Ethnoterritorial Concurrence in Spain', *Publius*, Vol. 27, No. 4, Autumn 1997, p. 65; and Robert Agranoff and Juan Antonio Ramos Gallarin, 'Towards Federal Democracy in Spain: An Examination of Intergovernmental Relations', *Publius*, Vol. 27, No. 4, Autumn 1997, p. 1.
46 Newton with Donaghy, 1997, p. 119. After the attempted coup and in an attempt to placate opponents of regional autonomy, the government changed the rules for regional autonomy. LOAPA, one of the

Agreements on Autonomy approved in July 1981, was an effort to contain the autonomy of the Basque and Catalan regions, reducing their autonomy to a level more comparable to that of the other regions. Clark, 1989, p. 236. See also Newton with Donaghy, 1997, p. 123; Goldie Shabad, 'After Autonomy', in Stanley Payne (ed.), *The Politics of Democratic Spain* (Chicago: Chicago Council of Foreign Relations, 1986), p. 118.

47 John Coverdale, 'Regional Nationalism and the Elections in the Basque Country', in Howard R. Penniman and Eusebio M. Mujal-Leon (eds), *Spain at the Polls 1977, 1979, and 1982* (Chapel Hill: Duke University Press, 1985), p. 227.

48 Zirakzadeh, 1991, p. 107.

49 Shabad, 1986, p. 125.

50 Quoted in George Miller, 'A Lesson Learned in Uruguay', *New Leader* Vol. 76, No. 10, 9 August 1993, p. 8.

51 Informe Gallup, 1970, p. 12. See also Gallup Uruguay OP 132/133.

52 Informe Gallup, 1970, p. 10. See also Gallup Uruguay OP 115/99.

53 Ronald H. McDonald, 'Electoral Politics and Uruguayan Political Decay', *Inter-American Economic Affairs*, Vol. XXVI, No. 1, Summer 1972, p. 36.

54 Instituto de Ciencias Sociales, *Uruguay: Poder, Ideologia y Clases Sociales* (Montevideo: Facultad de Derecho, 1970), pp. 66–7.

55 Instituto de Ciencias Sociales, 1970, p. 68.

56 Instituto de Ciencias Sociales, 1970, p. 72.

57 Instituto de Ciencias Sociales, 1970, p. 71.

58 Jellinek and Ledesma, 1979, Part 1, p. 10. See also *Cuadernos de Marcha* No. 47.

59 Mieres, 1991, p. 209.

60 Mieres, 1991, p. 210.

61 Davis, 1995, p. 36.

62 *Generals and Tupamaros*, p. 10.

63 *Generals and Tupamaros*, p. 20.

64 *Generals and Tupamaros*, p. 26. Within Uruguay, however, he had a strong reputation as a fascist, earned while in charge of the Montevideo police from 1963 to 1967. During that time Uruguayan students used to chant, 'Queremos a Aguerrondo, Colgado de un farol, y a todos sus secuaces con las tripas al sol' (We want Aguerrondo, hanging from a street light, and all his henchmen and their guts drying in the sun.)

65 Gillespie, 1991, p. 46.

66 *Generals and Tupamaros*, p. 64.

67 Ronald McDonald, 1972, p. 42, stated: 'Uruguay's democratic heritage was the strongest hallmark of its traditions and culture, but the apparent acquiescence, if not outright support, of public opinion for the military's action suggests that, in face of daily challenges to individual economic and personal security, political commitments can run a poor second'.

68 Graham, 1992, p. 84.

69 Wilson Jaime Barreto, *Marketing Político: Elecciones 1990* (Lima: Universidad del Pacifico Centro de Investigacion, 1991), p. 156.
70 Soldevilla, 1994, p. 36.
71 APOYO, *Informe de Opinion*, APOYO, November 1991 and May 1996.
72 DATUM, also in *Caretas*, 1119, July 1990.
73 FBIS LAT 88 207, p. 41.
74 DATUM, also in *Caretas*, 1119, July 1990.
75 FBIS LAT 88–239, p. 40.
76 Data taken from FBIS 90–FBIS 92 and *Pretextos*, Vol. 3, 1992, p. 43.
77 FBIS LAT 91 172, p. 55.
78 FBIS LAT 91 242. FBIS LAT 91 244, p. 27. For an extensive overview of the conflict, see Beth Simmons, *Territorial Disputes and Their Resolution: The Case of Ecuador and Peru* (Washington, DC: United States Institute for Peace, 1999).
79 The National Questionnaire about Violence, 1988, p. 23.
80 The National Questionnaire about Violence, 1988, p. 23.
81 Other churches were identified by 2.5 per cent, other 14.8 per cent, the Red Cross 2.2 per cent and no identifications 8.2 per cent. The National Questionnaire about Violence, 1988, p. 26.
82 FBIS LAT 91–180, p. 36.
83 Adrianzén, 1993, p. 30.
84 Adrianzén, 1993, p. 30.
85 Philip Mauceri, 'State Reform, Coalitions, and the Neoliberal Autogolpe in Peru', *Latin American Research Review*, Vol. 30, No. 1, Winter 1995, p. 22.
86 FBIS LAT 91 211, pp. 40–1.
87 FBIS LAT 91 222, p. 54.
88 FBIS LAT 91 211, pp. 40–1.
89 FBIS LAT 91 244, p. 27.
90 Centro de Investigaciones Sociológicas, 1977, Vol. 49, p. 248.
91 Centro de Investigaciones Sociológicas, 1977, Vol. 48, p. 348.
92 Gunther *et al.*, 1988, tables 26–7, p. 259.
93 Maravall, 1982, p. 123.
94 Maravall, 1982, p. 123.
95 Victor Pérez Díaz, 'Políticas económicas y pautas socials en la España de la transición: la doble cara del neocorporatismo', in Linz (ed.), *Un presente para el futuro* (Madrid: Instituto de Estudios Economicos, 1985), p. 37.
96 Linz, 1985, p. 39.
97 Peter McDonough, Samuel Barnes and Antonio López Pina, 'The Growth of Democratic Legitimacy in Spain', *APSR*, Vol. 80, No. 3, September 1986, p. 743.
98 *Marcha*, No. 1,264, 22 December 1972.
99 James Kohl and John Litt, *Urban Guerrilla Warfare in Latin America* (Cambridge: MIT Press, 1974), p. 302.

TESTING OF HYPOTHESES ONE AND TWO   169

100 Weinstein, 1988, p. 43.
101 McDonald, 1972, p. 40.
102 Porzencanski, 1973, p. 59. Some scholars, such as Cesar Aguiar, claim that the key to understanding the 1971 elections really has a foundation in 1958. In these elections, the Blancos achieved power. Aguiar points out that the social alliance of the rural forces of masses, small and medium producers, defeated a conglomeration of urban groups (Aguiar, 1981, p. 36). The Blancos, with a different set of alliances, won again in 1962. Aguiar characterizes this decade of one in which the state was unable to maintain stable, long-term policies. He states: 'the instability of the public policies is a manifestation of the representational incapacity of the state, which is a consequence of the accumulation of the clientelistic politics automatically supported, holding the political system prisoner'. (Aguiar, 1981, p. 39; my translation.) According to Aguiar, if the neobatllistas had been a faction of the Colorados, instead of the Blancos, the Frente Amplio would have developed as a further faction within them. Instead, the Frente Amplio formed with little possibility of an alliance with rural sectors. The split of 1958 made it difficult for any viable alliance with the vital rural modernizing sectors (Aguiar, 1981, pp. 40–5).
103 Gillespie, 1991, p. 44, citing *Informe de Opinion Publica*, No. 186–7, February 1972.
104 *Cuadernos de Marcha*, No. 47 in late 1971.
105 Jellinek and Ledesma, 1979, Part 1, p. 10. See also *Cuaderno de Marcha*, No. 47.
106 Labrousse, 1970, p. 53.
107 'We have encountered the dirtiest elections that are recorded in our memory ... They want us to get used to behaving ourselves like a herd, but the oriental republic [Uruguay] was not born for tameness! This means struggle, means organized popular resistance. The struggle and resistance will be stronger than yesterday!' My translation. Nelson Caulo and Alberto Silva, *Alto el Fuego* (Montevideo: Montesexio, 1986), p. 30.
108 'The government, Mr. Bordaberry, not only has not known how to correct the disorder, but has contributed to its aggravation. The government has been transformed into the main agent of the disorder from which society suffers. Mr. Bordaberry has not had the capacity or the will to correct the situation in which the country lives and has tried to hide his ineptitude by blaming the popular discontent. '... For these reasons, we believe that Bordaberry should resign'. My translation. Republica Oriental del Uruguay Junta de Comandantes en Jefe, Tomo 2, p. 133.
109 'I believe that all of this is a direct consequence of the weakness of the executive ... Uruguay needs a strong executive power through a broader political base and the growth of prestige. Is it possible with Mr. Bordaberry as the first magistrate?' My translation. Republica Oriental del Uruguay Junta de Comandantes en Jefe. Tomo 2, 1978, p. 133.
110 'When he [Bordaberry] made the emotional call, only twenty to twenty-five girls ... stopped themselves in the front path. But the public was not there'; *Opinion Nacionalista*, 15 February 1973, p. 8.
111 *Generals and Tupamaros*, p. 64.
112 'We are essentially in agreement with the proposed measures of the armed forces as an immediate solution for the situation in which the

Republic finds itself. Certainly, the proposed measures are not incompatible with the ideology of the working classes'. My translation. Jellinek and Ledesma, 1979, Part 2, p. 82.
113 The communists took over the unions in the 1960s. George Miller, 'A Lesson Learned in Uruguay', *New Leader*, Vol. 76, No. 10, 9 August 1993, p. 8.
114 *La opinión*, 29 June 1973.
115 The National Questionnaire about Violence, 1988, p. 24.
116 FBIS LAT 91 047, p. 44.
117 FBIS LAT 91 202, p. 38.
118 McClintock, 1989, p. 142.
119 Mauceri, 1996, pp. 8–10.
120 Guillermo Rochabrún, 'Deciphering the Enigmas', *NACLA*, Vol. XX, No. 1, July/August 1996, p. 20.
121 FBIS LAT 92 068, p. 23.
122 Sandra Macassi Levander, 'Cultura politica de la eficacia', *Socialismo y participación*, No. 58, June 1992, pp. 65–75.
123 FBIS LAT 92 072, p. 54.
124 Macassi Levander, 1992, pp. 65–75.
125 Because of the variation from 1980 to 1984, which coincides with socialist control of the government, they conclude: 'None of these results corroborate expectations about crisp demarcations between government and regime or between popularity and legitimacy. McDonough et al., 1986', p. 740.
126 McDonough et al., 1986, p. 743.
127 Ramón Montero, 'The Business Sector and Political Change in Spain', in Richard Gunther (ed.), *Politics, Society and Democracy: The Case of Spain* (Boulder: Westview Press, 1993), p. 166.
128 Gunther (ed.), 1993, pp. 146–7.
129 Alonso and Reinares, 1993, p. 502
130 Gallup, IG 600/122.
131 Lancaster and Prevost, 1985, p. 113.
132 'They do not accept separatist autonomies and they want a decentralized Spain, not a broken one. They do not accept the impunity of the assassin terrorists against those who apply the law. They do not accept a situation in which the prestige of Spain diminishes daily; they do not tolerate public insecurity that prevents us from living in peace'. My translation. Buaquats et al., 1981, p. 89.
133 Aguero, 1995, p. 175.
134 Lancaster and Prevost, 1985, p. 113.
135 Maravall, 1982, p. 98.
136 Penniman and Mujal-Leon, (eds), 1985, p. 301.
137 Penniman and Mujal-Leon, (eds), 1985, p. 301.
138 Gillespie, 1991, p. 37.
139 Gillespie, 1991, p. 48.
140 Gillespie, 1991, p. 35.

7
Conclusion

Introduction

This study focused on three pivotal events. In Uruguay, democratic institutions were dissolved in the slow coup by the Uruguayan military. In February 1973, the army and air force rebelled, forced President Bordaberry to create a new advisory committee, and demanded the appointment of a new minister of defence and a new marine commander. Bordaberry appealed to the public to defend the institutions. Less than one hundred people showed up to protest the military defiance. In June, the slow coup was completed when the military, with the approval of President Bordaberry, closed the National Assembly. In April 1992, Peruvian president Alberto Fujimori dissolved Congress and the judiciary with the support of the military. His actions were strongly supported by the public. Eighty per cent of those questioned approved of the *autogolpe*. In Spain, the troubled democracy survived an attempted coup in February 1981. Immediately after the attempted coup, large demonstrations broke out in major cities in favour of democracy. Support for democracy and rejection of possible coup attempts was clear in the polls. Over three out of four Spaniards rejected the coup and almost half said they would act to defend democracy. Less than 10 per cent supported the attempted coup. Why did Uruguayans and Peruvians withhold support for their democracies? Why did the Spaniards defend theirs?

In this study, it was asked what caused democratic breakdown in Uruguay and Peru. Also investigated was how Spain, a country with many of the same serious problems faced by

Uruguay and Peru, managed to avoid a democratic breakdown. The reactions of the citizens are crucial for understanding the fate of democracy. To discern these reactions, it is necessary to study both terrorist violence and the state reaction to the violence. The Aristotelian concept of purposes of the state illuminates how state and terrorist violence affected the citizens' support for democracy. Terrorist violence attacks both rudimentary purposes of the state: security and integration. An indiscriminate repressive state response further undermines the security and integration of the political community. As purposes of the state are undermined, levels of citizen confidence fall and democratic instability rises.

Alternative explanations

There are reasonable and helpful alternative explanations of regime breakdown and consolidation, such as political, leadership and international factors, which are important for understanding the general atmosphere of crisis. However, only a focus on the consequences of violence through the lens of the Aristotelian concept of purposes of the state can explain why Uruguayans declined to demonstrate in the streets in favour of democracy, why 80 per cent of Peruvians supported Fujimori's *autogolpe*, and why the Spaniards marched in record numbers in support of their democracy.

Political system and parties

Many scholars link democratic stability to political factors. Some scholars focus on the strength of political parties. Others focus on the type of political system to indicate future stability. A cursory discussion of the three cases of Uruguay, Peru and Spain indicates that although these theories may be useful in general, they do not help to understand the differing reactions of the publics in these countries.

Institutional strength or weakness of political parties

Some scholars make the connection between democratic stability and the strength of the political parties.[1] For example, Larry Diamond and Juan Linz state:

An important element in the institutional resilience of democracy has been the strength of the party system and the high degree of institutionalization and popular loyalty achieved by the major parties. All of our cases call attention to the institutional strength or weakness of parties as a determinant of success or failure with democracy, and each of them grapples with the problem of institutionalization in terms that inevitably recall Samuel Huntington's classic formula: coherence, complexity, autonomy, and adaptability.[2]

In two of the three case studies, the factor of strength or weakness of the political parties did not predict the ultimate outcome of democratic stability.

Uruguay had very well established political parties, the Blancos and Colorados. These two main political parties dominated Uruguayan politics from 1904 until 1971. Party affiliation was usually passed from parents to children. The groups have fairly coherent memberships. The Colorados are typically urban notables, Italian immigrant descendants, lawyers, intellectuals and businessmen. The Blancos are usually traditional elites and large landowners.[3] The two parties had been sufficiently flexible to adjust to the alteration between a unified executive and a Colegiado (nine-member executive). In the 1971 presidential elections, a new leftist coalition, the Frente Amplio party, gained one-third of the presidential votes in that year.

Peru's parties were poorly established compared with Uruguay's. Peru's APRA was established in 1930, but had been excluded from participation for much of its existence. The AP was founded in 1956 and the PPC in 1967. According to Adrianzén a party system does not exist in Peru. He points out that the last three presidents have been elected without a coherent programme, and that few party loyalties are generated.[4] Joseph Tulchin found a severe difficulty in crafting stable alliances in his analysis of Peru. For example, after the 1990 elections

> The lack of viable political intermediaries in the executive and in the Congress led to a cacophony of political demands (for resources, representation, recognition, influence and benefits) to rapidly shifting and unstable political alliances on specific issues, to improvisation and reactive political behaviour, and to conflicts and inflexible positions. All of this made it extremely difficult to agree on policies and strategies to confront

the explosive combination of problems faced by Peru at the beginning of the 1990's.[5]

This difficulty in forging alliances further complicated attempts to create majority coalitions in the Congress. The weakness of Peruvian political parties is highlighted by the success of a new independent party, Fujimori's Cambio 90 party, in the 1990 presidential election.

In Spain, after the death of Franco in 1975, more than two hundred groups emerged, proclaiming themselves political parties. Some of these parties had emerged from parties active during the Second Republic, but many more were completely new groups.[6] In the founding election, two parties dominated. The PSOE and the UCD were the main recipients of votes. The UCD was a newly formed centrist party, established in 1977, led by Adolfo Suárez. The UCD carried Spain through the first years of democracy. Three of the main parties, the PSOE, the PCE and the PNV had existed since the Second Republic. The parties continued underground under Franco. Another important party, the AP, comprised mostly former Francoist officials and was founded in 1976. Although there was some continuity among parties from the Second Republic, many major political forces from that period were not represented after 1975. For example, the bourgeois republican parties of the centre left, the anarchist parties and the conservative clerical party (the Confederación Española de Derecha Autónoma) had disappeared.[7] In spite of the emergence of two main political parties, the party system was unstable. According to Mario Caciagli,

> The fragility of the new democracy in Spain derived also from the insufficient penetration of the parties in society and the vagueness of their images. The rapid and profound changes in the choice of the Spanish voters, from one election to another until the cataclysm of 28 October 1982, confirmed the instability of the relationship between the two parties and the electorate.[8]

After 1982, the UCD lost its electoral support and was formally dissolved in February 1983. The newly reoriented socialist party, the PSOE, dominated elections after 1982 with the conservative AP (later the Partido Popular) as the major opposition party.[9] In addition to the immaturity and instability of the party system, the successful parties had not captured the political mobilization of the Spanish voters.

Caciagli states: 'party development in Spain has been top-heavy, for the individual parties have evolved more as institutional than socio-politico forces.'[10]

From this brief discussion of main political parties, it appears that the strength of party systems is not helpful in understanding the outcomes in Uruguay and Spain. In Peru, according to this factor, instability is expected. This is congruent with Fujimori's 1992 *autogolpe*. However, this factor predicts the opposite of what occurred in Uruguay and Spain. Uruguayan democracy, with its well-established party system, was overthrown. Spanish democracy, with an immature, unstable and top-heavy party system, survived.

The political system

Other scholars have tried to explain the Uruguayan and Peruvian breakdowns in terms of the failures of the political system. Both countries had multi-party presidential political systems that tended to produce presidents without stable majorities in the legislative bodies.[11] Moreover, both countries had unique aspects that further complicated presidents being elected with electoral majorities. In Uruguay, the culprit was the *lema* system (see below) that tended to produce electoral fragmentation. In Peru, the cause was the runoff elections.

Edy Kaufman blames the political system for the eventual demise of Uruguayan democracy. Kaufman finds fault with the *lema* system. Uruguay's unique double simultaneous vote (DSV) system entails a presidential election in which the equivalent of primary and presidential elections are held simultaneously. This DSV encourages party fragmentation, since the law allows factions to combine their votes in favour of the candidate who received the most votes. The more candidates a party has, the more votes the party can potentially receive. For example, in 1971 Bordaberry, a Colorado, became president even though Blanco leader Wilson Ferreira Aldunate received more votes. This occurred since the total of all votes for Colorado factions was greater than the total of the Blancos. In this case, Bordaberry, the leader of the dominant faction within the party receiving the most votes, the Colorados, would become president even if a Blanco faction received more votes than Bordaberry's. In addition, the party system in Uruguay had become increasingly fragmented. In 1946, there were only 45 lists for deputy in the Blanco party and 108 in the Colorado party. By 1971, there were 308 lists for the Blancos and 246 for the Colorados.[12] In nine years the number of lists for deputy increased by approximately one hundred for each party.

In Uruguay, the party system was institutionalized, autonomous and complex. However, according to Kaufman, the lack of party cohesion and increasing fragmentation, the authoritarian personality of Bordaberry and the emergence of the Frente Amplio, 'hampered the placement of a solid civilian obstacle to the military drive'.[13] In the case of Uruguay, President Bordaberry did lose his majority in the National Assembly before the coup. The military exploited Bordaberry's precarious political situation, making him more dependent on military support.[14] However, a fragmented political system does not explain the public apathy towards the dissolution of Uruguay's constitutional institutions in 1973.

In Peru, the party system was faulted for creating conditions that hindered stable and effective political control. For example, Maxwell Cameron notes that the Peruvian system of a runoff election between the two most popular candidates to ensure a president gains at least 50 per cent popularity also made it difficult to achieve a congressional majority.[15]

Cooperation

Other scholars focus on the presence or absence of cooperation among competing politicians. In Spain, the tendency towards conciliation among Spaniards and a fear of the previous faction were cited as a factor in the successful transition to democracy. Raymond Carr and Juan Pablo Fusi said, 'in 1977 and 1978 there existed an indubitable democratic consensus and a will to make democracy work, shared by the King and all the principal political leaders of the country.'[16] José Maravall emphasized three characteristics that influenced the stability of the new democracy. First, the deaths of Franco and Carrero Blanco created the opportunity for a transition in 1976. Second, the weakness of the democratic right 'obliged it to use the existing apparatuses of the state in order to build a party, and also to ally itself with "converted democrats" whose political background was in the *Movimiento* (single party under Franco).' Finally, the left was too weak to impose a full break with the previous regime.[17] These factors contributed to compromise in the new democracy. Maravall credits the inability of the major parties to impose their will, the increased industrialization and lack of polarized class relations with helping to create a favourable environment of conciliatory relations for democracy.[18]

Another scholar, Ramón Arango, believed that consociationalism was encouraged by the fear of a reactionary backlash, the lack of political dominance and the limitation of problems. According to Arango, consociationalism allowed for cooperation among elites. In addition, he credits both Suárez and King Juan Carlos with a skilful political manoeuvring during the transition.[19] Some cite the founding national election, the first election after approval of the new constitution, as a source of unity that encouraged cooperation. Juan Linz and Alfred Stepan cite a fortuitous ordering of founding elections that aided stability. 'We believe that if the first elections in Spain had been regional, rather than union-wide, the incentives for the creation of all-union parties and an all-union agenda would have been greatly reduced.'[20] Ronald Chilcote concurs:

> Suárez dissolved the Cortes and called for parliamentary elections for March 1979, to be followed by municipal elections in April. He was not going to repeat the mistake of Alfonso XIII in calling municipal elections first, and he was aware that the Left would be very strong in the municipal elections and did not want them to have momentum going into the general elections.[21]

The nationwide founding election helped to create a stable national politics that would be better positioned to reconcile the increasing demands of the different regions. Moreover, Spain is a parliamentary democracy. Linz would cite this as a form of constitution more stable than a presidential form. Linz believes presidentialism has exacerbated crises and increased polarization by the presence of a strong executive and a weak legislature.[22]

In Spain, there was much cooperation in regard to preserving the democracy.[23] In Uruguay, there was also much cooperation. In Uruguay, cooperation among the main political parties was common in regard to policy and to power. However, instead of stability, cooperation led to stagnation and crisis in Uruguay. Since the late nineteenth century there had been a tradition of peaceful sharing of political and informal bureaucratic power, including opposition presence in governments and the bureaucracy. The Uruguayan system of coparticipation, that had guaranteed stability for early Uruguay, may have become debilitating towards the end of democratic rule. According to Weinstein, *coparticipación* as 'an integrating mechanism was perverted by the sectarianism of party politics into jockeying for advantage by factions of the two traditional parties. What was left an orphan was the "national interest" and the effective policies to promote it.'[24] Ronald McDonald follows up on this reasoning, stating:

> Paradoxically, the Uruguayan political system with its checks, balances, controls and its extensive structural development, has 'stabilized' national government to the point of paralysis and stagnation ... The old system is so sluggish and preoccupied with its traditional Montevideo electorate that creative leadership toward new developmental politics is precluded by short-run political sensitivities. These sensitivities have been bred by a half-century specialization on allocative rather than developmental public policy.[25]

The extensive cooperation among politicians, instead of resulting in the successful mediation of conflict, resulted in an inability effectively to confront the crises facing the state.

Conclusion

The explanatory power of these political factors is mixed. In Spain, many parties were new, although others had been established prior to the civil war. However, Uruguayan democracy broke down in spite of a stable party system and Spain's democracy consolidated despite its unstable party system. A focus on political systems does predict trouble for Uruguay and Peru. Both democracies were multi-party presidential systems. The case of a successful, stable democracy, Spain, was a parliamentary system.

A focus on cooperation is unhelpful in the comparative context. The presence of cooperation to create and maintain democracy among political leaders may have aided democracy in Spain, but an excess of cooperation in regard to policy and power sharing frustrated problem solving in Uruguay. Although these separate focuses on political factors may help to explain each country individually, they do not illuminate the different outcomes in cases in this comparative study.

Leadership

Many scholars have followed the focus of Juan Linz by studying leadership. Linz asks, 'What causes a regime to move beyond its functional range to become a disrupted or semicoercive regime that ends in repudiation by large or critical segments of the population?'[26] Linz argues against deterministic analysis, stressing that factors create opportunities and constraints for the agents involved, while still leaving room for meaningful action. He argues that

> The democratic regimes under study had at one point or another a reasonable chance to survive and become fully consolidated, but that certain characteristics and actions of relevant actors – institutions as well as individuals – decreased the probability of such a development.[27]

Although he does state that the actions of leaders have a cumulative effect on the probability of regime survival, Linz notes, 'at any point in the process up to the final point chances remain, albeit diminishing chances, to save the regime.'[28] One difficulty with this style of analysis is that it is extremely difficult to define good or effective leadership before the fact. Without a prior definition of good or effective leadership, explanations based on leadership become tautological.

Uruguay

Some scholars have blamed poor leadership for Uruguay's troubles. With hindsight, leadership errors can be identified. Martin Weinstein identifies the dilemma as one of poor leadership. This is a sentiment echoed by General Liber Seregni, presidential candidate for the Frente Amplio, who during the 1971 elections called the Colorado and Blanco parties dead and void of leadership.[29] Charles Gillespie also believes that the individual politicians must take responsibility for much of the blame for the democratic breakdown. He states that the 'final complicity of the politicians was to abandon Bordaberry when he appealed for help during the military rebellion of February 1973.'[30] For example, on 7 February 1973, during the crisis, Blanco leader Wilson met and negotiated with military officials Generals Ventura Rodríguez and Cesar Martínez. Wilson proposed new elections within the year and the establishment of a broad national cabinet coalition until then. Kaufman commented, 'it endorsed the principle of military involvement within the government machinery.'[31] Wilson was not the only politician to court the military. Julio Sanguinetti, current President of Uruguay, has said, 'the Uruguayan left – especially the Communists, Socialists and Christian Democrats – encouraged the military advance, believing it was possible that the progressive tendencies hardly appearing would get stronger.'[32] Ronald McDonald also finds fault with the political leadership in the National Assembly:

> Aside from the presidential proclivity to rule by decree, the legislature became increasingly unable to respond to the obvious issues of economic and political decay, and the urgency for development. Amid an atmosphere of increasing violence, social instability, and censorship, legislative debate became less relevant to national decision-making.[33]

When Bordaberry appealed for help to support the institutions in face of military pronouncements, neither the public nor other politicians responded. Bordaberry accepted the military's terms.

Peru

In the study of Peru, some scholars have blamed Fujimori for the *autogolpe*. Jaime de Althaus concluded that Fujimori conducted his *autogolpe* to prevent the re-election of Alan García. Many, especially those in the business community, believed that if García were elected again, the neoliberal reforms of Fujimori would be ended before they had had sufficient time to succeed. Maxwell Cameron believes that Fujimori instituted a coup to eliminate Congress and García as rivals. Moreover, according to Cameron, Fujimori personally preferred to rule by decree, not by building coalitions.[34]

Spain

The astute leadership of King Juan Carlos is widely noted as an important explanation for the successful democratization of Spain. Joel Podolny credits Juan Carlos for the successful transition to democracy: 'The central argument . . . is that the behavior of Juan Carlos greatly facilitated the compromise, consensus, mutual trust and most importantly, the legitimacy which were essential for the consolidation of the parliamentary monarchy.'[35] His ties to the military were strong, since he had served in all three military branches. In addition, he cultivated a strong relationship with the military both publicly and privately.[36] Richard Gunther believes that the King's personal legitimacy was transferred to the new regime:

> Favorable reaction to the person demonstrated both active and tacit acceptance of the institution and ultimately evolved into a new rational-legal basis of legitimacy for the Crown – a democratically approved constitution. Paradoxically, the forward legitimation of the monarchy facilitated the backward legitimation of democracy with the non-reactionary conservative sectors.[37]

Charles Powell states, 'while in the thirties the establishment of democracy had forced the prior elimination of the monarchy, four decades later only the monarchy seemed capable of guaranteeing the continuation of democracy.'[38] Indeed, on the night of the attempted coup in February 1981, the King succeeded in securing the loyalty of many otherwise disgruntled and potentially seditious officers.

Summary

The focus on leadership as a primary means of explanation is tricky. A definition of good leadership is difficult to craft *a priori*. Moreover, the focus on leadership privileges the actions of the elites over those of the citizens. Elites are not leaders if people do not follow them.[39] In Uruguay and Peru, the public broadly supported, or at the very least calmly acquiesced to, the overthrow of their democracies. In Spain, the people demonstrated against the coup attempt. Although the actions of the elites were important, the granting or withholding of mass support from potential coups is very important to understand the success or failure of coups.

International influences

Some scholars privilege international influences to explain the breakdown or stability of democracies.[40] Many scholars of Uruguay blame the involvement of the United States for the breakdown of democracy. Foreign influence was also theorized to be important in Peru and in Spain. A brief discussion of international influences in the breakdown of Uruguay and Peru, in addition to the successful democracy in Spain, reveals an incompleteness of this factor as an explanatory cause.

Uruguay

International factors were blamed frequently in the Uruguayan breakdown. For example, Martin Weinstein cites a diffusion effect in the importance of international factors. He states:

> One shoe dropped for Uruguay when the dynamics of the bureaucratic authoritarian regime in Brazil brought hard-line elements to power in the late 1960's; the other dropped with the accentuated belief by successive military governments in Argentina that liberal, civilian run Uruguay provided too much of a safe haven for their domestic foes. Thus the breakdown of democracy, initiated after the 1966 elections and picking up momentum during the Gestido, Bordaberry and Pacheco Areco governments, took place in a country subjected to nearly irresistible pressures by neighbors with forty times and ten times its population and resources.[41]

Although there were rumours of a possible Brazilian intervention, actual linkages between Argentina and Brazil are unclear in causing Uruguayan breakdown. There is some evidence of an Argentine influence. For instance, in February 1971 Uruguayan President Pacheco met with Argentine President General Levingston to discuss how to deal with terrorists, in addition to economic matters.[42] On 9 June 1972, *Marcha* published the declaration of former policeman Nelson Benítez who revealed that Pacheco was cooperating with Argentina on the training of Uruguayan para-police groups in Argentina.[43]

A. J. Langguth and Wilson Fernández blame US involvement for the Uruguayan breakdown.[44] Others blame the influence of the National Security Doctrine for the demise of Uruguayan democracy. The United States gave Uruguay aid through the Agency for International Development (USAID), International Military Education and Training Program (IMET), the InterAmerican Police Academy (IPA) and through the training of Uruguayan officers. During 1962–70, through USAID's Office of Public Safety, Uruguay's police force received money and training. Also through USAID, the US gave an additional $225,000 in 1972.[45] The IPA was established to train police to fight communism wherever it existed.[46] US public safety technicians and consultants, including undercover CIA agents,[47] were hired to train Uruguayan police officers. As of 1971, 113 policemen had been trained in the United States, with an additional 700 trained in Uruguay by American advisers.[48] The total expenditure reached $285,000 in the form of police aid in 1970 and $619,000 in 1971. The total amount from 1961–71 was $1,936,000. From 1946–82, 920 Uruguayan officers attended courses at Fort Gulick in the Panama Canal Zone.[49] Uruguayan police were also sent to Los Fresno, Texas, where they were taught how to build bombs by US army Green Berets. US influence was also felt through officer training at the School of the Americas at Fort Sherman.[50] In addition, the United States gave significant amounts of aid through IMET. Between 1968 and 1972, it gave $1,703,000. The peak year of giving was 1971, with $423,000. In 1972, the US contributed only $323,000.[51] The United States was involved in the training of Uruguayan police and military, but how influential was the involvement?

Carina Perelli argues forcibly against attributing military interventions to the National Security Doctrine of the United States. She disagrees with the argument that the Doctrine of National Security was spread through the School of the Americas and the training courses attended by Latin American officers in the United States. Perelli rejects the contention that the adoption of this doctrine reinforced a historical tendency to intervene in politics. She states: 'by this view, the armed forces act as mindless instruments that simultaneously obey the dominant demands of their societies and of the creators of the doctrine.'[52] She calls for an examination of the context in which the military operated, noting the wide social unrest. She identifies that the changes in the societies led to a reexamination of the role of the military. She argues that the military intervened due to three factors. First, the divisions in the political class, scandal, inefficiency and corruption led to the existence of a belief in a void of power. In addition, the poor economic performance and use of violence primed the military to rethink its role and intervene.[53]

Two factors weaken the argument that the United States-influenced security doctrine was responsible for the Uruguayan breakdown. First, General Liber Seregni, who was later the presidential candidate for the Frente Amplio, had been director of the officer school, Instituto Military de Estudios Superiores. The fact that a progressive, constitutionalist officer was in charge of officer training for years casts doubt on this explanation, especially that of the National Security Doctrine. In addition, Uruguay's National Security and Defence School was established five years after the coup, instead of before a coup, such as in Brazil. Brazil's Escola Superior de Guerra was established before the coup.[54]

Peru

The effect of international factors in Peru is inconsistent. In Peru, instead of US involvement under the pretence of fighting subversion, as in Uruguay, in Peru US involvement was directed towards curbing the drug trade. However, unlike in Uruguay, among Peruvians, especially those in the military leadership, there was a distrust of US involvement. Economic and military aid to Peru from the United States was inconsistent and rife with negotiation of terms.

Parts of Peru are ideal for growing coca leaves and coca production is high. Consequently, the US views Peru as a main drug-producing country. Typically the coca leaves are grown in Peru and sent to Colombian traders for processing. Approximately 60,000 to 300,000 families grow coca in the Peruvian Huallaga Valley in addition to 10,000–20,000 in the rest of Peru.[55] In 1985 a new policy of drug interdiction was introduced, called 'Operation Condor,' in which US military pilots and Drug Enforcement Agency (DEA) officials cooperated with Peruvian officials. This policy was more effective in reducing the processing and trafficking capabilities, which then lowered the price for coca leaves, making it a less desirable crop to cultivate.[56] Under Peruvian President García, the United States was involved in drug enforcement through the DEA. The operation was called 'Operation Snowcap' and was developed in 1987. In this, DEA officials would help local police in crop eradications and drug interdiction. US army Green Berets were also involved in training and established a base in the Upper Huallaga Valley. However, late in García's term US President Bush announced the Andean plan, a five year $701,000,000 plan of economic and military assistance. The aid was conditional upon Peru's focusing on a military strategy. García refused the military assistance. Many in the state and in the military were hesitant to involve the military in the counter-drug operations.[57] After his election, Fujimori did not initially accept US aid in 1990 because of the US preoccupation with a military focus. Fujimori wanted more attention paid to the economic crisis. Eventually an agreement was signed in May 1991 that recognized Peru's security and economic needs in addition to the anti-drug campaign pushed by the United States.[58] The increase in military assistance in 1991 reflects the successful agreement between Fujimori and the United States that May.

The international reaction to the coup, including the US reaction, was negative and in fact encouraged Fujimori quickly to call new elections. The US suspended all aid. In addition, the IMF withheld a $222 million loan and the Organization of American States (OAS) released a declaration stating it 'profoundly deplored' the coup. International pressure succeeded in moving on Fujimori's plan for the reintroduction of elections. The Democratic Constituent Congress was elected on 13 November 1992. Municipal elections were held in February 1993, and a constitutional referendum was held on 31 October 1993.[59] Although US anti-drug policy exacerbated the problem with Sendero and encouraged a heavy-handed response to Peruvian problems, the US response to Fujimori's coup was strongly negative and pressured for the return to democratic governance. The US suspended all economic and military assistance and used its influence to delay loans from the Peru Support Group and the Inter-American Development Bank.[60]

Spain

International factors seemed to both help and hinder the new Spanish democracy. Spain began to integrate itself into European institutions after Franco's death. Spain tried to gain associate EEC membership in 1962, but was turned down since it was a dictatorship.

> [A]lthough the EEC Treaty said that 'any European State may apply to become a member of the Community,' democracy has – in practice – been a basic precondition. Spain was given a preferential trade agreement in 1970 ... but ... only with ... the death of Franco in Spain in 1975 was EEC membership [taken as a real possibility].[61]

In June 1977, Spain again applied for membership to the European Community. Two months later, in October 1977, it was admitted to the Council of Europe. In 1982, despite objections from the PSOE and negative public opinion, the UCD leader Leopoldo Calvo Sotelo gained approval of entry into NATO.[62] Some scholars, such as Richard Gillespie, credit this integration for an increasing stability. Gillespie states, 'the new regime benefited from EC solidarity and the process of European integration made it increasingly difficult for anti-democratic elements in Spain to offer a credible scenario for the future.'[63] In addition, the joining of NATO re-focused the future of the military to a more professional role in NATO. However, the influence of the United States is negative for democratic consolidation in Spain. Under Franco, in 1953, Spain signed an agreement with the United States to establish American bases in Spain in return for economic aid. Many cite this aid as crucial in sustaining Franco's regime when it may otherwise have failed. Through this agreement, the Spanish military had much contact with the US military. Moreover, even later, democratic Spain was not helped by the United States during its attempted coup.[64] During the crisis, US Secretary of State Alexander Haig commented that the attempted coup was an internal matter for Spaniards.[65]

Summary

Undoubtedly, international pressures account for opportunities and constraints on national events. Even for scholars who believe that international forces can influence democratic outcomes, there is an acknowledgement of the limitation of the effectiveness of international forces. For example, P. Nikiforos Diamandorus states,

> First, by mobilizing effectively in support of forces favoring a democratic outcome, nondomestic structures can enhance the democratization dynamic and thus contribute to eventual consolidation. Second, and perhaps more important, international influences play a role that can only be described as complementary and secondary to that of domestic forces.[66]

However, in our three cases, no consistent pattern of effect can be seen. Moreover, even if international factors affected military or political leaders, they cannot account for the different responses of the citizens of the respective countries. International factors cannot explain why Uruguayans and Peruvians abandoned their democracies and why Spaniards supported theirs.

The treatment of violence in the literature

One theme is recurrent in the literature. When violence is discussed as a possible threat to democratic stability, it is usually discussed in the context of legitimacy.[67] For example, in the case of Peru Carol Graham states that under García, 'the political violence emanating from within the ranks of the governing party clearly demonstrated the lack of agreement on commitment to democratic practices and principles within the party, undermined the legitimacy of the state and surely exacerbated the political polarization process.'[68] In the case of Uruguay, Charles Gillespie believed that labour unrest alone probably would not have toppled the regime, but that

> Labor militants had begun to scare managers and owners quite badly (especially when the factory occupations became violent and the Tupamaros began to kidnap businessmen). Uruguayan democracy became delegitimated in the eyes of businessmen for failing to protect their personal safety, liberty and property. Just as it appeared hollow to strike leaders who were detained in the barracks by the military.[69]

For Graham, the violence of the state undermined the legitimacy. For Gillespie, both the state violence and Tupamaro violence undermined legitimacy.

In the literature that discusses violence more generally, the tie to legitimacy is also important. Martha Crenshaw points out that, 'in examining both the causes and consequences of terrorism, a central question is the relation between terrorism and political legitimacy, particularly in democratic states.'[70] Typically in the literature, the democratic response is analysed in the following manner. According to Cynthia McClintock, terrorist violence affects legitimacy because

> Government officials perceive a contradiction between respect for human rights and the defeat of the subversives. Civilian

and military officials argue over the correct policy response. The democratic state loses its legitimacy both by reacting aggressively, without concern for the constitution, and by reacting more cautiously, and thereby possibly appearing ineffectual.[71]

In terms of the results of state violence, G. Bingham Powell also connects violence to legitimacy. Powell states:

> It is hard to escape the conclusion that the reactions of the democratic parties are at least as important as the terrorist strategies or the military sympathies. This point is emphasized when we consider another form of the use of violence: its employment by electoral parties or their supporters to intimidate opponents and mobilize backing ... Such electoral violence also undermines the claim of democracy to be able to manage conflict through peaceful electoral processes, justifying the use of various coercive resources by any groups possessing them.[72]

However, how exactly does violence affect legitimacy? Is legitimacy the best concept to address this question?

Why the purposes of the state is an appropriate concept

Legitimacy is usually recognized as based in belief, habit or rational calculation. Socialization and habit are very important for identifying options of regimes, but are not very helpful in explaining changes in citizen support. Moreover, in Peru and in Spain both authoritarian rule and democracy had existed, complicating the main source of habit-based legitimacy, time. In Uruguay, the country had had seventy years of solidly democratic rule. One would expect a well-established habit and belief in the legitimacy of a democratic form of constitution. To explain changes of citizen support, it would seem reasonable to look at rational calculation. Linz focuses on efficiency and efficacy in the basic functions of a state. He identifies the basic functions as economic and social policies, the 'maintenance of civil order, personal security, the adjudication and arbitration of conflicts, and a minimum of predictability in the making and implementation of decisions.'[73] However, Linz's attempt at identifying basic functions of a regime is unable to differentiate why Spaniards continued to support their democracy and why Peruvians and Uruguayans abandoned their democratic institutions. All three countries faced challenges of civil order and personal security, domestic conflict and economic crisis. Each democracy had minimally predictable systems of making and implementing decisions. The typical concepts of legitimacy cannot explain why Spaniards continued to support democracy despite the national problems and why Peruvians and Uruguayans did not. Without the concept of the purposes of the state, why citizens support or abandon their democracies is unclear.

Spaniards supported democracy in spite of rating many problems as worse since the transition to democracy. The public judged the state's performance as ineffective. The citizens overwhelmingly rated unemployment, delinquency, the economy, security and public order, and corruption as worse than before. The political situation and the quality of leaders were overall rated as better than before, but by slim margins. Thirty-nine per cent said the political situation was better and 38 per cent said it was worse. Thirty per cent felt there was better leadership and only 24 per cent thought it was worse. With such a tepid endorsement of democratic Spain, why did a majority of Spaniards say they would personally act to defend democracy? Why did only 10 per cent approve of the attempted coup? Only by examining public opinion data with the concept of the purposes of the state can this reaction be understood. The only areas where Spaniards rated state performance as better were citizen liberties (53 per cent better, 27 per cent worse), regional autonomy (48 per cent better and 20 per cent worse) and information (61 per cent better and 12 per cent worse). Interestingly enough, this corresponds to the restraint shown by the state in its response to terrorism. The state did not further undermine the purposes of the state by using indiscriminate repressive and violent measures. The three areas in which the state was assessed as better than before are areas that would have suffered if a repressive response had been chosen. These are the only areas where the state received high marks. Without that support, upon what basis would citizens support democracy? By analysing public opinion data according to the rudimentary purposes of the state, security and integration, it can be shown why Spaniards supported democracy and why Peruvians and Uruguayans did not. Uruguay and Peru faced the same difficulties. However, the state responses attacked security and integration, which were already undermined by terrorist violence. Security was undermined by the increase in state violence and repression. Integration was undermined by the suspension of individual liberties and the decrease in tolerance as levels of suspicion increased.

> **Hypothesis one**
>
> Terrorist violence threatens democratic stability by undermining both rudimentary purposes of the state, security and integration. As the purposes of the state are unfulfilled, citizen confidence in the state declines. As citizen confidence decreases, democratic instability increases.

In all three cases, Uruguay, Peru and Spain, terrorist violence was viewed as a serious threat to the state. In Uruguay, a strong majority of the population viewed the Tupamaros as a highly dangerous group. A concern about the violence was also evident in public opinion polls, with social disorder and instability a concern for many. In Peru, approximately seven out of ten people were afraid of the violence, viewed it as serious and were repulsed by it. Over half thought the country was in a state of civil war. In Spain, terrorism was consistently ranked as one of the top three problems facing the state. Moreover, citizens recognized terrorism as a threat to democracy. Interestingly, all three states received poor evaluations for their efforts to deal with the terrorist threat. In Uruguay, only approximately one out of eight citizens characterized the National Assembly as doing a good job. The Peruvian Congress had overwhelmingly low approval ratings. Every democratically elected leader except for Fujimori ended his term with extremely low approval ratings. In addition, traditional parties in both Uruguay and Peru lost support in the last election before the coup. Even in Spain, the successfully consolidated democracy received high marks of dissatisfaction in regard to the economy, unemployment, corruption, public order and security.

Clearly, terrorism was viewed by Uruguayan, Peruvian and Spanish citizens as a serious problem. As the threat continued unabated, the states were held accountable in public opinion for the failure to promote the two rudimentary purposes of the state: security and integration. Citizens were afraid and the violence was viewed as a threat in these countries.

> **Hypothesis two**
>
> State repression and violence also undermine the rudimentary purposes of the state, integration and security. Decreases in citizen confidence should follow a decrease in the fulfillment of the rudimentary purposes. Finally, as citizen confidence in the state decreases, increases in democratic instability should be identifiable.

In two of the three cases, Uruguay and Peru, the state responded to terrorist violence by indiscriminate repressive and violent means. In Uruguay, the state broadly suspended rights, practised censorship, instituted torture in investigations and used covert, state-sponsored violent groups to combat terrorist violence. In Peru, the state suspended rights in the areas under a state of emergency, forced many to participate in armed peasant groups, and used torture and extrajudicial executions in its counterinsurgency policy. Spain, on the contrary, pursued a policy of national reconciliation. The state restored political liberties, granted amnesty to political prisoners and allowed regional autonomy. Although there were scattered instances of allegations of torture, it was not a state policy. Some anti-terrorist legislation was introduced, but it was used sparingly. The citizens' reaction to the state was negative in Uruguay and Peru. The state policies of indiscriminate repression and violence further undermined the purposes of the state. Levels of citizen confidence and democratic stability declined. In Spain, however, the state's policy of national reconciliation helped to bolster the purposes of the state that were under attack from terrorist violence. Consequently, there is no evidence of a further degeneration in security due to state actions. Furthermore, the state actions seemed to improve integration.[74]

The indiscriminate state repression and violence further undermined the purposes of the state in Uruguay and Peru.

As the citizens faced threats from terrorist groups, instead of being confident in an appropriate proportionate response by the state to those responsible, all citizens suffered from the repressive measures instituted by the state. Citizens began to look at the state as a threat to their security and integration, in addition to the terrorist groups. Only the military, in Uruguay, and the military and Fujimori, in Peru, maintained positive citizen support. With the state presenting more of a threat than a solution, many citizens supported the coups in Uruguay and Peru, in hopes of achieving a more practicable form of government. In Spain, the state did not add to the violence. Instead, its policies of a rational reconciliation buttressed the security and integration that were attacked by the terrorist violence, instead of further weakening them. Consequently, the citizens remained supportive of democracy, believing it to be the most practicable constitutional form.

An answer to a possible objection

One objection that can be raised is the following question. Why did the people support the military in Uruguay and in Peru when the military was involved in the repressive policies? The answer to this rests on the development of factions within each military. Given these factions, citizens could support the military with different hopes for, and expectations of, a military-led state.

Uruguay

Four factions of military officers developed within the armed forces. The popular frontist group was composed of officers who supported the Frente Amplio, including its candidate, Liber Seregni. The second group was composed of traditional legalist members. These officers were basically members of the traditional parties and some were candidates for office, such as General Juan Ribas, who ran for president under the Colorado banner, and General Mario Aguerrondo, who ran for the Blanco party. This group also included Generals Gravina and Francese. A third group, the nationalist reformist group, viewed itself as similar to the Peruvian revolutionary military regime of 1968. It advocated intensive economic development and social change. A prominent member of this group was General Gregorio

Alvarez, who led the fight against the Tupamaros and who served as Secretary General of COSENA. Finally, there was the developmental or gorila group. This group of the extreme right favoured a takeover of the state. It also believed in the promotion of unrestricted foreign investment in Uruguay. Members included Commander-in-Chief of the army, General Hugo Chiappe Posse, and General Esteban Cristi, who advocated the military's responsibility to eliminate subversion and political corruption.

The influence of the traditional legalist officers waned quickly. In July 1972, 559 officers condemned the attempt by the National Assembly to name soldiers responsible for the death of a civilian publicly. Despite being warned by constitutionalist Commander-in-Chief General Florencio Gravina that the proposed resolution was 'inopportune and inappropriate', the officers continued. General Gravina also disapproved of the military's investigation of economic crimes. He resigned in October 1972 in protest.[75] These incidents mark the increase in power of the hard-line, developmental faction in the military.[76] By the time of the crisis in February 1973, most of the popular frontist and traditional legalist factions were out of the military. The few that remained lost influence shortly after the crisis.[77] The nationalist reformist group and the hard-line developmental group were mainly responsible for the slow coup. The nationalist reformist group remained visible and influential through the June dissolution of the National Assembly. This group was responsible for authorship of military communiqués four and seven. These communiqués called for the elimination of unemployment and subversion, the implementation of land reform and further benefits for citizens, such as health care and the pursuit of modernization and development, and called for the guarantees of sovereignty and security. One of the main nationalist reformist generals, General Gregorio Alvarez, was a leader of the February rebellion and the June dissolution of the National Assembly. He also served as Secretary-General of COSENA. The hard-line developmental group, including General Esteban Cristi, also participated in the slow coup and the dissolution of the National Assembly. With two contrasting factions conducting the slow coup, it seems plausible that citizens could have very different expectations of a military state.

Peru

In Peru, it must be remembered that the military succeeded in implementing significant, although not entirely successful, reforms under the military rule of General Velasco Alvarado (1968–75). In spite of the failures of the revolutionary military state of 1968–80, in 1988 Peruvians rated General Velasco as the best president since 1950.[78] The military had different possible traditions to follow.

Although the military had been placed in charge of the counterinsurgency policy, it was not given a policy to follow by the governments of Belaúnde and García. Paralleling the inconsistency in the governments of Belaúnde and García, there was a similar lack of unity among the generals charged with the elimination of the threat during those two presidencies. In terms of controlling the counterinsurgency policy, the military was in complete control. However, this military had been divided over how to solve the problem. For example, General Clemente Noel Moral, the first commander in Ayacucho, viewed the conflict as an internal war. 'One misses the fact that Sendero Luminoso, whatever its political variation, is the armed wing of a large movement which attempts to disrupt the established order to favor international communism, and nothing less'.[79] General Adrián Huamán, the only general to be discharged by President Belaúnde, was military commander of Ayacucho from 1983 until September 1984. Huamán attempted to create a new counterinsurgency strategy that nurtured the alliance between the people and the armed forces. He speaks fluent Quechua, was born in Apurimac and is the son of peasants. Huamán stated:

> Here the solution is not military, because if it had been military, I would have resolved it in minutes. If it were a question of destroying Ayacucho, the area would not exist for half an hour, nor would Huancavelica. We would be done with the problem. But that is not the answer. What is happening is that we are talking about human beings from the forgotten pueblos who have been crying out for 160 years, and no one has paid any attention to them. Now we are reaping the result.[80]

This disagreement among the generals was reflected in the seesaw-like policies of the military. In Ayacucho in 1988, General José Valdiva was in charge. He followed an internal war approach, complete with curfews and the prohibition of the presence of the Red Cross and other human rights organizations. The result was an increase in human rights violations. General Sinesio Jarama disagreed with those policies, stating in 1989 that the first thing that is needed to combat subversion is an examination of the political, economic, social and psychological context: 'Eso es la famosa estrategia contrasubversiva de la que tanto todos hablan y que no existe'.[81] Later, in 1989, a different general, General Howard Rodríguez, lifted many repressive measures and involved the military in civic action programmes. In 1990, General Petronio Fernández Dávila continued the programmes of Rodríguez, but added a psychological campaign, which was later dropped.[82] The same inconsistency due to the turnover of generals occurred in the Huallaga Valley, a coca-growing region with high levels of Sendero activity. General Alberto Arciniega reported on the battle for Huallaga in a *QueHacer* interview. The general communicated his sympathetic attitude towards the peasants.

> Tenemos que tener en cuenta que el productor de coca, el campesino cocalero, era acosado por la policía y por cuanta fuerza de orden existía, porque era considerado un delincuente ... Estamos hablando del 80 per cent de la población! Lo que hacemos, entonces, es modificar esta situación para evitar que el campesino cocalero – la base de la que nutria Sendero para realizar sus actividades – sea hostigado.[83]

The general denied that the peasant who grows the coca should be treated like a drug trafficker. General Arciniega succeeded in ending the alliance between insurgents and Sendero. When his term ended, his successor changed strategies, targeting the peasants who grow the coca. As a result, Sendero's activity increased in the region.[84] As in Uruguay, it seems plausible that citizens could have very different expectations of Fujimori's military-supported state.

Lessons learned from Uruguay, Peru and Spain

In-depth comparative case studies examining different responses to terrorism are rare. In the literature, there is a tension in major works on counter-terrorism. What is the best way to respond? Some scholars believe that a firm stance should be taken, at the expense of certain civil liberties if necessary. Others believe that the suspension of civil liberties only exacerbates the problem. One thing to remember is that almost all terrorist groups intend to provoke a repressive response to further their goals and ease their recruitment.

The advice of former Israeli Prime Minister Benjamin Netanyahu is representative of those who would recommend a more severe response to terrorism. He counsels states to take an active approach against terrorists. He states: 'there is little choice but to adopt an active posture against terror'.[85] Just what does an active posture mean for Netanyahu? Netanyahu believes that civil liberties should not be considered absolutes: 'In this regard, there is apparently a moment of truth in the life of many modern democracies when it is clear that the unlimited defense of civil liberties has gone too far and impedes the protection of life and liberty'.[86] His specific recommendation of loosening warrant requirements in terrorism cases, among others, is reminiscent of the experiences of Peru and Uruguay.

Two other scholars represent a view that is sensitive to maintaining the support of the people. Max Mainwaring believes that the outcome of any counterinsurgency effort will be determined by the legitimacy of the state, the unity of effort, the type of support for the targeted state, the ability to reduce outside aid to the insurgents, intelligence and, finally, the discipline and capabilities of the armed forces. He believes that the single most important factor is legitimacy.[87] Bard O'Neil suggests that the best way to deal with internal terrorism 'is to emphasize police work, good intelligence, and judicial sanctions'.[88] Sometimes experts recommend that the military be deployed or that local militias be established. However, O'Neil cautions that 'their effectiveness will be partly contingent on whether they constitute a disciplined force perceived to be a servant of the people . . . , or are instead ill-disciplined units guilty of excesses against the people'.[89] O'Neil recognizes that popular support is important for the state. He also recognizes the role of an effective, responsive state: 'No matter how hard insurgents try, they will be frustrated if the government has a competent and capable administration that dispenses services, controls the population, and effectively coordinates a multitude of political, economic and security policies'.[90] The emphasis on legitimacy and the political aspect of countering terrorism is echoed by J. Samuel Fitch. He warns:

> at a minimum, democratic governments must clearly delineate the lines between police and military roles in internal security. Insofar as possible, the armed forces should be removed from primary responsibility for internal security, without denying the need for trained counterinsurgency forces to intervene when antidemocratic forces attempt to establish a territorial base. Ultimately, democratic regimes will need to develop an alternative counterinsurgency doctrine that acknowledges that legitimacy and inclusiveness of democratic regimes to isolate and politically defeat violent anti-regime forces.[91]

The clear lesson from examining the Uruguayan, Peruvian and Spanish experiences from the Aristotelian perspective is that an indiscriminate, repressive state response undermines citizen support and harms the democracy that the state is supposedly acting to protect. Even today, Spain and Peru both struggle with terrorism. However, in Spain democracy did not suffer as a result of the actions to suppress it. In Peru, the democratic system established in 1980 was sacrificed. The temptation to resort to repressive means does not seem to be more effective than an approach that maintains civil liberties and is less damaging to democracy. When crafting a response to terrorism, it is necessary to consider the reaction within the broader context of democratic stability. Domestic terrorism is, above all, a political problem with security and military implications. The Aristotelian approach directs the discussion about possible responses to terrorism to consider not only the cessation of the terrorism, but also the preservation of the democracy which is under attack.

Notes

1 See Mainwaring, 1988, pp. 91–120; Samuel Huntington, *Political Order in Changing Societies* (New Haven: Yale University Press, 1969); Robert Dix, 'Democratization and the Institutionalization of Latin American Political Parties', *Comparative Politics*, Vol. 24, No. 4, January 1992, pp. 488–511; and Liliana de Riz, 'Política y partidos: Ejercicio de análisis comparado: Argentina, Chile, Brasil y Uruguay', *Desarrollo Económico*, Vol. 25, No. 100, January/March 1986, pp. 659–82.

2. Larry Diamond and Juan Linz, 'Introduction', in Larry Diamond, Juan Linz, and S. M. Lipset (eds), *Democracy in Developing Countries: Latin America* (Boulder: Lynne Rienner, 1989), pp. 20–1.
3. Gillespie, 1991, p. 18.
4. See Adrianzén, 1993.
5. Francisco Sagasti and Max Hernandez, 'Crisis of Governance', in Tulchin and Bland (eds), 1994, p. 26.
6. Bonime-Blanc, 1986, p. 27.
7. Mario Caciagli, 'Spain: Parties and the Party System in the Transition', in Pridham (ed.), 1984, p. 87.
8. Caciagli, 1984, p. 85.
9. For a more in-depth analysis of the Spanish party system see Gunther *et al.*, 1988.
10. Caciagli, 1984, p. 97.
11. See Mainwaring, 'Presidentialism, Multipartism, and Democracy – the Difficult Combination', *Comparative Political Studies*, Vol. 26, No. 2, July 1993, pp. 198–228, for the argument that the combination of a multi-party system and presidentialism is detrimental to a stable democracy. See also César Cansino, 'Party Government in Latin America: Theoretical Guidelines for an Empirical Analysis', *International Political Science Review*, Vol. 16, No. 2, 1995, pp. 169–82; and Juan Linz and Arturo Valenzuela (eds), *The Failure of Presidential Democracy* (Baltimore: Johns Hopkins University Press, 1994). For a more general discussion of party systems see Giovanni Sartori, *Parties and Party Systems: A Framework for Analysis* (Cambridge: Cambridge University Press, 1976).
12. Gillespie, 1991, p. 31. See also Aguiar 1981.
13. Kaufman, 1979, pp. 22–3. For a complete description and analysis of the Uruguayan electoral system, see Oscar Bottinelii, *El sistema electoral uruguayo: descripción y análisis*, Working Paper No. 1 (Montevideo: PIETHO, 1991).
14. Kaufman, 1979, pp. 26–7.
15. Cameron, 1995, p. 197.
16. Carr and Fusi, 1981, p. 237.
17. Maravall, 1982, pp. 204–5.
18. Maravall, 1982, p. 208.
19. Arango, 1995, p. 131. Other scholars focusing on cooperation include Donald Share; see Share, 1986.
20. Juan Linz and Alfred Stepan, 'Political Identities and Electoral Sequences: Spain, the Soviet Union, and Yugoslavia', *Daedalus*, Vol. 121, No. 2, spring 1992, p. 127.
21. Fred A. Lopez III, 'Bourgeois State and the Rise of Social Democracy in Spain', in Ronald Chilcote (ed.), *Transitions from Dictatorship to Democracy* (New York: Crane Russak, 1990), p. 57. See also Richard Gunther, P. Nikiforos Diamandouros and Hans-Jurgen Puhle (eds), *The Politics of Democratic Consolidation* (Baltimore: Johns Hopkins University Press, 1995).
22. See Linz, 1978, pp. 71–4.

23 See also Omar Encarnacion, 'Social Concertation in Democratic and Market Transactions: Comparative Lessons from Spain', *Comparative Political Studies*, Vol. 30, No. 4, August 1997, p. 387 and Paloma Aguilar, 'The Memory of the Civil War in the Transition to Democracy: The Peculiarity of the Basque Case', *West European Politics*, Vol. 21, No. 4, October 1998.

24 Weinstein, 1988, p. 34.

25 McDonald, 1972, p. 44.

26 Linz, 1978, p. 10.

27 Linz, 1978, p. 10.

28 Linz, 1978, p. 11.

29 General Liber Seregni, *Discursos* (Montevideo: Bolsilibros ARCA 86, 1971), p. 14.

30 Gillespie, 1991, p. 44.

31 Kaufman, 1979, p. 28.

32 *La Opinión*, 18 July 1973.

33 McDonald, 1972, p. 34.

34 Cameron, 1995, pp. 150–3.

35 Joel Podolny 'The Role of Juan Carlos I and the Consolidation of the Parliamentary Democracy', in Gunther (ed.), 1993, p. 90.

36 Podolny, 1993, p. 95.

37 Podolny, 1993, p. 104.

38 Charles Powell, *El piloto del cambio* (Barcelona: Editorial Planeta, 1991), p. 17. See also Charles Powell's book, *Juan Carlos of Spain* (Oxford: St. Anthony's College, 1996).

39 This criticism is analogous to Daniel Levine's criticism of the focus on elite pacts in the literature on redemocratization, such as in Guillermo O'Donnell, Phillippe Schmitter, and Laurence Whitehead's *Transitions from Authoritarian Rule: Prospects for Democracy* (Baltimore: Johns Hopkins University Press, 1986). For example, 'the stress on pacts as antidemocratic manipulation ignores the ties that link the elites who make the pacts to popular groups, and thus obscures the reasons why the latter give them a grant of legitimacy.' Daniel Levine, 'Paradigm Lost: Dependence to Democracy', *World Politics*, April 1988, p. 379.

40 For example, George Lopez, 'The National Security Ideology as an Impetus to State Terror', in Michael Stohl and George Lopez (eds), *Government Violence and Repression* (New York: Greenwood Press, 1986).

41 Weinstein, 1988, p. xiii.

42 *Generals and Tupamaros*, 1974, p. 21.

43 Inter-Church Committee on Human Rights in Latin America, 1978, p. 16.

44 See Wilson Fernández, *El Gran Culpable: La responsabilidad de los E.E.U.I. en el proceso militar uruguayo* (Montevideo: Ediciones Atenea, 1986) and Langguth, 1978.

45 Porzencanski, 1973, p. 54.

46 Langguth, 1978, p. 131.

47 William Cantrell, Adolfo Saenz and later Dan Mitrione.

48 Porzencanski, 1973, p. 53.
49 Weinstein, 1988, p. 48.
50 Langguth, 1978, pp. 242, 96.
51 Fernández, 1986, p. 175.
52 Perelli, 1993, pp. 25–6.
53 Perelli, 1993, p. 31.
54 Gillespie, 1991, p. 53, n. 11.
55 Cynthia McClintock, 'The War on Drugs: The Peruvian Case', *Journal of Interamerican Studies and World Affairs*, Vol. 30, No. 23, Summer/Autumn 1988, pp. 128–9.
56 However, this policy also alienated the coca growers, creating ripe conditions for an alliance with Sendero. McClintock, 1988, p. 132. This alliance nets Sendero as much as $30,000,000 annually, see Henry Dietz, 'Peru's Sendero Luminoso As a Revolutionary Movement', *Journal of Political and Military Sociology*, Vol. 18, Summer 1990, p. 136. Not only did the policy result in a lucrative alliance for Sendero, it failed to reduce the amount of coca grown. Since 1988, the growers have shifted their activities north and anti-drug activity has become more dangerous for the individuals in the anti-drug campaign. The amount of coca produced has again increased. Another strategy was proposed in which strong herbicides would be sprayed on coca fields. However, this strategy met with resistance due to fears of reprisals on the South American operations of the companies that produced the herbicide and possible product liability. McClintock, 1988, p. 133.
57 Kenneth Roberts and Mark Peceny, 'Human Rights and United States Policy toward Peru', in Maxwell Cameron and Philip Mauceri (eds), *Peruvian Labyrinth: Polity, Society, and Economy* (University Park: Pennsylvania State University Press, 1997), pp. 213–17.
58 Palmer, 1992, p. 73. For a complete overview of the amount of economic and military aid, see James W. Wilke (ed.), *Statistical Abstract of Latin America, Volume 23* (Los Angeles: UCLA Latin American Center Publications) p. 885.
59 Cameron, 1995, pp. 154–61.
60 David Scott Palmer, 'Collectively Defending Democracy in the Western Hemisphere', in Tom Farer (ed.), *Beyond Sovereignty: Collectively Defending Democracy in the Americas* (Baltimore: Johns Hopkins University Press, 1996), p. 273.
61 John McCormick, *The European Union: Politics and Policies* (Boulder: Westview Press, 1999), p. 59.
62 Newton with Donaghy, 1997, p. 6.
63 Richard Gillespie, 'The Continuing Debate on Democratization in Spain', *Parliamentary Affairs*, Vol. 46, October 1993, p. 536.
64 Gregory Treverton, *Spain: Domestic Politics and Security Policy* (Adelohi Papers 204, London: International Institute for Strategic Studies, 1986), p. 6.
65 Krasikov, 1984, p. 165.
66 P. Nikiforos Diamandorus, 'Southern Europe: A Third Wave Success Story', in Larry Diamond, Marc Plattner, Yun-han Chu and Hung-mao Tien (eds), *Consolidating the Third World Democracies* (Baltimore: Johns Hopkins University Press, 1997), p. 7.

67 Some scholars have discussed the plausibility of violence as a cause of democratic breakdown in Uruguay, Peru and Spain within the context of a combination of factors which weakened democracy. Three scholars in particular have examined Uruguay in this way. For example, see Kaufman, 1979, p. 95; Ronald McDonald, 'The Rise of Military Politics in Uruguay', *Inter-American Economic Affairs*, Vol. XXVII, No. 4, Spring 1975, p. 27; and Charles Gillespie, 1991, p. 34. See also Cameron, 1995, pp. 147–8; Maravall, 1982, p. 62; Howard Wiarda, *The Transition to Democracy in Spain and Portugal* (Washington, DC: American Enterprise Institute for Public Policy Research, 1988), p. 14; and Aguero, 1995. In general, one recent study has addressed the consequences of repression. Will Maore, in 'Repression and Dissent: Substitution, Context and Timing', *American Journal of Political Science*, Vol. 42, No. 3, July 1998, pp. 851–73, finds that dissidents will substitute violent protest for nonviolent protest and vice versa when faced with government repression. He found no evidence that contextual factors of authoritarian or democratic regimes affect this relationship or that there is a difference in effectiveness of repression in the short or long term.

68 Graham, 1992, p. 137.

69 Gillespie, 1991, p. 39.

70 Martha Crenshaw, 'Thoughts on Relating Terrorism to Historical Contexts', in Crenshaw (ed.), *Terrorism in Context*, p. 7.

71 McClintock, 1989, p. 129.

72 G. Bingham Powell, *Contemporary Democracies: Participation, Stability and Violence* (Cambridge: Harvard University Press, 1982), p. 167.

73 Linz, 1978, p. 20.

74 My results are confirmed by a different analysis from G. Bingham Powell. Powell concludes,

> I have suggested that party involvement in violence is particularly dangerous to the survival of the democratic regime ... In this decade [1967–76], at least, deadly violence was virtually a precondition for the suspension of democratic politics ... The special role of party involvement in violence is also evident. In countries where the major parties presented a united front against the use of violence and kept themselves and their supporters from engaging in it, the democratic processes continued unchecked. Where violence involved the parties themselves, even in a limited way, it was much more difficult – for a variety of reasons, including the weakening of the regime's legitimacy and the inability of the democratic forces to join forces in defense of the regime – to sustain a democracy. (Powell, 1982, p. 169)

In Powell's regression analysis the numbers of deaths (+.29) and the involvement of parties (+.62) were significant at the .05 per cent level. In his study, when including only cases with more than one death per year, the two variables account for 80 per cent of the variance in the continuity of the democratic regime (Powell, 1982, p. 263, n. 27).

75 Kaufman, 1979, p. 58.

76 *Generals and Tupamaros*, pp. 48–9.

77 Kaufman, 1979, pp. 58–9.

78 *Caretas*, 4 April 1988.

79 Moral, quoted in Mauceri, 1991, p. 91.

80 Bourque and Warren, 1989, p. 26 also *La República* 27 August 1984.

81 'This context is what has still not been defined. It is the famous counterinsurgency strategy that so many speak of and which still does not exist'. My translation. Guillermo Denegri, 'Entrevista al General Sinesio Jarama', *Debate*, No. 55, March–May 1989, p. 9.

82 Mauceri, 1991, p. 98.

83 'We must keep in mind that the peasants who grow the coca were accosted by the police and by whatever force of order existed, because they were considered a delinquent ... We are talking about 80 per cent of the population! What we need to do, then, is to modify this situation to prevent the harassment of the peasants growing the coca, the base Sendero needs to support its activities, by the government'. My translation. *QueHacer*, December 1989–January 1990, No. 62, p. 39.

84 Mauceri, 1991, p. 99.

85 Benjamin Netanyahu, *Fighting Terrorism: How Democracies Can Defeat Domestic and International Terrorists* (New York: Farrar Straus Giroux, 1998), p. 28.

86 Netanyahu, 1998, p. 33.

87 Stephen Sloan, 'Introduction', in Edwin Corr and Stephen Sloan (eds), *Low Intensity Conflict: Old Threats in a New World* (Boulder: Westview Press, 1992), p. 12.

88 Bard O'Neil, *Insurgency and Terrorism* (New York: Brassey's, 1990), p. 128. See also John McCuen, *The Art of Counter-Revolutionary Warfare* (Harrisburg, Pa: Stackpole Books, 1966).

89 O'Neil, 1990, p. 130.

90 O'Neil, 1990, p. 154.

91 J. Samuel Fitch, *The Armed Forces and Democracy in Latin America* (Baltimore: Johns Hopkins University Press, 1998), pp. 132–3.

8
Epilogue

Introduction

Although the focus of this study is on the breakdown of Uruguayan democracy in 1972, the dissolution of Peruvian democracy in 1992 and the attempted coup in Spain in 1981, a brief discussion in the context of recent terrorism will be discussed in this epilogue. The purpose of this chapter is to extend the argument to a discussion of prospects for stability in these countries into more recent years.[1] The violence in Uruguay is over; however, many Uruguayans desire a reckoning of human rights violations during the military coup. In Peru, the violence of Shining Path continues, although the group has lost many of its main leaders and has broken into factions. In Spain, the violence of ETA continues, although Spain has recently experienced a time of peace. Moreover, two international factors have changed. In Peru, the OAS has become a more active force for democracy in the region. Other non-governmental agencies and countries have continued to pressure Peru to maintain the integrity of its democratic process. In Spain, membership of the EU has strengthened Spain's ability to prosecute ETA and has also symbolized democratic progress and modernization to both Spanish elites and citizens.

Uruguay (1973–98)

After the dissolution of the National Assembly, and contrary to the expectations of many, a period of intense repression began. Seven years later, in 1980, the Uruguayan military held a referendum to institutionalize its rule. The plebiscite failed, receiving only 43 per cent of the vote. The military announced its plans for a controlled liberalization of the regime, called the *cronograma*. Primaries were held and the traditional parties were allowed to participate. In August 1984, representatives from the Colorado party, the Frente Amplio party and the Unión Cívica, a Catholic party affiliated with the military, met to discuss the transition. The Blanco party did not participate. In accordance with these talks, the military regime passed Institutional Act 19, which returned the country to its pre-1973 democratic institutions. Eventually, elections were held in 1984 and the country was returned to democracy in 1985. In 1984, Colorado party leader Julio Maria Sanguinetti was elected president, serving from 1985–90 and again from 1995–2000.[2] Although the main political parties won the presidency in the first three elections, the leftist Frente Amplio party has gained support, becoming a legitimate challenger. In 1989, the socialist Tabaré Vasquez was elected Mayor of Montevideo. In 1994, he lost the presidential election by only 35,000 votes.[3] Sanguinetti had served in the National Assembly and as a minister of education in the previous democratic regime. He led the democratic delegation in the 'Club Naval' talks with the military in 1984.

One issue that was not settled in the Club Naval talks was that of human rights violations during the military regime.[4] Under the military regime, there were 4,000 long-term prisoners in Uruguay, whose average length of detention was 6.8 years. The total number of prisoners during the period reached 600,000.[5] During the military regime of 1973 to 1985, virtually all political prisoners were tortured.[6] Although the number of people killed by the regime was relatively low at 168,[7] Uruguay had the highest proportion of political prisoners in the world. Amnesty International estimated that 1 out of 600 Uruguayans were jailed under the military regime.[8]

Civil–military relations were smoothed by President Sanguinetti, who did not call for either trials or investigations. In March 1985, the National Assembly approved an amnesty law that freed political prisoners, except those who had intentionally committed homicide. However, this bill did not include an amnesty for members of the military or state security forces. Thus a different amnesty bill was passed in August 1986, although the government maintained the right to investigate abuses. This 1986 'Expiry' law exempted all military and police personnel from liability for human rights violations during the dictatorship.[9] Many citizens challenged this amnesty, gathering over 600,000 signatures to force a plebiscite on the law. However, their efforts to annul the law failed. The law was approved in the 1989 plebiscite, 56 per cent to 43 per cent.[10] The government, the main political parties and the military are content to honour the 1989 plebiscite. Despite this, significant numbers of Uruguayans still want the issue to be discussed. For example, in May 1996 50,000 people participated in a silent march held in remembrance of the disappeared.[11] During Sanguinetti's first term, civil–military relations were normalized under civilian supremacy. During the presidency of Lacalle (1990–95), new service commanders of the navy and air force were appointed against the wishes of the military command.[12]

Economically, Uruguay faces problems typical for the region. Inflation picked up after the restoration of democracy, and continues to increase at a moderate rate. The new democracy faced sluggish growth from 1988 to 1990 and again in 1995. Despite this fluctuation, the current troubles are better than the twenty year stagnation experienced prior to 1973. Recently, steady growth has returned (table 8.1).

The outlook for Uruguayan democracy is positive. The country has not faced additional violence since the restoration of democracy. Despite a polarization of the public in regard to the amnesty for the military and security forces, the country is again tranquil. Since the transition, military and civilian relations have remained stable and citizen support of democracy is strong.

Peru (1992–99)

Fujimori restored Peru to a democratic system after his *autogolpe*. Although there is a large domestic opposition to Fujimori's new democracy, recently he has made efforts to rectify a few of the most egregious shortcomings of the

Table 8.1 Uruguay: economic indicators, 1980–99

	CPI rate (%)	GDP rate (%)	Unemployment
1980	63	6	NA
1981	34	2	NA
1982	19	−9	NA
1983	49	−6	NA
1984	55	−1	NA
1985	72	1	NA
1986	76	9	10.7
1987	64	8	9.1
1988	62	0	8.6
1989	80	1	8
1990	112	1	8.5
1991	102	3	9
1992	68	8	9
1993	54	3	8.3
1994	45	6	9.2
1995	42	−2	10.2
1996	28	5	11.9
1997	20	5	11.9
1998	11	5	
1999	7	3.5	

Sources: Inter-American Development Bank <http://www.iadb.org/int/sta/ENGLISH/staweb/index.htm>. IMF.

new institutions. The country has recovered from the economic disaster of the 1980s. However, the recovery has yet to reduce the stubbornly high rates of poverty in the country. The violence of Shining Path continues, although at a lower rate. Moreover, the international environment, specifically the OAS, has changed, allowing for a more robust defence of democracy in the region.

Some scholars, for example Abraham Lowenthal, have noted the importance of international organizations, especially the actions of the OAS, in pressuring for a return to electoral politics in Peru, Guatemala and Haiti.[13] Previously, the OAS had been committed to a doctrine of non-intervention. In the OAS charter, the principle of nonintervention is clearly specified. Article 18 states:

> No State or group of States has the right to intervene, directly or indirectly, for any reason whatever, in the internal affairs of

any other State. The foregoing principle prohibits not only armed force but also any other form of interference or attempted threat against the personality of the State or against its political, economic and cultural elements.

Article 19 states: 'No state may use or encourage the use of coercive measures of an economic or political character in order to force the sovereign will of another State and obtain from it advantages of any kind'.[14] In June 1991, Resolution 1080 requested the OAS to respond to 'violations of the democratic process' and the General Assembly responded with a change in the policy and what has now become known as the Santiago Commitment to Democracy. It laid the foundations for procedures in which, after an interruption of the democratic institutional process, OAS foreign ministers would be called to an emergency meeting to decide on a collective action. Moreover, with the Protocol of Washington of 1993, the OAS has been changed to allow the suspension of delinquent states.[15] Moreover, the OAS has issued resolutions on restoring democracy in Haiti, Peru and Venezuela. It stated in its resolution that 'representative democracy can be promoted and defended only by democratic means, any other course being rejected as contrary to the fundamental principles established in the Charter of the OAS'. It resolved to hold Fujimori to his pledge of calling elections for a Constitutional Congress and to urge Peru to respect the separation of powers, human rights and the rule of law, and offered to provide electoral observation.[16] The results of OAS actions have been uneven. The OAS condemned the attempted coup in Guatemala and the coup attempt failed eight days later when Serrano was ousted by the military and a new president was installed. In Haiti, the OAS failed to convince the military to restore President Aristide. In Peru, critics accuse the OAS of being a 'midwife to a process by which an authoritarian system is being established under the guise of formal democracy'.[17]

A new constitution was created and ratified in a referendum in October 1993 by 52.3 per cent of the population. Fujimori was reelected in 1995 with 65 per cent of the vote. His party, Cambio 90/Nueva Mayoria holds 69 seats of the 120-member Congress. The new democracy, however, lacks an effective balance of power among different branches and many aspects of the constitution are problematic.

The new judiciary is weak in relation to the executive. A preponderance of judges and prosecutors are provisional, appointed and controlled by Fujimori. Without a tenured, permanent position, the judges are more vulnerable to political pressure. For example, in 1997 only 403 of the 1,473 judges had permanent appointments. This occurs in the Supreme Court as well. Half of the Supreme Court judges have temporary or provisional status.[18] In December 1997, Congress granted provisional judges the same authority as tenured judges in the National Electoral Board (JNE), thus allowing them the right to vote and to participate in the JNE.[19] However, in response to critics, in 1996 two new institutions were created: the Defender of the People and the Constitutional Tribunal. However, the power of the Constitutional Tribunal is limited since there must be six out of seven votes for a law to be deemed unconstitutional.[20]

Another troubling aspect of the new constitution was article 173. This article created separate military courts. In addition, due to presidential decrees, these courts were presided over by anonymous judges. Individuals accused of terrorism were tried in faceless civilian courts and those accused of treason were tried in faceless military courts. These decrees also allowed extended times of police detention and a restriction of the right to a defence.[21] Moreover, the majority of these judges were military officers with little or no legal training. The trials were secret and the actions of defence attorneys limited. Human Rights Watch estimated that at least 10 per cent of those convicted by the faceless courts were innocent. After intense criticism by human rights groups, the faceless courts were abolished in October 1997.

The new legislature is very weak compared with the executive branch. Congress is now unicameral with 120 members elected at large. Moreover, rarely does Congress invoke its powers of oversight. It has consistently refused to investigate cases of alleged wrongdoing. One commission was formed in May 1996 after more than forty requests.[22] In addition, critics complain that the legislature is little more than a rubber stamp body. For example, in 1996 Congress passed the law of 'authentic interpretation' declaring that the limitation of two presidential terms does not apply to Fujimori since the 1993 constitution was not in force at the time of his first election in 1990.[23] Congress acted despite broad public rejection of the prospect of allowing Fujimori to run for a third term in 2000.

The lack of balance of powers is clear in the case of the drive to force a referendum on the issue of Fujimori's attempt to run for a third term. The importance of the dependence of individual judges was highlighted in 1997 when Congress removed three of the judges from the constitutional tribunal who had voted against the 'authentic interpretation' law of 1996. Because of this, the tribunal could not function because of a lack of quorum. As of June 2000, the tribunal is still inactive.[24] In response to the passage of the 'authentic interpretation' law, a grassroots effort formed to force a referendum on the issue. At least 1.4 million signatures were gathered. However, the National Board of Elections ruled that a referendum would occur only if forty-eight members of Congress voted for it. On 27 August 1998 only forty-five members voted for it. In short, the constitutional right to a referendum was undermined by Congress with no opportunity for judicial review.[25] This case signifies why many in the opposition believe that Fujimori has undermined the rule of law in Peru.

In general, Peru continues to face economic challenges (table 8.2). However, inflation has been contained, down from the massive increases of the late 1980s. As inflation

Table 8.2 Peru: economic indicators, 1988–99

	CPI (%)	Strikes	GDP
1988	1722.3	814	−8.3
1989	2775.3	667	−11.7
1990	7649.6	613	−5.4
1991	139.2	315	2.8
1992	56.7	219	−1.4
1993	39.5	151	6.4
1994	15.4	168	13.1
1995	10.2	102	7.3
1996	11.8	77	2.4
1997	6.5	66	6.9
1998	6.0	58	0.3
1999	3.7	NA	3.8

Source: INEI, <http://www.inei.gob.pe/>.

fell, so did the number of strikes. By 1996, strikes were ten times less frequent than in 1988. Fujimori was also successful in restarting economic growth, especially during the first three years after the *autogolpe*. However, growth rates slowed significantly in 1998 and 1999. Despite Fujimori's success in containing inflation and restarting growth, poverty remains very high. In 1998, half of Peruvians lived in poverty. Moreover, 14.7 per cent lived in extreme poverty, unable to access the basis necessities of sufficient food and water.[26] In response to the poverty, Fujimori founded a programme called the Fondo Nacional de Compensación y Desarrollo Social (FONCODES) in 1991. Spending dramatically increased in the two years preceding the 1995 elections. By the end of 1995, more than $650 million had been spent on 17,000 local projects. Included were the rebuilding of schools, clinics, water systems, electricity and agricultural projects.[27]

Shining Path after the *autogolpe*

Since the capture of Abimael Guzmán in September 1992, Oscar Ramirez Durand, better known as 'Feliciano', and Miguel Aranda Montanez have taken over the leadership roles of the Shining Path. The incarcerated Guzmán proposed peace talks in 1993. The government allowed Guzmán to read his proposal on television. Shining Path was divided over the issue of whether or not to heed the call of their imprisoned leader. A faction called 'Red Path', led by Feliciano, called for continued fighting. It rejected Guzmán's calls from prison for an end to violent action and a peace accord.[28] The original Shining Path, now led by Aranda Montanez, reiterated its desire to begin peace talks in December 1997. The group also promised to crush the dissident Red Path.[29]

The capture of Guzmán seemed to affect the operations of the group. After his arrest in 1992, the number of actions began to decline (table 8.3). However, the Red Path faction of Shining Path continues to operate and kill. In addition, peasant leaders are still targeted. In 1997, Shining Path killed twelve peasant leaders.[30] The figure for 1 January to 30 June 1998 was 158.[31] Shining Path is still active in the Upper Huallaga Valley, and in the Departments of Piura, La Libertad and Ayacucho. It is attempting to regain control of parts

Table 8.3 Peru: actions by armed groups, 1989–98

	Actions by armed groups (APRODEH)[1]	Actions by armed groups (INEI)[2]	Deaths from subversive and countersubversive actions (INEI)[2]
1989	1349	3149	1971
1990	1456	NA	NA
1991	1458	NA	NA
1992	1577	2995	1718
1993	1409	NA	NA
1994	408	NA	NA
1995	267	1232	428
1996	311	883	211
1997	490	681	130
1998	NA	310	83

Sources: [1]APRODEH, <gopher://gopher.rcp.net.pe/11/otros-gopher/nacionales/aprodeh/violencia>. [2]INEI <http://www.inei.gob.pe/>.

of Lima. The state continues to make progress in arresting leaders. In December 1998, a top military leader of Shining Path, Juan Carlos Rios, was captured in the slums of Lima.[32] In July 1999, Red Path leader 'Feliciano' was captured and in November was sentenced to life in prison. According to both government (Instituto Nacional de Estadistica e Informática) and independent (APRODEH) sources, terrorism continues to decline and the number of those killed yearly is significantly lower than before the *autogolpe*.

The other main group, the MRTA, is active mainly in Junin. However, its last major campaign took place on 17 December 1996. On this day, the MRTA took hostages in the Japanese embassy. Special forces finally stormed the complex on 22 April 1997. Seventy-two of the hostages were freed and one died in the process. Of the special forces, two were killed. All fourteen MRTA members were killed in the action. Reports allege that many were summarily executed.

State reaction after the autogolpe

Under Fujimori, the state continued to pursue a tough strategy to combat terrorism. States of emergency were declared, anti-terrorism laws were passed, and general amnesties were granted to the military and police. In addition, some attempts have been made to confront accusations of human rights violations of the accused.

After the establishment of the new constitution, much of the country remained under a state of emergency. In 1994, almost half of the population, 48 per cent, was living under a state of emergency.[33] By 1997, 16 per cent of the country and over 20 per cent of the population remained under a state of emergency.[34] Interestingly, many of the areas still under decree did not have a major guerrilla presence.[35] By 1999, only 6 per cent of the country was under a state of emergency.[36]

Due to the passage of anti-terrorism (DL 25475) and treason (DL 25659) laws, 5,003 people were jailed for terrorism as of 1994 (about 25 per cent of the prison population). About 66 per cent are members of Shining Path and 10 per cent are members of the MRTA. The affiliation of the rest is undetermined. Peruvian human rights groups are concerned that the cases in which the affiliations of the prisoners are unclear really indicate unjust imprisonment.[37]

Since 1995, Peru has both granted amnesty to its military and has responded to criticisms from international human rights groups. In June 1995, Laws 26479 and 26492 were passed, granting amnesty to members of the armed forces from responsibility for the human rights abuses that occurred from 1980–95.[38] In the same year, Decree Law 26248 was passed, restoring the right of habeas corpus to people charged under anti-terrorism laws.[39] In addition, the office of the Defensor del Pueblo, or Human Rights Ombudsman, was created and the Court of Constitutional Guarantees was reactivated.[40] In 1996, the Ad Hoc Pardons Commission was formed to investigate charges of unjust incarceration. By the close of 1998, a total of 462 prisoners had been released. In that year, the Commission's mandate was expanded until the end of 1999 to look at those who had been convicted of terrorism and treason but who had repented.[41] In February 1999, the state seemed to be moving away from the condoning of torture, which was made a specific offence in the Peruvian legal code. In 1998, there were no cases of disappearances. This compares favourably with the total of 2,371 people reported as disappeared during the internal conflict as recognized by the Human Rights Ombudsman.[42]

Despite the institutional and legal improvements, problems are still common. Torture is still commonly practised. In addition, charges of illegal monitoring of prominent Peruvians and journalists are frequent. For example, former UN Secretary-General Javier Perez de Cuellar was allegedly the target of wiretaps. The Peruvian media investigate and report these charges, even though they occasionally receive anonymous threats for doing so.[43] Human rights groups such as APORDEH have also reported harassment.

In terms of public opinion measured by the polling group APOYO, there is a declining trend of concern with terrorism. Months after the *autogolpe* and after the capture of Guzmán, only one out of four Peruvians listed terrorism as one of the country's main problems. As Shining Path regrouped, concern increased. However, as incidents decrease through time, less concern has been reported. In October 1992, the most pressing problem was terrorism. By late 1996, the focus had changed to the ongoing high unemployment and recession (53 per cent), cost of living (25 per cent) and poverty (30 per cent). Only 12 per cent of those polled believed that terrorism was one of the top three problems facing the country. The confidence of Peruvians that terrorism would decrease also vastly increased after Guzmán's capture.[44] However, fear of increases of terrorism in the future returned in 1997, after some increase in the amount of terrorist actions. In that year, according to APOYO, the population was almost evenly split among believing that terrorism would increase (35 per cent), decrease (29 per cent) or stay the same (31 per cent). Although the number of disappearances and extrajudicial executions also decreased, interestingly concern for human rights violations remain somewhat steady. This concern is also reflected in a growing distrust of the National Police. In August 1993, 44 per cent trusted the National Police and 42 per cent distrusted them. By the summer of 1997, only one out of every three Peruvians trusted the National Police, almost two out of three reported distrust. This corroborates the steady concern with human rights in Peru during this time.[45]

Fujimori enjoyed high levels of citizen confidence in the early period of state restructuring. However, the ratings of Fujimori and his institutions began to drop precipitously in 1996. Two months after the coup, at the beginning of June,

Fujimori's support was still strong. In a Lima-based poll, 65 per cent of those questioned still approved of the coup. Among middle-class adults and young adults, support reached 70 per cent. Fujimori's personal approval rating was 76 per cent, and among the middle class and young adults, that number increased to 83 per cent. The opposition received a 69 per cent disapproval rating.[46] In July, Fujimori's rating fell to 60 per cent. Carmen Rosa Balbi attributed this drop in approval to the increase of terrorist violence.[47] After the capture of Guzmán, Shining Path's master computer files and some key subordinates[48] on 12 September 1992, Fujimori's approval rating rose to 74 per cent and the approval of the antisubversive policy rose to 66 per cent.[49] In the same May APOYO poll, opposition leader Máximo San Roman received a positive rating of only 10 per cent, with a 79 per cent disapproval rating.[50] The June APOYO poll occurred the day after Fujimori announced a date for new elections. New congressional elections were held in 1992. Elections for a new constituent assembly were held in 1993. However, Fujimori's popularity began to drop after his reelection in 1995. In 1997, his average approval rating slipped to 34 per cent. By that year, Fujimori and his top adviser, SIN adviser Vladimiro Montesinos, ranked at the top of the most disliked officials in Peru.[51] APOYO reported that Montesinos was chosen as the most disliked by 26 per cent and Fujimori by 20 per cent. Roughly the same trend can be seen in the levels of confidence in institutions. As Fujimori's approval ratings drop in 1997, so does confidence in the institutions that are affiliated with him, according to APOYO polls. The approval of the military dropped from 57 per cent in 1992 to 38 per cent in 1997. Approval of the National Police also slid from 48 per cent to 32 per cent. The approval of the institution of the presidency dropped from 54 per cent to only 35 per cent. By 1997, the only institutions with positive ratings were the Catholic Church, the provincial and district governments, and the media. Confidence in Congress, the council of ministers and the judiciary had dropped to under 30 per cent. Political parties were only held in confidence by 14 per cent.[52]

This trend of a lack of confidence is also reflected in the decline in support for Fujimori's party. Fujimori's party, Vamos Vecino, lost in the municipal elections of October

1998. Incumbent major Alberto Andrade beat Fujimori's Juan Carlos Hurtado Miller in Lima's mayoral election. Other pro-Fujimori candidates won in only seventy-nine provinces while opposition candidates won in one hundred. Moreover, protests against Fujimori running for a third term continued to grow. In polls conducted by APOYO in the autumn of 1998, Peruvians were asked whom they would vote for in 2000 if Fujimori were allowed to run. Only 22 per cent said they would vote for Fujimori, 43 per cent said an independent and 21 per cent a member of the opposition.[53] On the eve of the 2000 election, Fujimori was the candidate with the most support, but was projected to lose a close race in the second round, against opposition candidate Toledo.[54] However, citing continued electoral irregularities and Fujimori's refusal to postpone the second-round elections to correct the problems, Toledo withdrew from the race in May 2000.

As support for and confidence in Fujimori decline, more Peruvians describe him as dictatorial. In an APOYO study, Peruvians were asked their opinion of his government. Although 52 per cent of those polled believed that Fujimori's government was democratic one month after his *autogolpe*, by June 1997 only one-third of those asked described him as democratic. A strong majority, 59 per cent, described him as dictatorial.[55]

Despite the frustration with the regime of Fujimori, support for democracy in general continues to grow. APOYO asked Peruvians what kind of regime they preferred, a democracy, a dictatorship or a revolutionary regime. By June 1997, 90 per cent of those questioned preferred democracy. This is an increase from 72 per cent in 1992. This affirmation of support for a democratic regime does not benefit Fujimori, who is predominantly viewed as dictatorial. The possibility of further instability is very real to many Peruvians. When APOYO asked Peruvians about the probability of a military coup, approximately one-third of the population believed it was a strong possibility. By June 1997, the belief in the probability of a coup reached its highest point since 1994, with 36 per cent believing that it was probable. However, still over half disagreed.[56]

Before the 2000 elections, Fujimori was mobilizing state resources to support his reelection. FONCODES resources are allocated according to the expected political benefit to Fujimori, as opposed to objective need.[57] Moreover, it has been charged that the government food distribution agency, PRONAA, tied the supply of aid to support for Fujimori in the 2000 elections.[58] In addition, the Carter Center has reported that the 2000 presidential election is widely believed to be flawed. There are numerous reports of a lack of media fairness, harassment of opposition candidates and the use of public resources to support the incumbent Fujimori.[59] Moreover, it has been reported by the Peruvian newspaper *El Comercio* that one million of the signatures used to register Fujimori for a third term were forged.

All the indicators point to a loss of support for both Fujimori and his regime. There is an increasing belief in the probability of a coup in Peru. Undoubtedly, any attempt to remove Fujimori's regime would have to have the support of at least part of the armed forces. However, as discussed in chapter 3, it must be remembered that the Peruvian military historically contains very progressive elements. However, when Fujimori first assumed the presidency, he took control over the institution, politicizing it and making it his political ally. However, coups are usually started by colonels, not generals. If he succeeds in winning an unprecedented third consecutive election, some further instability may be very possible indeed.

Spain (1986–2000)

Since 1986, Spain's democracy has continued to succeed. The economic performance has been stable. Civil–military relations have continued to improve. Incidents of ETA violence are becoming less frequent; however, recently concern about terrorism has continued to grow. ETA has found itself increasingly isolated from mainstream Basques. In 1998, it declared a cease-fire that lasted a year and a half, until January 2000. However, the continued growth of the European Union bodes well for effective, eventual control of ETA.

In accordance with the state's policy of preventing military intervention while mollifying the military, the state

Table 8.4 Spain: economic performance, 1987–98

Year	CPI (%)	GDP growth (%)	Unemployment (%)
1987	4.5	6	20.5
1988	6	5	19.5
1989	6.5	5	17.3
1990	5.8	4	16.3
1991	5.5	2	16.4
1992	5	1	18.4
1993	4.5	−1	22.7
1994	4.5	2	24.2
1995	3.5	3	22.9
1996	2	3	22.2
1997	2	3	20.8
1998	2	4	–

Sources: Instituto Nacional de Estadística, <http://www.ine.es/>. IMF.

acted to appease military members after the coup attempt. A reform package including early retirement with full pay and additional promotions was put into practice to reduce the number of officers.[60] This expensive plan was successful without aggravating relations with the military. In addition, due to military pressure an emergency powers law was passed, although it was later modified to stress civilian control. At the same time, a law 'for the defence of the constitution' was passed, making it an offence to apologize for terrorists or plot against the constitution.[61]

Economically, the country has been doing well. Since 1989, inflation has slowed. In addition, since 1987 there has only been one year of negative economic growth (table 8.4). Overall, Spanish economic performance has maintained reasonable performance.

Violence

Despite the successful continuation of democracy and the granting of autonomy to all the communities of Spain, violence continues. ETA continues to operate with kidnappings and killings. Each year from 1987 to 1997, ETA kidnapped one person a year, with the exception of 1996, in which two individuals were kidnapped.[62] These victims were later released, after being held for an extensive amount of time. For example, Jose Antonio Ortega, a Spanish prison officer,

Table 8.5 Spain: people killed by ETA, 1987–2000

1987	1988	1989	1990	1991	1992	1993
52	19	19	25	46	26	14
1994	1995	1996	1997	1998	1999	2000
12	15	5	13	6	0	4

Source: Spanish Ministry of the Interior, 2000 data includes up to May 7, <http://www.mir.es/oris/>.

was held for 522 days. A better indication of the trend of ETA's activity can be seen in the number of people killed by the organization between 1987 and 1998 (table 8.5).

The years 1987 and 1991 were the bloodiest. After 1991, a general decrease in deaths due to ETA occurred. However, ETA remained dangerous. For example, in 1995 ETA almost killed opposition leader and future Prime Minister José Maria Aznar of the Partido Popular in a car bomb. In addition to the actions of ETA, there has been an increase in ETA youth activity, specifically the actions of the ETA youth wing Jarrai, consisting of hooded youths, which caused millions of dollars worth of damage in 1997. Typically these members utilize molotov cocktails, setting afire homes, businesses, political offices and cars.[63] Street violence is more prevalent than higher-intensity violence. As of 1998, ETA's strength was estimated to be limited to forty gunmen, eighty more individuals ready to be trained and five hundred active supporters.[64] Despite the reduction in killings, the actions of ETA continue to cause an uproar among the majority of Spaniards.

Spanish rejection of ETA is well illustrated by the case of twenty-nine-year-old small-town councilman Miguel Angel Blanco. ETA kidnapped him in 1997, demanding the transfer of five hundred prisoners from all over Spain to the Basque country in exchange for his release. The Spanish state refused the demand. The Pope and Amnesty International called for his safe release. Its demands rejected, ETA executed the young politician and abandoned his body. In response, approximately six million Spaniards marched to protest his assassination. At the same time, ETA's political party, HB, led a march of 30,000 in support of ETA and independence from Spain.

In October 1997, the Spanish government accused the leaders of HB of being little more than a front for ETA. They were charged with condoning terrorism. The charges were precipitated by HB's distribution of an ETA video during the 1996 general election campaign. The leaders were arrested and sent to trial. The twenty-three leaders of the party were tried and convicted. Each was sentenced to seven years in prison.

Despite the imprisonment of HB's leaders, the violence did not end. Although the numbers killed were quite low, the targets were very salient. In a region normally insulated from ETA violence in southern Spain, in the city of Seville, ETA killed a local politician, Alberto Jimenez Becerril, and his wife on 30 January 1998. Jimenez Becerril was the first town councillor killed outside the Basque country. The same month, another councilman was killed by a bomb in Zarauz on the northern coast of the country. Later that year in June, another town councillor was killed by ETA in Renteria in northern Spain.[65]

Concern about ETA terrorism remained high. According to Gallup España polls, interestingly, concern was much higher in 1997, even though fewer people were killed than in 1995.[66] However, two of those killed were from Seville, a city usually immune from ETA activity. The concern about terrorism had more than doubled since 1986, increasing from 28 to 61 per cent. It was the most concerning issue of 1997.

Later in 1998, ETA decided to try a different strategy. ETA declared its first unconditional cease-fire on 16 September 1998, shortly before the elections. This cease-fire followed talks between ETA and the PNV, which culminated in the 12 September Declaration of Lizarra. This declaration proclaimed the right of the Basque people to determine their own future. Prime Minister Aznar rejected the call for a referendum and instead called for ETA to disarm and renounce violence before any talks between parties could begin.[67]

In November 1998, Prime Minister Aznar approved talks with groups linked to ETA. ETA organized its demands around five points: the end to police prosecution in Spain and in France; the transfer of ETA prisoners to the Basque country; a solution for ETA members in exile; the easing of conditions for prisoners who have completed most of their sentences; and the improvement of conditions for the imprisoned leaders of HB.[68] The truce was broken by ETA in January 2000. In response, an estimated one million Spaniards protested in the streets.

The EU

One factor that is positive for prospects for democracy in Spain is the European Union. The EU symbolizes progress, in the context of democracy, to the Spanish elite and citizens. Moreover, with the integration of security and crime fighting, it is easier for Spain to apprehend and investigate terrorism abroad and to extradite suspects. In addition, the EU has chastised countries that utilize internal repression. Ultimately, however, the ability of the EU to impose its influence is limited by an implementation deficit. The strength of its effects seem to be on the symbolic effect and commitment to the organization on the part of Spaniards.

Originally, Spain applied for EU membership in 1962. However, the request was rejected because of the authoritarian nature of the Franco regime. Membership was finally allowed in 1986. The symbolism of this membership was very important to Spanish democracy. According to Carlos Closa, it meant 'a return to the western world... The EC had a legitimizing effect on the new Spanish democracy because of Community members' permanent criticism and rejection and occasional condemnation of Franco's regime'.[69] The symbolism of the Spaniards was equalled by the expectations of the other Europeans. Despite problems with Spain's membership, such as its relative poverty, controversy over fishing rights and fear of excessive worker migration, 'the EEC felt membership would encourage democracy in the Iberian Peninsula and help link the two countries more closely to NATO and Western Europe'.[70]

After Spain joined the EU, it participated in the attempts to create a coordinated security and defence policy and integration. The admission into NATO, under a socialist government, also added to these pressures for integration. One of the reasons that the socialists changed their policy towards NATO was the desire to 'democratize military thinking through international contact'.[71] In addition to desires to reeducate the military, pressures for modernization came from budgetary and technological concerns, which helped to convince many European governments, including the Spanish, that cooperation can increase efficiency.[72] The Common Foreign and Security Policy commits member states 'to defining and implementing a common policy that includes all questions related to the security of the Union, including the eventual framing of a common defense policy'.[73]

Summary

In addition to cooperation in terms of external security, significant gains have been made in internal security, including the control of terrorism and other crimes. Recently, member states have agreed to cooperate in the investigation and prosecution of criminals who are participating in a criminal organization.[74] To that end, Europol has been directed to deal with crimes 'committed or likely to be committed in the course of terrorist activities against life, limb, personal freedom or property'.[75] One of the objectives of Europol is to increase the effectiveness of cooperation among different authorities in combating and preventing terrorism when there is evidence that two or more member states are involved. Since 1993, countering terrorism and other organized crime has been given top priority, even when the different countries lack the same legal provisions making an action an offence. Now, different legal traditions or specific differences in legal provisions are insufficient to prevent extradition. In effect, an exception has been made to previous requirements of dual criminality.[76] In addition, efforts to improve the cooperation among member states to combat terrorism have been recently highlighted in a Council Recommendation of 9 December 1999; specifically, the sharing of intelligence, creation of joint initiatives and participation by Europol were discussed. The importance of these actions should not be understated. Spain was able to prosecute ETA members more effectively when France started to cooperate with the Spanish authorities, no longer allowing ETA members to flee to safety in southern France.

In addition to helping with law enforcement, joining the EU also set certain standards of conduct. In the Single European Act, signed in February 1986 and implemented in July

1987, the promotion of democracy, human rights and the fundamental freedoms, including equity and social justice, were prominently placed in the Preamble.[77] These standards have recently been reaffirmed in actions taken against Indonesia and Yugoslavia to prohibit the sales of items that could be used for repression or state terror.[78]

Despite these precedents and treaties, the EU suffers from what some have called an 'implementation deficit'. Member states that do not comply with EU policies can be tried before the European Court of Justice and can be fined. However, the EU lacks a coherent and powerful administration that is capable of enforcing and implementing policies. Instead, the EU relies on the national and sub-national administrations to enforce EU policies. In cases where local officials do not support the policies, chances are that they will not be satisfactorily implemented.[79]

Spain remains one of the most enthusiastic member states of Europe. Moreover, its citizens share in this enthusiasm, more so than the average citizen of the EU. For example, in *Eurobarometer 50* of autumn 1998, 63 per cent of the Spaniards questioned thought that membership in the EU was a good thing. This is higher than the EU average of 54 per cent. Moreover, a majority of Spaniards, 58 per cent, tend to believe that Spain has overall benefited from EU membership, compared with the EU average of 49 per cent. Finally, Spaniards desire that the process of unification and building of Europe proceed as quickly as possible. On a scale of one to seven with one representing a standstill and seven representing as fast as possible, the average score of Spaniards was a speedy 5.45, compared with a more moderate pace of 4.04 in the EU average.[80]

Spain's democracy continues to strengthen. In fact, approval of the main institutions has been increasing in recent years, according to Gallup España. The monarchy remains the most popular institution in Spain. However, most of the other institutions have been gaining the public's confidence in recent years, especially after 1994. Most scholars consider its democracy to be fully consolidated. The violence of ETA is decreasing. The basis of support for violence is also decreasing. Moreover, the new institutions and cooperation of the EU may help to suppress any new eruptions of ETA violence.

Notes

1 Instead of reapplying an argument about democratic stability, some scholars would advocate the use of the term 'democratic consolidation'. A typical definition of consolidation is that 'a political regime in which democracy as a complex system of institutions, rules, and patterned incentives and disincentives has become, in a phrase, "the only game in town"'. Juan Linz and Alfred Stepan, 'Toward Consolidated Democracies', in Diamond et al. (eds), 1997, p. 15. However, none of the main theorists of consolidation believe that consolidated democracies are invincible. As Linz and Stepan (p. 16) note, 'we do not preclude the possibility that at some future time it could break down'. Because of this, some scholars have questioned the utility of such a concept. As Guillermo O'Donnell stated, 'I see little analytical gain in attaching the term "consolidated" to something that will probably though not certainly endure'. Guillermo O'Donnell, p. 44 'Illusions about Consolidation' in Diamond et al. (eds), 1997. Moreover, the continuation of arguments of stability is consistent with an Aristotelian approach. Aristotle noted that, 'to know the causes which destroy constitutions is also to know the causes which ensure their preservation' (Pol., p. 225).

2 Blanco leader Lacalle served as president from 1990–95.

3 Peter Winn, 'Frente Amplio in Montevideo', NACLA, Vol. XXIX, No. 1 July/August 1995, p. 20.

4 For an in-depth discussion of the contentious issue of human rights during the transition in Uruguay, see Alexandra Barahona de Brito, Human Rights and Democratization in Latin America (Oxford: Oxford University Press, 1997).

5 David Pion-Berlin, 'To Prosecute or to Pardon? Human Rights Decisions in the Latin American Southern Cone', Human Rights Quarterly, Vol. 16, No. 1, February 1994, pp. 105–30.

6 Servicio Paz y Justicia, Uruguay: Nunca Más (Philadelphia: Temple Press, 1992).

7 Servicio Paz y Justicia, 1992, pp. 417–30.

8 Servicio Paz y Justicia: Uruguay, 1986, p. 66.

9 Amnesty International, AI Report 1998: Uruguay; see <http://www.amnesty.org/ailib/aireport/ar98/amr52.htm>.

10 Luis Roniger and Mario Sznajder, 'The Legacy of Human Rights Violations and the Collective Identity of Redemocratized Uruguay', Human Rights Quarterly, Vol. 19, No. 1, February 1997, pp. 55–77.

11 US Department of State, Uruguayan Country Report on Human Rights Practices for 1996, released by the Bureau of Democracy, Human Rights and Labor, 30 January 1997.

12 Felipe Agüero, 'Toward Civilian Supremacy in South America' in Diamond et al. (eds), 1997, p. 184.

13 Abraham Lowenthal, 'Battling the Undertow in Latin America' in Diamond et al. (eds), 1997, pp. 58–9.

14 Tom Farer, 'Collectively Defending Democracy in the Western Hemisphere: Introduction and Oveniew', in Tom Farer (ed.), Beyond Sovereignty: Collectively Defending Democracy in the Americas (Baltimore: Johns Hopkins University Press, 1996) p. 7.

15 Claudio Grossman, 'The Organization of American States and the Protection of Democracy' in Farer (ed.), 1996, p. 133.
16 'OAS Resolutions', *US Department of State Dispatch*, Vol. 3, No. 26, 29 June 1992, pp. 525–8.
17 Richard J. Bloomfield, 'Making the Western Hemisphere Safe for Democracy? The OAS Derfense of Democracy Regime', *Washington Quarterly*, Vol. 17, No. 2, Spring 1994, pp. 157–70.
18 US Department of State, *Human Rights Practices*, 1997, <http:www.state.gov/www/global/human_rights/drl_reports/:html>.
19 Human Rights Watch, *World Report 1999*, <http://www.hrw.org/worldreport99/>.
20 Coordinadora Nacional de Derechos Humanos Perú, *Informe Sobre la Situación de los Derechos Humanos en el Perú en 1996* (Lima: CNDDHH, 1997).
21 For a complete analysis of the faceless courts see Human Rights Watch, *Peru: Presumption of Guilt* (Washington: Human Rights Watch, 1996).
22 Maxwell Cameron, 'Self-Coups: Peru, Guatemala, and Russia', *Journal of Democracy*, Vol. 9, No. 1, 1998, p. 130.
23 Cameron, 1998, p. 130.
24 Miguel Jugo, 'Panoram sobre derechos humanos', *Actualidad Peruana*, Vol. 8, No. 1. <http://elcelco.rcp.net.pe/aprodeh/public/acpe99ap0199.htm>.
25 US Department of State, *Human Rights Practices*, 1998, <http:www.state.gov/www/global/human_rights/drl_reports/.html>.
26 Coordinadora Nacional de Derechos Humanos Perú, *Informe Anual 1998* (Lima: Coordinadora Nacional de Derechos Humanos, 1999). <http://www.cnddhh.org.pe/98_indice.htm>.
27 Kenneth M. Roberts and Moises Arce, 'Neoliberalism and Lower Class Voting Behavior in Peru', *Comparative Political Studies*, Vol. 31, No. 2, April/May 1998, pp. 217–47.
28 Human Rights Watch, *Peru: Presumption of Guilt* (Washington, DC: Human Rights Watch, 1996), p. 31.
29 Jo-Marie Burt and Jose Lopez Ricci, 'Report on the Americas', *NACLA*, Vol. 28, No. 3, November 1994, p. 6.
30 Human Rights Watch, *World Report 1999*.
31 APRODEH, <gopher://gopher.rcp.net.pe:70/00/otros-gopher/nacionales/aprodeh/violencia/01>.
32 'World Briefing', compiled by Christopher S. Wren, *New York Times*, 5 January 1999.
33 US Department of State, *Human Rights Practices*, 1994, <http:www.state.gov/www/global/human_rights/drl_reports/.html>.
34 US Department of State, *Human Rights Practices*, 1997.
35 Human Rights Watch, *World Report 1999*. See also US Department of State, *Human Rights Practices*, 1998.
36 US Department of State, *Human Rights Practices*, 1999. <http:www.state.gov/www/global/human_rights/drl_reports/.html>.
37 Human Rights Watch, 1996, pp. 2–5. See also Coordinadora Nacional de Derechos Humanos, *Informe Sobre la Situación de los Derechos*

Humanos de el Perú en 1995 (Lima: Coordinadora de Derechos Humanos, 1996) and APRODEH et al., *Los Inocentes Tienen Nombre* (Lima: Grafimace S.A., 1995).
38 Coordinadora Nacional de Derechos Humanos, 1997. <http://www.cnddhh.org.pe/96informe.htm>.
39 Human Rights Watch, *Torture and Political Persecution in Peru* (New York: Human Rights Watch, 1998).
40 Human Rights Watch, 1996, p. 3.
41 US Department of State, *Human Rights Practices*, 1997.
42 US Department of State, *Human Rights Practices*, 1998.
43 US Department of State, *Human Rights Practices*, 1997.
44 APOYO, *Informe de Opinión*, September 1997.
45 APOYO, *Informe de Opinión*, August 1997.
46 FBIS LAT 92 117, p. 38.
47 *Pretextos* Docūmentos de trabajo (Lima: DESCO, División de Investigaciones), Vol. 3, p. 43.
48 Palmer, 1996, p. 72.
49 *Pretextos*, Vol. 3, p. 46.
50 FBIS LAT 92 097, p. 43.
51 FBIS LAT 97 363.
52 APOYO, *Informe de Opinión*, September 1997.
53 Angel Paez, 'Official Candidates Defeated in Peruvian Municipal Elections, *NACLA*, Vol. 32, No. 3, Nov.–Dec. 1998.
54 Poll conducted in Lima by Instituto de Investigaciones Económicas y Sociales, Universidad Nacional de Ingeniería. 18 March 2000.
55 APOYO, *Informe de Opinión*, June 1997.
56 APOYO, *Informe de Opinión*, July 1997.
57 Norbert Shady, 'Seeking Votes: The Political Economy of Expenditures by the Peruvian Social Fund (FONCODES), 1991–1995', *Latin American Research Review*, Vol. 33, No. 1, 1998, pp. 88, 99, 101.
58 'Mecánica naranja' *Caretas* 24 June 1999.
59 Carter Center, 'Statement of the NDI/Carter Center February 2000 Pre Election Delegation to Peru' Lima February 11, 2000, <http://www.cartercenter.org/reports/perustatement.html>.
60 Stanley Payne 'Modernization of the Armed Forces', in Payne (ed.), 1986, p. 188.
61 Lancaster and Prevost, 1985, p. 114.
62 Spanish Ministry of the Interior, <http:www.mir.es/oris/infoeta/esp/p9c-esp.htm>.
63 US Department of State, Spain Country Report on Human Rights Practices for 1997, <http:www.state.gov/www/global/humanrights/1997_hrp_report/spain.html>.
64 Adela Gooch, 'ETA Youths Test Ceasefire', *The Guardian*, 28 September 1998.
65 Adela Gooch, 'Terror Campaign: ETA Gunman kills Couple in Serille', *The Guardian*, 31 January 1998 and Adela Gooch, 'ETA Ceasefire', *The Guardian*, 18 September 1998.

66 Gallup, Spain, November 1997, OPP 302.
67 Patty Li Peiyin, 'Will It Hold?' *Harvard International Review*, Vol. 21, No. 1, Winter 1998/1999, pp. 10–11.
68 Emma Daly, 'Spain's Basques See N. Ireland as Peace Model', *Christian Science Monitor*, 13 November 1998.
69 Carlos Closa, 'Spain: The Cortes and the EU – A Growing Together', *Journal of Legislative Studies*, Vol. 1, No. 3, Autumn 1995, p. 136.
70 McCormick, 1999, p. 59.
71 Richard Gillespie, 'Regime Consolidation in Spain', in Geoffrey Pridham (ed.), *Securing Democracy: Political Parties and Democratic Consolidation in Southern Europe* (London: Routledge, 1990), p. 132.
72 William Wallace, 'Rescue or Retreat? The Nation State in Western Europe, 1945–1993', in Peter Gowan and Perry Anderson (eds), *The Question of Europe* (New York: Verson, 1997), p. 42.
73 McCormick, 1999, p. 266.
74 Joint Action of 21 December 1998 adopted by the Council on the basis of article K.3 of the Treaty on European Union, on making it a criminal offence to participate in a criminal organization in the member states of the European Union. *Official Journal*, L 351 29/12/1998 pp. 0001–0003.
75 Council Decision of 3 December 1998. Article 1, EU Document 399D0130(02). See also EU Document 497Y0623(01).
76 Article 3, Convention Relating to Extradition between the Member States of the European Union – Explanatory Report. *Official Journal*, C 191, 23/06/1997 pp. 0013–0026.
77 'Preamble to the Single European Union Act', in Brent Nelsen and Alexander C.-G. Stubb (eds), *The European Union: Readings on the Theory and Practice of European Integration* (Boulder: Lynne Rienner, 1994), p. 46.
78 See EU proposal 6.20.1999.
79 Tanja A. Borzel, 'Shifting or Sharing the Burden? The Implementation of EU Environmental Policy in Spain and Germany', *European Planning Studies*, Vol. 6, No. 5, 1998, pp. 537–40.
80 *Eurobarometer 50*, October–November 1998, tables 3.1a, 3.2a and 3.4.

Select bibliography

Abel, Christopher and Nissa Torrents (eds), *Spain: Conditional Democracy*. New York: St. Martin's Press, 1984.

Adrianzén, Alberto, *Democracia, etnicidad y violencia política en los países andinos*. Lima: IEP, 1993.

Agranoff, Robert and Juan Antonio Ramos Gallarin, 'Towards Federal Democracy in Spain: An Examination of Intergovernmental Relations', *Publius*, Vol. 27, No. 4, Autumn 1997, p. 1.

Aguero, Felipe, *Soldiers, Civilians, and Democracy*. Baltimore: Johns Hopkins University Press, 1995.

Aguiar, Cesar, *Uruguay de los setenta: balance de una decada*. Montevideo: CIEDUR, 1981.

Aguilar, Paloma, 'The Memory of the Civil War in the Transition to Democracy: The Peculiarity of the Basque Case', *West European Politics*, Vol. 21, No. 4, October 1998.

Alisky, Marvin, *Uruguay: A Contemporary Survey*. New York: Praeger Press, 1969.

Alisky, Marvin, *Latin American Media: Guidance and Censorship*. Ames: Iowa State University, 1981.

Alzaga, O. et al. (eds), *Entre Dos Siglos: Reflexiones Sobre la Democracia Española*. Madrid: Alianza Editorial, 1996.

Americas Watch, *A Certain Passivity: Failing to Curb Human Rights Abuses in Peru*. New Haven: Yale University Press, 1987.

Americas Watch, *Tolerating Abuses: Violations of Human Rights in Peru*. New Haven: Yale University Press, 1988.

Americas Watch, *Peru Under Fire*. New Haven: Yale University Press, 1992.

Amnesty International, *Peru: Violations of Human Rights in the Emergency Zones*. New York: Amnesty International, 1988.

Amnesty International, *Peru: Human Rights in a State of Emergency*. New York: Amnesty International, 1989.

Amnesty International, *Peru: Human Rights in a Climate of Terror*. New York: Amnesty International, 1991.

Amnesty International, *Peru: Human Rights During the Government of Alberto Fujimori*. New York: Amnesty International, 1992.

Amnesty International, *AI Report 1998: Uruguay*. New York: Amnesty International, 1998.

APRODEH, <gopher://gopher.rcp.net.pe:70/00/otros-gopher/nacionales/aprodeh/>.

APRODEH et al., *Los Inocentes Tienen Nombre*. Lima: Grafimace S.A., 1995.

Arango, E. Ramón, *Spain: Democracy Regained*. Boulder: Westview Press, 1995.

Aristotle, *Metaphysics*. Translated by Richard Hope. Ann Arbor: University of Michigan Press, 1952.

Aristotle, *The Politics of Aristotle*. Translated by Ernest Barker. Oxford: Oxford University Press, 1958.

Aristotle, *Nicomachean Ethics*. Translated by Martin Ostwald. New York: MacMillan Press, 1962.

Aristotle, *Nicomachean Ethics*. Translated by David Ross. Oxford: Oxford University Press, 1992.

Arteche, Miguel Castells, *Radiografía de un model represivo*. San Sebastían: Ediciones Vascas, 1982.

Balcells, Albert, *Catalan Nationalism*. New York: St. Martin's Press, 1996.

Banon, Rafael and Manuel Tamayo, 'The Transformation of the Central Administration in Spanish Intergovernmental Relations', *Publius*, Vol. 27, No. 4, Autumn 1997, p. 85.

Barahona de Brito, Alexandra, 'Truth and Justice in the Consolidation of Democracy in Chile and Uruguay', *Parliamentary Affairs*, Vol. 46, No. 4, October 1993, pp. 579–93.

Barahona de Brito, Alexandra, *Human Rights and Democratization in Latin America*. Oxford: Oxford University Press, 1997.

Barnhurst, Kevin, 'Contemporary Terrorism in Peru: Sendero Luminoso and the Media', *Journal of Communication*, Vol. 41, No. 4, Autumn 1991, pp. 75–90.

Bell, David, *Democratic Politics in Spain*. New York: St. Martin's Press, 1983.

Bethel, Leslie (ed.), *Cambridge History of Latin America. Volume VIII: Spanish South America*. Cambridge: Cambridge University Press, 1991.

Bethel, Leslie (ed.), *Cambridge History of Latin America. Volume VI: Latin America since 1930: Economy, Society and Politics*. Cambridge: Cambridge University Press, 1994.

Bonime-Blanc, Andrea, *Spain's Transition to Democracy*. Boulder: Westview Press, 1986.

Bonino, Luis Costa, *Crisis de los Partidos Tradicionales y Movimiento Revolucionario en el Uruguay*. Montevideo: Ediciones de la Banda Oriental, 1984.

Bordaberry, Juan Maria, *Las Opciones*. Montevideo: Impresa Rosgal, 1980.

Borzel, Tanja A., 'Shifting or Sharing the Burden? The Implementation of EU Environmental Policy in Spain and Germany', *European Planning Studies*, Vol. 6, No. 5, 1998.

Bourque, Susan C. and Kay B. Warren, 'Democracy Without Peace: The Cultural Politics of Terror in Peru', *Latin American Research Review*, Vol. 24, No. 1, 1989, p. 9.

Buaquets, Julio, Miguel Angel Aguilar and Ignacio Puche, *El Golpe*. Barcelona: Editorial Ariel, 1981.

Cameron, Maxwell, *Democracy and Authoritarianism in Peru*. New York: St. Martin's Press, 1995.

Cameron, Maxwell, 'Self-Coups: Peru, Guatemala, and Russia', *Journal of Democracy*, Vol. 9, No. 1, 1998, pp. 125–39.

Canseco, Javier Diez, *Democracia, militarización y derechos humanos en el Perú 1980–1984*. Lima: Asociación Pro Derechos Humanos: Servicios Populares, 1985.

Carr, Raymond and Juan Pablo Fusi, *Spain: Dictatorship to Democracy*. London: Unwin Hyman, 1981.

Carter Center, 'Statement of the NDI/Carter Center February 2000 Pre Election Delegation to Peru', Lima, 11 February, 2000.

Castillo Ochoa, Manuel, 'Fujimori and the Business Class', *NACLA*, Vol. XXX, No. 1, July/August 1996, pp. 25–30.

Caula, Nelson and Alberto Silva, *Alta el Fuego: FFAA y Tupamaros*. Montevideo: Montesexto, 1986.

Centro de Investigaciones Sociólogicas, 'Encuesa y Sondeos del Centro de Investigaciones Sociólogicas', *Revista Española de la Opinion Publica*. Madrid: Instituto de la Opinion Publica.

Ceresole, Norberto (ed.), *Perú: Sendero Luminoso, Ejercito y Democracia*. Buenos Aires: Biblioteca Hispanoamericana, 1987.

Chang-Rodríguez, Eugenio. *Opciones Políticas Peruanas*. Trujillo, Peru: Editorial Normas Legales S.A., 1987.

Chilcote, Ronald (ed.), *Transitions from Dictatorship to Democracy*. New York: Crane Russak, 1990.

Chirinos Soto, Enrique, *Alan García: Análisis de su gobierno*. Lima: Centro de documentación Andina, 1986.

Clark, Robert, *The Basques: The Franco Years and Beyond*. Reno: University of Nevada Press, 1979.

Clark, Robert, 'The Basques, Madrid, and Regional Autonomy: Conflicting Perspectives between Center and Periphery in Spain', in William D. Phillips, Jr and Carla Rahn Phillips (eds), *Marginated Groups in Spanish and Portuguese History*. Minneapolis: Society for Spanish and Portuguese Historical Studies, 1989.

Clark, Robert P, *Negotiating with ETA: Obstacles to Peace in the Basque Country, 1975–1988*. Reno: University of Nevada Press, 1990.

Clark, Stephen, *Aristotle's Man*. Oxford: Clarendon Press, 1976.

Closa, Carlos, 'Spain: The Cortes and the EU – A Growing Together', *Journal of Legislative Studies*, Vol. 1, No. 3, Autumn 1995, pp. 136–50.

Collier, Ruth Berins and David Collier, *Shaping the Political Arena*. Princeton: Princeton University Press, 1991.

Comisión Especial de Investigación y Estudio sobre la Violencia y Alternativas de Pacificación en el Perú, *Violencia y Pacificación*. Lima: Senado de la República, 1989.

Comisión Especial de Investigación y Estudio sobre la Violencia y Alternativas de Pacificación, *Violencia y Pacificación en 1991*. Lima: Senado de la República, 1992.

Coordinadora Nacional de Derechos Humanos, *Informe Sobre la Situación de los Derechos Humanos de el Perú en 1995*. Lima: Coordinadora de Derechos Humanos, 1996.

Coordinadora Nacional de Derechos Humanos, *Informe Sobre la Situación de los Derechos Humanos en el Perú en 1996*. Lima, CNDDHH, 1997.

Coordinadora Nacional de Derechos Humanos, *Informe Sobre la Situación de los Derechos Humanos en el Perú en 1997*. Lima, CNDDHH, 1998.

Coordinadora Nacional de Derechos Humanos, *Perú, Informe Anual 1998*. Lima: Coordinadora Nacional de Derechos Humanos, 1999.

Corr, Edwin and Stephen Sloan (eds), *Low Intensity Conflict: Old Threats in a New World*. Boulder: Westview Press, 1992.

Cowan, Andrew, 'The Guerrilla War Against Franco'. *European History Quarterly*, Vol. 2, No. 2, April 1990, pp. 227–53.

Crabtree, John, *Peru Under Garcia*. Pittsburgh: University of Pittsburgh Press, 1992.

Craven, Carolyn, 'Wage Determinism and Inflation in Uruguay', *Journal of Developing Areas*, Vol. 27, No. 4, July 1993, pp. 457–69.

Davis, William, *Warnings from the Far South: Democracy versus Dictatorship in Uruguay, Argentina, and Chile*. Westport: Praeger, 1995.

del Campo, Salustiano (ed.), *Tendencias Sociales en España*. Bilbao: Fundacion BBV, 1993.

del Campo, Salustiano (ed.), *Tendencias Sociales en España Volumen III*. Bilbao: Fundacion BBV, 1993.

Diamond, Larry, Marc Plattner, Yun-han Chu and Hung-mao Tien (eds), *Consolidating the Third World Democracies*. Baltimore: Johns Hopkins University Press, 1997.

Dietz, Henry, 'Peru's Sendero Luminoso As a Revolutionary Movement', *Journal of Political and Military Sociology*, Vol. 18, Summer 1990, pp. 123–50.

Douglass, R. Bruce, Gerald M. Mara and Henry S. Richardson (eds), *Liberalism and the Good*. New York: Routledge, 1990.

Douglass, William and Joseba Zulaika, 'On the Interpretation of Terrorist Violence: ETA and the Basque Political Process', *Comparative Studies in Society and History*, Vol. 32, No. 2, April 1990, pp. 238–48.

Encarnacion, Omar, 'Social Concertation in Democratic and Market Transactions: Comparative Lessons from Spain', *Comparative Political Studies*, Vol. 30, No. 4, August 1997, p. 387.

Escalante, María and Ana María Vidal, *Los Decretos de la Guerra*. Lima: IDS Minilibros, 1993.

Farer, Tom (ed.), *Beyond Sovereignty: Collectively Defending Democracy in the Americas*. Baltimore: Johns Hopkins University Press, 1996.

Finch, Henry (ed.), *Contemporary Uruguay*. University of Liverpool, Institute of Latin American Studies, Working Paper No. 9, 1989.

Finch, M. H. J., *A Political Economy of Uruguay Since 1870*. New York: St. Martin's Press, 1981.

Finley, M. I., *Politics in the Ancient World*. Cambridge: Cambridge University Press, 1983.

Fishman, Robert, *Working Class Organization and the Return to Democracy in Spain*. Ithaca: Cornell University Press, 1990.

Fitch, J. Samuel, *The Armed Forces and Democracy in Latin America*. Baltimore: Johns Hopkins University Press, 1998.

Fitzgibbon, Russell, *Uruguay: Portrait of a Democracy*. New Brunswick: Rutgers University Press, 1954.

Fitz-Simons, Daniel W., 'Sendero Luminoso: Case Study in Insurgency', *Parameters*, Vol. 23, No. 2, Summer 1993, pp. 64–73.

Forgues, Rolando (ed.), *Perú: entre el desafío de la violencia y el sueño de lo posible*. Lima: Minerva, 1993.

Gallup, *Informe Gallup 1970: Futuro Inmediato y Previsible del Uruguay*. Montevideo: Gallup Uruguay, 1970.

'García's Peru', *NACLA*, June 1986, pp. 34–46.

Gardels, Nathan and Abraham Lowenthal, 'Saving the State in Peru', *New Perspectives Quarterly*, Autumn 1993, pp. 10–12.

Gellner, Ernest, *Legitimation of Belief*. London: Cambridge University Press, 1974.

Generals and Tupamaros: The Struggle for Power in Uruguay 1969–1973. London: Latin American Review of Books, 1974.

Gillespie, Charles Guy, *Negotiating Democracy: Politicians and Generals in Uruguay*. Cambridge: Cambridge University Press, 1991.

Gillespie, Richard, 'The Continuing Debate on Democratization in Spain', *Parliamentary Affairs*, Vol. 46, October 1993, pp. 534–48.

Glewwe, Paul and Gillette Hall, 'Poverty, Inequality, and Living Standards During Unorthodox Adjustment: The Case of Peru, 1985–1990', *Economic Development and Cultural Change*, Vol. 42, No. 4, July 1994, pp. 689–718.

González Casanova, Pablo and Marcos Roitman Rosenmann (eds), *La Democracia en América Latina: actualidad y perspectivas*. Mexico D.F.: La Jornada, 1995.

Gorriti, Gustavo Ellenbogen, *Sendero. Historia de la guerra milenaria en el Perú*. Lima: Editorial APOYO, 1990.

Gowan, Peter and Perry Anderson (eds), *The Question of Europe*. New York: Verso, 1997.

Graham, Carol, *Peru's APRA*. Boulder: L. Rienner Publishers, 1992.

Gunther, Richard (ed.), *Politics, Society and Democracy: The Case of Spain*. Boulder: Westview Press, 1993.

Gunther, Richard, Giancomo Sani and Goldie Shabad, *Spain After Franco*. Berkeley: University of California Press, 1988.

Gunther, Richard, P. Nikiforos Diamandouros and Hans-Jurgen Puhle (eds), *The Politics of Democratic Consolidation*. Baltimore: Johns Hopkins University Press, 1995.

Gutiérrez, Gustavo, *A Theory of Liberation: History, Politics and Salvation*. Maryknoll: Orvis Books, 1973.

Handelman, Howard, 'Labor–Industrial Conflict and the Collapse of Uruguayan Democracy', *Journal of Interamerican Studies and World Affairs*, Vol. 23, No. 4, November 1981.

Harrison, Joseph, *The Spanish Economy in the Twentieth Century*. London: Croom Helm, 1985.

Herz, John (ed.), *From Dictatorship to Democracy*. Westport: Greenwood Press, 1982.

Hispania Service, *La imagen de las instituciones políticas en la opinión pública*. Madrid: Hispania Service, 1981.

Human Rights Watch, *Peru: Presumption of Guilt*. Washington, DC: Human Rights Watch, 1996.

Human Rights Watch, *Torture and Political Persecution in Peru*. New York: Human Rights Watch, 1998.

Human Rights Watch. *World Report 1999*.

Instituto Nacional de estadistica e informatica. *Perú en Cifras*.

Instituto Nacional de estadistica e informatica, *Peru: compendio estadístico 1995–6*. Lima: Dirección Ejecutiva de Coyuntura, 1996.

Instituto de Ciencias Sociales, *Uruguay: Poder, Ideologia y Clases Sociales*. Montevideo, Facultad de Derecho, 1970.

Inter-Church Committee on Human Rights in Latin America, *Violations of Human Rights in Uruguay (1972–1976)*. Toronto: Inter-Church Committee on Human Rights in Latin America, 1978.

Janke, Peter, *Spanish Separatism: ETA's Threat to Basque Democracy*. London: Institute for the Study of Conflict, 1980.

Jellinek, Sergio and Luis Ledesma, *Uruguay: Del Consenso Democratico a la Militarismo Estatal*. Part 1, Paper No. 19, November 1979. Stockholm: Institute of Latin American Studies, 1979.

Jellinek, Sergio and Luis Ledesma, *Uruguay: Del Consenso Democratico a la Militarismo Estatal*. Part 2, Paper No. 19, November 1979. Stockholm: Institute of Latin American Studies, 1979.

Jugo, Miguel, 'Panoram sobre derechos humanos', *Actualidad Peruana*, Vol. 8, No. 1, February 1999. <http:// ekeko.rcp.net.pe/aprodeh/public/acpe99/ap0199.htm>.

Kaufman, Edy, *Uruguay in Transition: From Civilian to Military Rule*. New Brunswick: Transaction Books, 1979.

Klaren, Peter, 'Peru's Great Divide', *The Wilson Quarterly*, Vol. 14, No. 3, Summer 1990, pp. 23–33.

Kohl, James and John Litt, *Urban Guerrilla Warfare in Latin America*. Cambridge: MIT Press, 1974.

Krasikov, Anatoly, *From Dictatorship to Democracy: Spanish Reportage*. Oxford: Pergamon Press, 1984.

Kraut, Richard, *Aristotle on the Human Good*. Princeton: Princeton University Press, 1991.

Labrousse, Alain, *The Tupamaros: Urban Guerrillas in Uruguay*. Harmondsworth: Penguin Books, 1970.

Lancaster, Thomas D. and Gary Prevost (eds), *Politics and Change in Spain*. New York: Praeger, 1985.

Langguth, A. J., *Hidden Terrors*. New York: Pantheon Books, 1978.

Lannon, Frances and Paul Preston (eds), *Elites and Power in Twentieth-Century Spain: Essays in Honour of Sir Raymond Carr*. Oxford: Clarendon Press, 1990.

Levander, Sandro Macassi, 'Cultura politica de la eficacia', *Socialismo y participacion*, Lima, No. 58, June 1992, pp. 65–75.

Linz, Juan (ed.), *Un presente para el futuro*. Madrid: Instituto de Estudios Economicos, 1985.

Linz, Juan, 'Church and State in Spain from the Civil War to the Return of Democracy', *Daedalus*, Vol. 120, No. 2, Summer 1991, pp. 159–79.

Linz, Juan and Alfred Stepan, 'Political Identities and Electoral Sequences: Spain, the Soviet Union, and Yugoslavia', *Daedalus*, Vol. 121, No. 2, Spring 1992, pp. 123–40.

Linz, Juan and Alfred Stepan, (eds), *Problems of Democratic Transition and Consolidation: Southern Europe, South America and Post-Communist Europe*. Baltimore: Johns Hopkins University Press, 1996.

Llera, Francisco J., José M. Mata and Cynthia L. Irvin, 'ETA: From Secret Army to Social Movement – the Post Franco Schism of the Basque National Movement', *Terrorism and Political Violence*, Vol. 5, No. 3, Autumn 1993, pp. 106–34.

López Pintor, *La Opinión Pública Española del Franquismo a la Demcracia*. Madrid: CIS, 1982.

Loveman, Brian, '"Protected Democracies" and Military Guardianship: Political Transitions in Latin America', *Journal of Interamerican Studies and World Affairs*, Vol. 36, Summer 1994, pp. 105–89.

MacIntyre, Alasdair, *After Virtue*. Notre Dame: University of Notre Dame Press, 1984.

Mainwaring, Scott, 'Political Parties and Democratization in Brazil and the Southern Cone', *Comparative Politics*, Vol. 21, No. 1, October 1988.

Maravall, José, *The Transition to Democracy in Spain*. London: St. Martin's Press, 1982.

Masterson, Daniel, 'In the Shining Path of Mariategui, Mao Zedong or Presidente Gonzalo? Peru's Sendero Lumirioso in Historical Perspective', Journal *of Third World Studies*, Vol. 11, No. 1, Spring 1994, pp. 154–79.

Mauceri, Philip, 'Military Politics and Counter-Insurgency in Peru', *Journal of Interamerican Studies and World Affairs*, Vol. 33, No. 4, Winter 1991, pp. 83–109.

Mauceri, Philip, 'State Reform, Coalitions, and the Neoliberal Autogolpe in Peru', *Latin American Research Review*, Vol. 30, No. 1, Winter 1995, pp. 256–66.

Mauceri, Philip, *State Under Siege: Development and Policy Making in Peru*. Boulder: Westview Press, 1996.

Mayer, Enrique, 'Patterns of Violence in the Andes', *Latin American Research Review*, Vol. 29, No. 2, 1994, pp. 141–71.

McClintock, Cynthia, 'The Prospects for Democratic Consolidation in a "Least Likely" Case: Peru', *Comparative Politics*, Vol. 21, No. 2, January 1989, pp. 127–49.

McClintock, Cynthia and Abraham F. Lowenthal (eds), *The Peruvian Experiment Reconsidered*. Princeton: Princeton University Press, 1983.

McClintock, Cynthia, 'The War on Drugs: The Peruvian Case', *Journal of Interamerican Studies and World Affairs*, Vol. 30, No. 23, Summer/Autumn 1988, pp. 127–42.

McCormick, John, *The European Union: Politics and Policies*. Boulder: Westview Press, 1999.

McDonald, Ronald H, 'The Rise of Military Politics in Uruguay', *Inter-American Economic Affairs*, Vol. XXVII, No. 4, Spring 1975, pp. 25–44.

McDonald, Ronald H. 'Electoral Politics and Uruguayan Political Decay', *Inter-American Economic Affairs*, Vol. XXVI, No. 1, Summer 1972, pp. 25–46.

McDonald, Ronald, 'Confrontation and Transition in Uruguay', *Current History*, Vol. 84, February 1985.

McDonough, Peter, Samuel Barnes and Antonio López Pina, 'The Growth of Democratic Legitimacy in Spain', *APSR*, Vol. 80, No. 3, September 1986.

Medrano, Juan Díez, *Divided Nations: Class, Politics, and Nationalism in the Basque Country and Catalonia*. Ithaca: Cornell University Press, 1995.

Méndez, Juan, *Human Rights in Peru after President Garcia's First Year*. New York: Americas Watch Committee, 1986.

Mieres, Paolo, 'Elecciones de 1989 en Uruguay', *Sintesis*, Vol. 13, April–June 1991, pp. 205–28.

Miller, George, 'A Lesson Learned in Uruguay', *New Leader*, Vol. 76, No. 10, 9 August 1993.

Moreno, Luis, 'Federalization and Ethnoterritorial Concurrence in Spain', *Publius*, Vol. 27, No. 4, Autumn 1997, p. 65.

Muller, Edward Henry Dietz and Steven Finkel, 'Discontent and the Unexpected Utility of Rebellion: The Case of Peru', *American Political Science Review*, Vol. 85, No. 4, December 1991, pp. 1261–83.

Nef, Jorge and J. Vanderkop, 'The Spiral of Violence: Insurgency and Counter-Insurgency in Peru', *Canadian Journal of Latin American and Caribbean Studies*, Vol. 9, No. 17, 1988, pp. 53–72.

Nelsen, Brent and Alexander C.-G. Stubb (eds), *The European Union: Readings on the Theory and Practice of European Integration*. Boulder: Lynne Rienner, 1994.

Nelson, Caulo and Alberto Silva, *Alto el Fuego*. Montevideo: Montesexio, 1986.

Newton, Michael T. with Peter J. Donaghy, *Institutions of Modern Spain*. Cambridge: Cambridge University Press, 1997.

Nussbaum, Martha, 'Human Functioning and Social Justice: In Defense of Aristotelian Essentialism', *Political Theory*, Vol. 20, No. 2, May 1992, pp. 202–46.

Nussbaum, Martha and Amartya Sen (eds), *The Quality of Life*. Oxford: Clarendon Press, 1993.

Obando, Enrique, 'Fujimori and the Military: A Marriage of Convenience', *NACLA*, Vol. XXX, No. 1, July/August 1996, pp. 31–6.

Palmer, David Scott, 'Rebellion in Rural Peru', *Comparative Politics*, Vol. 18, No. 2, January 1986.

Palmer, David Scott, '"Fujipopulism" and Peru's Progress', *Current History*, February 1996.

Palmer, David Scott, 'Peru, The Drug Business and Shining Path: Between Scylla and Charybdis?', *Journal of Interamerican Studies and World Affairs*, Vol. 34, No. 3, Autumn 1992, pp. 65–89.

Paloma Roma Marugan. *Cronología*.

Payne, Stanley, *Basque Nationalism*. Reno: University of Nevada Press, 1975.

Payne, Stanley (ed.), *The Politics of Democratic Spain*. Chicago: Chicago Council of Foreign Relations, 1986.

Payne, Stanley, 'Political Violence During the Spanish Second Republic', *Journal of Contemporary History*, Vol. 25, 1990, pp. 269–88.

Pease García, Henry, *America Latina 80: Democracia y Movimiento Popular*. Lima: Centro de Estudios y Promocion del Desarrollo, 1981.

Peckenham, Nancy, 'Ayacucho Under Siege', *NACLA*, Vol. 19, No. 3, May/June 1985.

Penniman, Howard R. and Eusebio M. Mujal-Leon (eds), *Spain at the Polls 1977, 1979, and 1982*. Chapel Hill: Duke University Press, 1985.

Perelli, Carina, 'From Counterrevolutionary Warfare to Political Awakening: The Uruguayan and Argentine Armed Forces in the 1970's', *Armed Forces and Society*, Vol. 20, No. 1, Autumn 1993, pp. 25–49.

Pérez-Díaz, Víctor (ed.), *El Retorno de la sociedad civil*. Madrid: Instituto de Estudios Económicos, 1987.

Pérez-Díaz, Víctor M., *The Return of Civil Society*. Cambridge: Harvard University Press, 1993.

Pion-Berlin, David, *Human Rights Quarterly*, Vol. 16, No. 1, February 1994, pp. 3–4.

Poole, Deborah (ed.), *Unruly Order: Violence, Power and Cultural Identity in the High Provinces of Southern Peru*. Boulder: Westview Press, 1994.

Poole, Deborah and Gerardo Renique, 'The New Chroniclers of Peru: US Scholars and their "Shining Path" of Peasant Revolution', *Bulletin of Latin American Research*, Vol. 10, No. 2, 1991, pp. 133–91.

Porzencanski, Arturo, *Uruguay's Tupamaros*. New York: Praeger, 1973.

Powell, Charles, *El piloto del cambio*. Barcelona: Editorial Planeta, 1991.

Powell, G. Bingham, *Contemporary Democracies*. Cambridge: Harvard University Press, 1982.

Pridham, Geoffrey (ed.), *The New Mediterranean Democracies*. London: Frank Cass, 1984.

Pridham, Geoffrey, *Securing Democracy: Political Parties and Democratic Consolidation in Southern Europe*. London: Routledge, 1990.

'Report on Peru', *NACLA*, Vol. XX, No. 1 July/August 1996.

Report on the Situation of Human Rights in Peru. OAS, 1992.

Republica Oriental del Uruguay Junta de Comandantes en Jefe. *La Subversion*. Montevideo: Las Fuerzas Armadas al Pueblo Oriental, 1977.

Republica Oriental del Uruguay Junta de Comandantes en Jefe. Tomo 2. *El Proceso Politico*. Montevideo: Las Fuerzas Armadas al Pueblo Oriental, 1978.

Rial, Juan, 'Los Partidos Traditionales: restauración o renovación', Documentos de Trabajo CIEDSU/DT 77/84, Montevideo, CIESU.

Roberts, Kenneth M. and Moises Arce, 'Neoliberalism and Lower Class Voting Behavior in Peru', *Comparative Political Studies*, Vol. 31, No. 2, April/May 1998, pp. 217–47.

Roniger, Luis and Mario Sznajder, 'The Legacy of Human Rights Violations and the Collective Identity of Redemocratized Uruguay', *Human Rights Quarterly*, Vol. 19, 1997, pp. 55–77.

Rorty, Amelie Oksenberg (ed.), *Essays on Aristotle's Ethics*. Berkeley: University of California Press, 1980.

Ross, Chris, 'Nationalism and Party Competition in the Basque Country and Catalonia', *West European Politics*, Vol. 19, No. 3, July 1996, pp. 488–506.

Salkever, Stephen, 'Aristotle's Social Science', *Political Theory*, Vol. 9, No. 4, November 1981, pp. 479–508.

Salkever, Stephen, *Finding the Mean: Theory and Practice in Aristotelian Political Philosophy*. Princeton: Princeton University Press, 1990.

Santos, Julia, Javier Pradera and Jaoquin Prieto (eds), *Memoria de la transicion*. Madrid: Taurus, 1996.

Savater, Fernando and Gonzalo Martínez-Fresneda, *Teoría y presencia de la tortura en España*. Barcelona: Editorial Anagrama, 1982.

Schmidt, Gregory, 'Fujimori's 1990 Upset Victory in Peru', *Comparative Politics*, April 1996.

Schmitter, Phillippe, 'Interest Intermediation and Regime Governability in Contemporary Western Europe and North America', in Suzanne Berger (ed.), *Organizing Interests in Western Europe*. Cambridge: and New York Cambridge University Press, 1981, pp. 285–327.

Seregni, General Liber, *Discursos*. Montevideo: Bolsilibros ARCA 86, 1971.

Servicio Paz y Justicia: Uruguay. *Nunca Más: Human Rights Violations, 1972–1985*. Philadelphia: Temple University Press, 1986.

Shady, Norbert, 'Seeking Votes: The Political Economy of Expenditures by the Peruvian Social Fund (FONCODES), 1991–1995', *Latin American Research Review*, Vol. 33, No. 1, 1998.

Share, Donald, *The Making of Spanish Democracy*. New York: Westport, 1986.

Shifter, Michael, 'Human Rights: Peruvian Responses', *Hemisphere*, Winter/Spring 1990, pp. 6–9.

Shub, Joyce Lasky and Raymond Carr (eds), *Spain: Studies in Political Security*. New York: Praeger, 1985.

Soldevilla, Fernando Tuesta, *Perú Político en Cifras*. Lima: Fundacion, 1994.

Sosnowski, Saúl and Lousie Popkin (eds), *Repression, Exile, and Democracy: Uruguayan Culture*. Durham: Duke University Press, 1993.

Starn, Orin, 'To Revolt Against the Revolution: War and Resistance in Peru's Andes', *Cultural Anthropology*, Vol. 10, No. 4, November 1995, pp. 547–81.

Starn, Orin, Carlos Ivan Degregori and Robin Kirk (eds), *The Peru Reader: History, Culture, Politics*. Durham: Duke University Press, 1995.

Stokes, Susan, *Cultures in Conflict*. Berkeley: University of California Press, 1995.

Strauss, Leo, *The City and Man*. Chicago: University of Chicago Press, 1964.

Strauss, Leo, *Natural Right and History*. Chicago: University of Chicago Press, 1965.

Tamames, Ramon, *Una Idea de España*. Madrid: Plaza & Janes Editores, 1985.

Tezanos, José Feliz, Ramón Cotarelo and Andrés De Blas Guerrero, *La Transición Democrática Española*. Madrid: Editorial Sistema, 1989.

Treverton, Gregory, *Spain: Domestic Politics and Security Policy*. Adelphi Papers 204, 1986.

Tucker, H. H. (ed.), *Combating the Terrorists: Democratic Responses to Political Violence*. New York: Facts of File, 1988.

Tulchin, Joseph and Gary Bland (eds), *Peru in Crisis: Dictatorship or Democracy*. Boulder: Lynne Rienner, 1994.

United Nations Development Programme, *Human Development Report 1999*. New York: Oxford University Press, 1999.

Uruguay, Ministro del Interior, *Siete Meses de la Lucha Antisubversiva*. Montevideo: Ministro del Interior.

US Government, *Uruguay: A Country Study*. Washington, DC: Federal Research Division, Library of Congress, 1990.

US Department of State. *Human Rights Practices*. 1994, <http:www.state.gov/www/global/human_rights/drl_reports/.html>.

US Department of State. *Human Rights Practices*. 1996, <http:www.state.gov/www/global/human_rights/drl_reports/.html>.

US Department of State. *Human Rights Practices*. 1997, <http:www.state.gov/www/global/human_rights/drl_reports/.html>.

US Department of State. *Human Rights Practices*. 1998, <http:www.state.gov/www/global/human_rights/drl_reports/.html>.

US Department of State. *Uruguayan Country Report on Human Rights Practices for 1996* (Washington, DC: US Government Printing Office).

US Department of State. *Spain Country Report on Human Rights Practices for 1997*.

US House of Representatives and Committee on Foreign Relations. *Report Submitted to the Committee on International Relations, 1978–1986* (Washington, DC: US Government Printing Office).

US Senate. *Committee Report of Human Rights Practices 1979–1986* (Washington, DC: US Government Printing Office).

Villanueva, Victor, 'Peru's New Military Professionalism: The Failure of the Technocratic Approach', in Peter Gorman (ed.), *Post Revolutionary Peru*, Boulder: Westview, 1982.

Watters, R. F., *Poverty and Peasantry in Peru's Southern Andes, 1963–1990*. Pittsburgh: University of Pittsburgh Press, 1994.

Weinstein, Martin, *Uruguay: Democracy at the Crossroads*. Boulder: Westview Press, 1988.

Werlich, David, 'Peru: The Shadow of the Shining Path', *Current History*, Vol. 83, February 1984, pp. 78–84.

Weyland, Kurt, 'Latin America's Four Political Models', *Journal of Democracy*, Vol. 6, No. 4, October 1995, pp. 125–40.

Wiarda, Howard, *The Transition to Democracy in Spain and Portugal*. Washington, DC: American Enterprise Institute for Public Policy Research, 1988.

Wilson, Fernández, *El Gran Culpable: La responsabilidad de los E.E.U.I. en el proceso militar uruguayo*. Montevideo: 1986.

Wilson, Ferreira Aldunate, *El exilio y la lucha*. Montevideo: Ediciones de la Banda Oriental, 1986.

Wilson, Jaime Barreto, *Marketing Político: Elecciones 1990*. Lima: Universidad del Pacífico Centro de Investigacion, 1991.

Woy-Hazleton, Sandra and William A. Hazleton, 'Sendero Luminos and the Future of Peruvian Democracy', *Third World Quarterly*, Vol. 12, No. 2, 1990, p. 29.

Yack, Bernard, 'Natural Right and Aristotle's Understanding of Justice', *Political Theory*, Vol. 18, No. 2, May 1990, pp. 216–37.

Yack, Bernard, *The Problems of a Political Animal: Community, Justice and Conflict in Aristotelian Political Thought*. Berkeley: University of California Press, 1993.

Yehude, Simon Munaro, *Estado y Guerrillas en el Peru de los '80*. Lima: EES Asociación Instituto de los Estudios Estratégicos y Sociales, 1988.

Zirakzadeh, Cyrus, *A Rebellious People: Basques, Protests and Politics*. Reno: University of Nevada Press, 1991.

Index

Note 'n' after a page reference indicates a note number on that page.

Aldunate, Ferreira Wilson 153, 179, 180
Alfonso XIII, king of Spain 48
Alianza Apostólica Anticomunita (AAA) 87
Alianza Popular Revolucionaria Americana (APRA) 42–3, 45, 99, 103, 173
amnesty
  Spain 106
  Peru 212
Antiterrorismo ETA 87
Arce, Liber 92, 136
Aristotelian approach 2, 12–32
'authentic interpretation' law of 1996, 209
autonomy 106, 130

Bardesio, Nelson 81, 96
Barrionuevo, José Luis 109
Belaúnde, Fernando 45, 84, 98–9, 101, 140, 155, 194
Belmont Cassinelli, Ricardo 139
Boiso Lanza agreement 41
Bordaberry, Juan Maria 39, 40, 42, 82, 151–2, 176, 179, 180

Carrero Blanco, Admiral Luis 49, 61, 176
Catalan Convergence and Union (CiU) 50
Caza Tupamaro 82, 96
Central Intelligence Agency (CIA) 7
Centro de Estudios Militares de Peru (CAEM) 43

Chiappe Posse, General Hugo 41, 193
citizen confidence 30
  Peru 138–43
  Spain 144–7
  Uruguay 134–48
Club Naval talks 204
Colegiado 37, 173
Comando Rodrigo Franco 103
Communist Party
  Peru 43
  Spain 49, 52, 62, 124, 174
Consejo de Seguridad Nacional (COSENA) 42, 193
constitution 39, 45, 55, 138
coup
  Peru 45–7, 156, 171
  Spain (attempted) 53–4, 160, 171
  Uruguayan 'slow coup' 40, 42, 79, 153–4, 171, 179, 203
Cristi, General Esteban 41, 42, 193

Dahl, Robert 13, 26
Declaration of Lizarra 219
democratic consolidation 223n1
democratic stability
  Peru 154–8, 162–3
  Spain 158–62, 63–4
  Uruguay 150–4, 161
desencanto 149, 153
DSV *see lema* system
Durand, Oscar Ramirez ('Feliciano') 210–11

INDEX

economic performance
  Peru 65–7, 209
  Spain 67–8, 217
  Uruguay 63–5, 205
ELP (National Liberation Army) 43
Ertzaintza 107
ESMACO 42
Estatuto de Guernica 106
European Economic Community, European Union 185–6, 216, 220–2
Euzkadi ta Askatasuna (ETA) 49, 60–2, 86–7, 107, 123, 217–18
'Expiry' law 205

faceless courts 2–8
'Feliciano' *see* Durand, Oscar Ramirez
Fondo Nacional de Compensacion y Desarrollo Social (FONCODES) 210, 215
Francese, General Antonio 40–1, 124, 127, 192
Franco, General Francisco 6, 48–9, 51, 67–8, 86, 105, 108, 131, 147, 159, 176, 186
Frente Amplio 81, 136, 151, 173, 179, 184, 192, 204
Frente Democrático (FREDEMO) 139
Fujimori, Alberto 4, 7, 17, 45–7, 65–7, 84–5, 100, 103, 139, 140–1, 143, 156, 180, 185, 205, 207–10

GAL 109
Garcia, Alan 45, 65–6, 84, 98–101, 103, 138, 140, 156, 180, 184, 187, 194
Generalitat 130
Gestido, Oscar 137
González, Felipe 50
Grupos de Resistencia Antifascista Primero de Octobre (GRAPO) 62–3, 86
Gutiérrez Mellado, General Manuel 52
Guzmán, Abimael 58, 85–6, 210, 214

Herri Batasuna (HB) 50, 60, 109, 219

Integration 29
  Peru 126–30
  Spain 130–1
  Uruguay 124–6

Játiva conspiracy 52
Juan Carlos I, king of Spain 5, 49, 53–4, 147, 177, 180–1
JUJEM 52
Junta de Comandantes en Jefe 42
Juventud Uruguaya de Pie (JUP) 96

'Law for the Defence of the Constitution' 108
Law of Political Reform 49
Law of State Security 94
leadership 179–81
legitimacy 13–15, 20, 187–8
lema system (DSV) 175
Linz, Juan 6, 13–14, 26, 172–3, 177, 179, 188

MANO 117
Miláns de Bosch, General Jaime 52, 54
military
  Peru 43–7, 185, 194–5, 212
  Spain 51–4, 216–17
  Uruguay 38–40, 137, 153, 183, 192–3, 204–5
MIR (Movement of the Revolutionary Left) 43
Mitrione, Dan 57
Moncloa Pact 50–1
Montesinos, Vladimiro 46, 214
Movimiento Revolucionario Tupac Amaro (MRTA) 59–60, 84–6, 100, 103–4, 118, 211–12
MPS (prompt security measures) 39, 91, 93–4, 110n4, 135

National Security Doctrine 7, 182, 183
North Atlantic Treaty Organization (NATO) 220–1

Organization of American States (OAS) 206–7
Operation Galaxia 53
Operation Zen 108
Otero, Alejandro 95

Pacheco Areco, Jorge 91, 93, 137–8, 182
pact of *chinchulín* (pork barrel pact) 64
party system 38, 172–5
Pérez, General José 41
PNV 50, 60–1, 162, 174
political system 175–8

Primo de Rivera, General Miguel 48
PSOE 50, 174
purposes of the state 20-2, 26-8, 30-1, 188-90

regionalism 130, 144
repression 21, 27, 30
 Peru 98-105, 211-13
 Spain 107, 109
 Uruguay 90-8, 203
rondas 101-4, 112n67, 121

Sanguinetti, Julio 180
Second Republic 48
security 29
 Peru 118-21
 Spain 121-4
 Uruguay 116-18
Sendero Luminoso 4, 6, 46-7, 58-9, 84-6, 103-4, 118-19, 126-9, 210-11

Seregni, General Liber 151-2, 179, 183, 192
Shining Path *see* Sendero Luminoso
SINAMOS 43-4
'Sinchis' 99
state 12, 13, 15, 19
state of emergency 99-102, 211-12
state of internal war 93
state of siege *see* MPS
'strategic hamlet' plan 6, 102
Suárez, Adolfo 49, 50, 52-3, 147, 173, 177

Tejero, Lt. Colonel Antonio 54
teleology 17-18
Tupamaros 3, 39, 55-8, 81-3, 95-8, 116, 125, 150-1

Union of the Democratic Centre (UCD) 50, 52, 122, 173
United States 182-6